Praise for
Filthy Beasts

"A vivid and compelling portrait of a dysfunctional family . . . Hamill is a gifted storyteller, crafting scenes and dialogue that read like a riveting novel. . . . The author absorbingly narrates a complicated story fraught with betrayal, abandonment, and grief, and he shows us—via his own recovery—that beauty, pain, and love can all coexist in the same space. . . . A stunning, deeply satisfying story about how we outlive our upbringings."

—*Kirkus Reviews* (starred review)

"Written with brutal and complex honesty, Hamill navigates the painful yet powerful path toward self-acceptance and love in a story that is, at its core, one of survival."

—Moda Operandi

"An astonishing memoir . . . Readers will appreciate his dry wit and compassionate lens while admiring the survival instincts that led Hamill to proudly assert himself as a gay man deserving of romantic love. . . . A gifted storyteller shares the humor and pathos of growing up in a dysfunctional family where the adults relate better to children once they've reached drinking age."

—*Shelf Awareness*

"Hamill's honesty in questioning past choices and their consequences as well as his slow realization that he's gay will emotionally engage readers, as telling unvarnished truths about his family, he provides a unique look into a world unknown to most of us. . . . [For] fans of *Wild Game* by Adrienne Brodeur and *A Forever Family* by Rob Scheer."

—*Booklist*

"Sharp [and] thoughtful . . . In smooth prose, Hamill's narrative moves gracefully without ever being precious. Fans of difficult family memoirs will want to take a look."

—*Publishers Weekly*

"Shades of *Grey Gardens*."

—*New York Post*, "Best of Summer Books for 2020"

"There are few coming-of-age stories with so many highs and lows as Hamill's, and he makes such a roller coaster irresistible reading. *Filthy Beasts* reminds us how hard it is to let go of your family, especially your mother, no matter how they betray or disappoint us."

—Amy Sutherland

"Kirkland Hamill's memoir is brilliantly, sharply, and unsettlingly new. Reading *Filthy Beasts* reminded me of inhaling Sedaris for the first time—that humor, that voice—only the work is tenderer and friendlier, an invitation not just to laugh and marvel but to truly understand."

—Beth Macy

"A complex and unflinching account of a family's undoing told with style and a mordant humor that will keep you reading until the final page. I closed the book not in awe of Hamill's talent (although I am), but rather of the mere fact that he survived."

—Steven Rowley

Filthy Beasts

a Memoir

Kirkland Hamill

AVID READER PRESS

New York London Toronto Sydney New Delhi

AVID READER PRESS
An Imprint of Simon & Schuster, Inc.
1230 Avenue of the Americas
New York, NY 10020

First Avid Reader Press trade paperback edition June 2021

AVID READER PRESS and colophon are
trademarks of Simon & Schuster, Inc.

For information about special discounts for bulk purchases,
please contact Simon & Schuster Special Sales at 1-866-506-1949
or business@simonandschuster.com.

The Simon & Schuster Speakers Bureau can bring authors to
your live event. For more information or to book an event,
contact the Simon & Schuster Speakers Bureau at 1-866-248-3049
or visit our website at www.simonspeakers.com.

Interior design by Kyle Kabel

Manufactured in the United States of America

1   3   5   7   9   10   8   6   4   2

Library of Congress Cataloging-in-Publication Data has been applied for.

ISBN 978-1-9821-2276-8
ISBN 978-1-9821-2277-5 (pbk)
ISBN 978-1-9821-2278-2 (ebook)

To my fellow filthy beasts, Robin and Monty:
You are the bravest people I know. I love you.
To my mother—ferocious, fearless, and funny.
You taught me how to survive you.

Filthy Beasts

Prologue

When I tell people stories about my mother, as I tend to do, people sometimes ask me how long she's been gone. I think back to the spring day in 1982 when I asked her to drive me into town and she got into the car with a full glass of scotch, wearing the sunglasses that she never took off, and she chewed her nails nervously as she tried to figure out how to start the engine.

And I remember years later when I called her condo in Florida because I hadn't heard from her in a while, and she said "I call you every week," and I said "No you don't," and she said "I leave a message at your dorm," and I said "I have a phone in my room," and she said "Is your math class getting any better," and I said "I'm not in boarding school anymore. I went to college this year."

And I remember the day, a year before she died, when I put down the phone after speaking with her, and that familiar tornado of sadness—a panic attack, really, that always started as a pinprick in my gut and swirled like a funnel cloud before traveling up my stomach and into my throat, where it swallowed my words until I hacked it out in heaving sobs—lost its power and I didn't cry for her anymore.

And I remember it was a hot June day in Bermuda when my younger brother Monty and I flew in from opposite ends of the Eastern Seaboard to join our older brother Robin and our stepfather by her bedside to say goodbye. I leaned over her bed, the only one of the assembled capable of being face-to-face with her at the end, and asked "Are you scared?" as three nurses scurried around her, one to pull out the breathing tube, one to administer the morphine, and one to shut off the machines. And I remember that she looked up at me with her bright green eyes, the only part of her body that hadn't fallen apart, and shook her head dismissively—as if I had just asked if she wanted a cup of tea.

And I remember the day, a few days after my mother stopped breathing, when my brothers and I were eating lunch with my stepfather overlooking a private beach at Castle Harbor. The sun was warm, and the salty sea breeze was blowing up the corner of my white linen napkin in a way that made me think it was waving at me. In the distance the whitecaps hit the top of the reefs and broke apart so that the low waves came in lazily and lapped up gently onto the pink beach. And I closed my eyes and smiled, and for a moment the anxiety and sadness of the past twenty-five years was gone.

But then the tornado swirled up again, stronger this time—and I turned to Robin and told him that I didn't feel well and was going to the bathroom. But his eyes met mine and he blurted out "What's wrong?" as the sides of his mouth dipped and he shifted in his seat. He looked like a little boy whose blanket had been snatched away. And Monty, who had been laughing the second before, stopped and looked at me, and then at Robin, and became quiet. So I swallowed hard, looked at my brothers reassuringly, and settled back into my seat, knowing that it wasn't my turn to cry yet. "I'm okay, just a little hot. Nothing's wrong," I said.

Part I

Chapter 1

I remember them laughing.

I was a four-year-old boy dressed in a pink halter top and miniskirt with pearls and heels, a cardboard "Gay Liberation" sign hanging around my neck. I wasn't sure what to make of the laughter. I was making people happy, but it seemed like their sharp cackles betrayed something other than joy. It was the first time that I had been the subject of adult laughter, and there was something sinister about it. The laughter spiked when I wiggled my hips as instructed, making it difficult to stay balanced on my mother's two-inch heels. My seven-year-old brother, Robin, wearing a dark suit, his hair combed down like a Wall Street banker's, walked beside me. My mother laughed the loudest.

It was the annual Labor Day skit at our Adirondack hunting and fishing club. More than a hundred people lined both sides of the enormous main room of the clubhouse to watch individual family camps perform cute skits using props like deer antlers and fishing rods. Puns like "there's something *fishy* going on" or "that was un*bear*able" accompanied lighthearted stories acted out by loving parents who swam after their kids in fake trout fins or chased them draped in grizzly pelts.

Earlier, at our family's camp, my mother had kneeled down to dress me, giggling like a naughty schoolgirl. My father rifled through his closet, trying to find a necktie that would fit my older brother.

"But I don't *want* to," I kept saying.

"Oh, hush," my mother said. "It will be fun."

I was bouncing up and down and twisting my body back and forth.

"Hold still, Kirkland," she said, her giggles elevating, "you're going to lose your—oh my God—you're going to lose your top! Bobby, you've got to come in here!"

"*There's* my pretty little boy," my father said as he walked into the bathroom.

"I'm not pretty!" I yelled.

"You look like a hooker," my father told me proudly.

"His boob's sticking out!" my mother cried.

"It's not *funny*!" I said, stamping my foot, yet at the same time cracking a tentative smile. I didn't know what "gay liberation" meant. But on some level I knew that I had been chosen over Robin to be "the girl." It felt like a warning, and a little bit of a punishment, and I sensed the injustice of being made a prop for my mother's amusement. But I delighted in how happy it made her.

MY MOTHER WAS BEAUTIFUL. Most people are understandably dubious of this claim, probably assuming that as a son, I see her how I want to see her. But she *was* beautiful, indisputably. People compared her to Grace Kelly and Candice Bergen, but it was the comparisons to Jackie Kennedy Onassis that she liked the best.

Even as her son, I was as in awe of her as the rest of the world seemed to be. I appreciated how the expression of her beauty changed with her moods, how her bright green eyes sparkled innocently when she was telling a funny story, or held somebody's gaze as she listened to them. She had fair skin and naturally blond, shoulder-length hair that fell in wisps in front of her eyes or from behind her ears in endless variations. Her smile was lit from a source deep inside of her, candid and genuine, so it was easy for me to tell when she was faking one. Her high cheekbones didn't lift, the smile looked more like a scowl, but it was the eyes that gave her away. I always knew how my mother felt by looking into her eyes.

My father was not lit from the inside. He would have been considered cosmetically good-looking, with dark curly hair and dimpled cheeks. He had the kind of aristocratic frame that was both athletic and sexless, like many men of his ilk, a blank canvas onto which was painted Nantucket-red pants, Gucci loafers, and nondescript button-down, short-sleeve shirts.

His side of the family was pure white-Anglo-Saxon-protestant, *Mayflower*-descendant, white-butler rich. The butler's name was Eugene, and in my memory he wore a tuxedo all day long, but it might have just been a suit. We had many portraits of bygone relatives hanging throughout our house—one of my great-grandfather looking like Teddy Roosevelt, reading studiously with pince nez hanging off his nose, and a second great-grandfather in a suit standing upright with a cane, both men humorless, and commanding. Perhaps the painting of my grandfather, showing him looking relaxed behind the helm of one of his three yachts, is telling of the family fortune that would be lost under his watch. My parents and one of his many girlfriends were usually the only guests included on my grandfather's yachting trips up the Maine coast every summer (he left my grandmother at home).

We lived in Cedarhurst, a quiet Long Island suburb, on a dead-end street lined with enormous maple and oak trees that created a protective canopy over the neighborhood. Three homes made up our family compound. The three-story, four-thousand-square-foot house we lived in had been a wedding present from my father's parents. On one side of us was my great-aunt Peg's house, a thirteen-thousand-square-foot mansion called "Lauderdale," that my great-grandfather Henry Hobart Porter had built in the late 1800s. On the other side lived Peg's son, Seton (named after another ancestor, Mother Seton), and his family. I asked my aunt once if my grandmother's middle name, Delano, indicated any relation to FDR. She scowled and said, "Grandfather never liked to talk about that cousin. He was a *Democrat*."

On the weekends, my grandfather would host us for dinner at the Long Island Rockaway Hunting Club that was just down the street from our house, where we would order steaks ("Pittsburgh rare"—meaning seared on both sides and raw in the middle) with insider names like Delmonico and Porterhouse. The adults would greet the club staff as if they were family. The club had a gaming room with multiple backgammon boards (you only played for money) surrounded by framed photos of the past club presidents, my grandfather and great-grandfather included. There were men's-only bars that smelled of cigars and scotch. The club logo was a fox surrounded by guns and golf clubs assembled together to look like the crest of some English earl's estate. The fox hunting part of the club had ceased long before I was born, but the name remained, ensuring that people knew we were the type of people who would dress in red, mount thoroughbred horses, and follow screeching hounds chasing a fox to its death if we still could. Breakfast at the club had only two items, runny eggs and crisp bacon. Being rich back then meant that you could have anything you wanted, but you limited choices to ensure that the new rich people who wanted omelet stations and bottomless mimosas would never even try to join. Whenever we drove to the clubhouse, we passed the rows and rows of grass tennis courts. Occasionally there would be two women who looked to be the same age as my mother playing on the court closest to the clubhouse, in their short white skirts and frilly underwear.

By the time my parents married, my father's family had secured a seemingly permanent foothold in society's upper echelons. They owned Park Avenue apartments and second homes right outside the city. They drank a lot. They often didn't have jobs and the ones they did have they didn't need. They cheated on their wives with the wives of their closest friends.

My father was the youngest of four (the next oldest was ten years his senior) and the only boy. His parents didn't think child care had anything to do with them, so the nannies and kitchen staff looked after him until he went to boarding school when he was seven. He saw his parents on school vacations, if they happened to be in the country, and was expected to dress for breakfast in jacket and tie when they were in town.

My grandfather went to Yale, served on the boards of Pan American Airways and the Metropolitan Life Insurance Company, and was the president of my great-grandfather's engineering company. My father wasn't a strong student, which is what one says about spoiled offspring who don't feel like they have to work at anything. He would not have been accepted to Yale even in the days when the progeny of graduates were almost guaranteed admission. So he was encouraged by his father to bypass higher education altogether. "Not to worry," my grandfather told him. "The only reason people go to college is to get a job, to make money. And *you* will never have to worry about money." Knowing my father as I do now, I imagine he was relieved to find that there was no expectation that he should live up to his father's success, and that he could instead skip straight to living the life that had already been earned for him. But first, he had to find the right partner.

My mother was from a working-class family in Bermuda, born to a stay-at-home English mother and a Scottish father who worked as a traveling hardware salesman. My mother rarely talked about her life before my father, but when she did I was left with the impression that she was concealing an undisclosed wound, deep enough to want to escape into my father's far more complicated world. I have a vague memory of once seeing my grandfather standing near his company van, the open double doors revealing an assortment of hanging tools, containers full of nails and screws, and various prepackaged boxes. I remember feeling loneliness on his behalf, thinking of him driving to new neighborhoods in his van, knocking on strangers' doors, trying to sell them products for which they hadn't asked. I equated what he did with some character in an old movie who was turned away time and again, each scene ending with a door shut in his face and a slow, dejected walk back to the van. Like a lot of the impressions I formed when I was younger, this one resembled nothing of his actual experience. I've since learned he knew his customers well. They requested not only the items he brought to them but his expertise in using them.

My mother had one sister, Gail, who was four years older. According to my mother, Gail was jealous of my mother's beauty, her popularity, and her relationship with their father— and their mother took Gail's side in disputes, at the expense of fairness, to balance out the deficit. My mother told us that her father was the only one who ever stood up for her, although I can't imagine she received more than the occasional stoic grunt that she interpreted as support.

My mother's younger brother, Derek, was absent from the early versions of my mother's narrative. My grandparents adopted him as a baby, but at seventeen years old he was kicked out of their house for unknown crimes and sent to England. When I first heard about Derek, I remember thinking his adopted status explained the seeming ease with which they erased him from their lives. When I was older, I began to question my mother more about him, needing to understand what he could have done that would justify total banishment. She refused to talk about it, saying only that she had loved him and felt protective of him when they were growing up, but she never wanted to see him again. Derek died in England in his forties, possibly of a drug overdose—my mother wasn't sure.

My mother met my father in the spring of 1963, when she was nineteen and he was twenty-three. He had brought five of his closest friends to stay at his parents' vacation home in Bermuda for a last hurrah before they all enlisted to fight in Vietnam. (Apparently my father had suggested to his friends that enlisting early would ensure that they would get in and out of the war before the worst of the fighting began; he wasn't the type of person to be moved by patriotism.)

My father asked a girl he knew to round up five of her friends, one of whom was my mother, and the group spent the entire week together—most likely at various social occasions held at the exclusive Mid Ocean Club in Tucker's Town, to which my father's family belonged. The club was right across from their house, "Happy Days," which overlooked Tucker's Town Bay. In the early sixties, the only way to access Tucker's Town was through a gate manned twenty-four hours a day, even though most of the development was on public land. When I was young, we would drive up and the gatekeeper would open the gate without knowing who we were or why we were there, presumably because we looked like we belonged.

My father told us that he and his friends were all captivated with my mother. Only he was able to return to the island to claim her after being rejected from the army for flat feet and a bad back. They were engaged within six months and married soon thereafter, a union welcomed by both sets of parents. My mother's beauty and exotic heritage and my father's pedigree checked everyone's boxes. A year after that, when my mother was twenty-one years old and my father was twenty-five, my mother gave birth to my older brother, Robin. I was born two and a half years later.

THE FIRST SIX YEARS OF MY LIFE followed the path predestined by the social stratum that I was born into. In my father's family, children were to be seen and not heard, and should any of us exhibit a malfunction, servants whisked us away to sort it out. My father was not interested in the intricacies of our emotional lives, in the same way that his parents had not been interested in his.

My mother was more conflicted. Not having come from my father's world, and having been so young when she entered it, she was simultaneously unfamiliar with the ways of the New York social elite and easily influenced by them. She integrated seamlessly with my father's friends, charming the women and captivating the men. My mother had a way of seeming vulnerable and impenetrable at the same time, a quality that made people feel protective of her. "There was something so innocent about your mother," a friend of my parents said later, "and yet you always had the feeling that there was so much more going on beneath the surface. It was a very appealing combination."

For the most part, the ease with which she acclimated to her new life, guided by the grounding that her old life provided, allowed her to be open and very much herself in a context where many others were trying to be something more. And yet there were times, most often around older women she admired or feared, when she changed in a way that she never did with men, no matter how powerful or intimidating. I was four years old when I met this formal version of my mother. She was sitting up straight on one of the floral armchairs in the living room we never used. When my older brother and I arrived at the door, escorted by our nanny, my mother opened her left arm theatrically and summoned us forward with a big fake smile and an exaggerated "Come here, darlings." My mother never called us "darling" when we were young, and her summons made me wary of the woman in the room. To my mother, I was always "Cuzzy wuzzy" or "Cuzzy iz" because I craved her affection and snuggled up next to her at every opportunity. Robin was "Robinski"—an ethnic version of his name meant to highlight how proudly ethnic we weren't.

"Kirkland, say hello to Mrs. Sippi," my mother commanded. (I would learn later that this was the real name of one of my father's parents' friends, and not one of the cutesy names that old-money matriarchs assume to conceal how terrifying they are.) Robin and I held out our hands to Mrs. Sippi, who looked us up and down and smiled, at which point my formal and strangely angry mommy issued a stern directive meant to ensure our hasty and orderly exit. I complied, not wanting to embarrass her in front of a woman who apparently had the power to change who my mother was.

ALTHOUGH HE HAD HELD VARIOUS ODD JOBS in his late teens and early twenties, and sold high-end yachts now and then, accompanying my grandfather on his many yachting trips up the Maine coast and to the family home in Bermuda was my father's primary job. (Though they were not close when he was young, in my family your value increased the closer you approached drinking age, peaking when you could imbibe freely and appreciate off-color humor.) My mother joined many of their outings, leaving us at home with nannies.

I didn't know the home we lived in was part of a family compound. I didn't know that not everyone had nannies or went to private clubs where grown men in uniforms treated you the way you were supposed to treat adults. I didn't know that my family split people into tiers, those who were catered to, those who did the catering, and the "no come-froms" who sat somewhere in the gray, vast middle. There were no black people, or people of any other color, in our world besides our nanny, Cathy, and the staff of the hunting club. The thing about growing up wealthy and white is that nobody puts it into context for you. Nobody tells you that the Jews your father keeps talking about have the same thoughts and feelings as other people; nobody mentions that there are black people who don't wear tuxedo jackets and fix you dinner. You're dropped into a reality that you need to make sense of on your own, among people whose love for you serves as a shroud over their distaste for people who are not like you, so that it's hard to see their distaste as wrong. If the rest of my life had turned out like the lives of many of my peers, I might never have strayed too far from this path. But it didn't. Eventually my evolving understanding of the world came into direct conflict with many of the values that I had been taught, spurring an internal awakening, a lifeboat launched from a ship that didn't know it was already sinking.

Chapter 2

On the day I was born, March 4, 1968, my father entered my mother's hospital room to see me for the first time, took one look, and said, "That cannot possibly be our son." I was a large baby—almost nine pounds, five pounds of which was cone head.

"I don't understand, Wendy. We are *very* good-looking people," my father said.

"He has a face only a mother could love," she replied.

I had red hair that popped out of the top of my enormous head like Bert's from *Sesame Street*. According to my mother, when I started crawling, I would balance my head on my shoulders as a circus performer might balance another circus performer while riding a unicycle. I started out with a big smile, but the slow and steady drifting of my head to the carpeted floor would stop my forward momentum. "Your little neck could only take so much," she told me once, "but you were a determined little guy. Your father and I used to watch your arms and legs slipping and sliding on the carpet, trying to budge your boulder head. God, we laughed."

When I was six months old, my parents grew concerned about the enormity of my head and consulted a pediatric neurosurgeon to see if there might be a problem. "His brain is growing too fast for his skull," the doctor warned. "If it doesn't stop, we may need to cut the top of his head open to create more room." Hearing this story retold, I was always surprised that this was the only solution, even in 1968, that my skull was the crust of a pot pie that needed venting. "We never had to go through with it," my mother said. "Not that we would have, even if your brain had kept growing. Your head was already freakishly big, for Christ's sake."

FROM THE MOMENT WE COULD WALK, my brother Robin and I were assigned household chores. I delivered the ice bucket for evening cocktails, a nightly pre-bedtime ritual that started when I was around three years old. The nanny filled the bucket and directed me to the bar on the other side of the house with a wave of the hand and a comrade-like bidding of good luck. Part of the fun for my parents was watching me from the study as I dragged it across the carpeted floor, stopping every few minutes to catch my breath and reestablish my grip.

"Mommy's thirsty, Cuzzy," my mother encouraged from the couch, "so put a nickel in it, sweetheart."

"And don't drop any," my father would add. "Nobody likes a fuzzy ice cube."

My father gave me a sip of his scotch when I reached the threshold of the study. I snuggled with my mother, and played "beep beep" on her breasts, before being handed off to the nanny. I cried as she carried me up the stairs.

I felt loved by my mother. While some other mothers parented like they were being evaluated, my mother expressed little awareness that anyone but my brothers and I existed when she was with us. She cried out loudly when we fell, as if she was the one who'd hit the ground. She held me close and whispered in my ear, the beating of her heart lulling me to sleep. My mother was safety, and occasionally danger, but she was always a base to come back to that felt like home.

Our nanny, Cathy, was the second love of my life. She was an obese Jamaican woman who never smiled unless she beamed, her face transforming from stern to euphoric in an instant, often in response to something I said or did. She ambled around the house talking to herself in perturbed whispers, smelling of what I thought of generically as "laundry." I don't remember a time before Cathy.

I thought Cathy was magic, not only because she looked exotic, with her jet-black skin offset by a light blue housedress, but also because she spoke as if she were conjuring up dark spells over a cauldron, even when she was saying something benign. "You don't want to be rollin' dose peas around on your plate, young man," she would warn. "The Lord created them for eatin'." Although she never explained the consequences of forsaking the Lord's pea plans, they sounded dire, potentially apocalyptic, so I complied. Adding to Cathy's allure was her ability to dislodge her teeth with a swipe of the tongue before excavating them from her mouth to chase us playfully around the house, dentures clacking behind us like a chatty skeleton.

I spent many nights pushing hard on my own teeth, wondering what special incantation would loosen them.

Cathy was superstitious, and warned my mother about evil spirits and haunted rooms. She didn't like my father, and thought Robin had the devil lodged inside of him. Both she and my mother were suspicious of Robin's impact on people— like he was a prince certain of the kingdom he would one day inherit—and often took my side in disputes, knowing that the world would favor him as we got older. Robin was the obvious suspect whenever there was something knocked over in the dining room or spilled in the kitchen, and a simple head tilt in his direction led to him being dragged off to his room as he shouted his innocence and vowed revenge. I pretended to be scared, and ran to my mother or Cathy for comfort as he was dragged away, pointing and crying, "Look! He's smiling! He did it!"

Robin and I were as chemically opposite as you can get in siblings. He was adorable—compact and symmetrical from every angle, olive-skinned and lithe. He was also a cranky, twitchy bastard—a foot-stomping, fist-pounding, red-faced, screaming little shit. I watched with awe as he would twirl himself into a frenzy, wondering where all the energy and anger came from. When he was three and I was six months old, he tried to drown me in my crib by pouring a bucket of water over my head. My mother said she found me laughing and splashing in the crib, with Robin glaring at me through the bars.

I followed him around, even though I just wanted him to stay still. Photos of me as a toddler show me in a medley of seated positions: swallowing the white pebbles from our roundabout driveway, covered in apple sauce and ketchup at the kitchen counter, or propped up against an inanimate object. By contrast, everyone around me appears in motion— my brother striking an action pose, projectile in hand; one of my parents in conversation with a relative or friend while sipping from plastic tumblers. It didn't matter how strategically I stationed myself among the people surrounding me. They all just kept moving.

Andrew, Robin's best friend, visited often. The two of them played in the pebbled driveway while I followed them around like a sullen Secret Service agent, which they tolerated much like sharks tolerate remoras. My mother told them to include me in everything they did, I suspect more to keep me occupied than to inspire brotherly bonding. Robin's anger escalated until his bottom teeth jutted upward over his upper lip like a bull-dog's when he didn't get his way. I could never summon such fury, but discovered over time that I could see into his future in ways that he couldn't.

One particular spring day, when I was five and Robin was seven, he chased me around the driveway until I ended up just inside the back door to our house, my hand resting lightly on the doorknob. The top of the door was covered in glass panes. He paused before running toward me, his eyes furious. He didn't register that I had stayed put, and I closed the door when he lifted his hands to grab my neck. I don't remember the expression on his face, or the sound of shattering glass. I didn't see both of his arms poking through the jagged panes or witness the moment when he pulled them back and the shards shredded his forearms. I only remember walking in the opposite direction as I listened to him shrieking, and then, later, seeing white towels covered in blood and my brother lying on the ground in the front hall as my mother frantically yelled at my father to call somebody. I remember that Robin stopped making noise at some point before he was taken away. Once he was gone, a huge red stain on my mother's cream-colored carpet was all that was left. I faced no repercussions. My parents may have assumed it was an accident; Robin may have looked at me more warily thereafter. I've never asked him about it. I would like to think that at this moment he began to appreciate that there were powerful forces in the world besides his anger, and that he needed to become aware of them.

MY YOUNGER BROTHER, MONTY, was born three and a half years after I was. For the first year he was just a disembodied cry from the other room that summoned my mother's attention and took it away from me. As he hit toddlerhood, I noticed that he was more adorable than Robin and more easygoing than I was. He had an infectious, joyous laugh. His existence displaced me as the youngest, and slotted me into the squishy role of middle child, pulling my parents' focus away, not to be replaced.

Monty worshipped me, and I loathed him. This dynamic was altered in some ways, and cemented in others, when we left Cedarhurst for upstate New York—the year I turned seven—and our family's dormant demons were rustled from their slumber.

Chapter 3

In the summer of 1975, my father relocated us to Clinton, a quaint college town in upstate New York. He didn't consult my mother about the move. As a young child, I perceived a vague anxiety that permeated our lives after the successive deaths of both of my father's parents, my grandmother's in 1973 followed by my grandfather's in 1974. They weren't a part of our daily lives, so their passing registered only in how it unsettled our parents, who increasingly talked behind closed doors in urgent and angry whispers. We had no way of knowing that my grandparents' deaths had revealed that the massive inheritance my father had planned on was mostly gone. My grandfather's lavish spending and poor financial decisions would require my father to now think of long-term financial sustainability in a way he'd never had to before. Our mother became sullen and withdrawn right before the move. Her mood didn't improve afterward.

My father purchased Sky Step Farm, a seventy-acre horse farm that boarded up to seventy horses. I never asked why he chose a horse farm, especially since he knew nothing about horses or farming, but my suspicion is that he felt he could adjust to the necessity of a downgraded lifestyle as long as it fit within the accepted parameters of his social station. Besides alpacas or some other more exotic animal, boarding horses fit the bill. Moving to Clinton also brought us closer to our Adirondack summer camp, now just an hour away, which ensured at least some proximity to a world which seemed to be moving out of our reach.

We took up residence in an old, white house at the top of a long driveway that overlooked the farm made up of three horse barns, a riding facility, and acres of grazing fields. Our new house was smaller than our Cedarhurst home, but not by much. Robin and I still shared a bedroom, while Monty had his own at the top of the stairs that separated our family room from the front foyer, which led to a more formal living and dining area, and a covered patio on the side of the house. My parents had a full wing to themselves, and there was one guest bedroom, also on the second floor. Most of the Cedarhurst furniture and artwork moved with us, so it didn't feel as though much had changed, aside from the lack of other mansions nearby, or private clubs, or neighbors of any kind.

Robin and I rode the bus back and forth to the local public school, took horse-riding lessons in the afternoons and on the weekends, and occasionally traveled to regional horse shows where we competed against other riders in our age group. I loved sitting beneath the enormous weeping willow tree in our front yard on windy afternoons. I enjoyed walking through the barns to visit each of the horses on weekend mornings, especially in the moments right after the stalls had been mucked out and the air smelled of fresh straw mixed with leather, saddle soap, and the dark-green, pungent aroma of horse feed. Over time, I learned the personalities of the animals. Some were skittish or aggressive, but the majority would poke their heads over the half door in anticipation when they heard my footsteps, hoping that I was carrying an apple, a carrot, or a sugar cube.

Cathy warned my mother that our new house was haunted. I remember her cowering at the bottom of the stairs, refusing to climb them until she had prayed to herself, and even then, she would pause on each step and look up, expecting something to appear. "There are bad spirits in this house," she would say, looking toward the second-floor landing. I would sometimes stand at the bottom of the steps and stare upward, thinking if I were quiet enough one of these spirits would appear. When one did, the second and last summer that my brothers and I lived in the house, it came in a different form than expected.

I was suited to life on the farm only in so much as it provided me with acres of land to roam around and dream of being somewhere else. That nagging feeling that I didn't belong hadn't abated with the move, and the threat of being asked to do some kind of manual labor in dirty places surrounded by hardened men and humorless women only exacerbated my sense of alienation. I wore my jeans high over my belly button to account for a husky frame. My hair had transformed from red to bright white and flopped daintily to one side, accentuated by a cowlick. I constantly ran my fingers through my hair, loving the softness of it. When I spoke, I tilted my head to the side coyly, and my hand would find its way to my hip.

Robin adjusted effortlessly to life on the farm. He worked hard in the stables, became an accomplished equestrian, and began winning multiple ribbons at every horse show he entered. Blue and red first- and second-place ribbons, and the multicolored, extra-long "best in show" ribbons, covered his side of the room, while my side was a sea of limpid yellow third-through green sixth-place awards. I wasn't in competition with him. I didn't feel the need to work that hard. He had already cornered the market on the responsible son.

MONTY WAS FOUR YEARS OLD when we moved to the farm, and as such, he still mostly lived a separate life from Robin and me. He didn't speak much, having suffered from an early hearing problem that wasn't diagnosed until he was three years old. It was difficult for him to pronounce words properly, especially words with an "r" in them. For breakfast, he liked "woo woos" (Froot Loops), and he called me "Cock," which would make my parents laugh. I didn't understand what was so funny. Of course, Monty delighted in pleasing our parents, and so called me "Cock" over and over again and laughed along with them. It felt as if an alliance had been formed, and I was on the outside of it.

Monty was largely kept from the barn, but for his fourth birthday present our parents bought him a miniature pony named Jigsaw. On the morning of his birthday, my father blindfolded Monty and led him down to the barn while the rest of us followed closely behind. As we approached, Jigsaw stood with his head resting on the stall door, looking like an oversized stuffed animal come to life. My mother, Robin, and I stood back as my father deposited Monty in front of Jigsaw's stall. Monty opened his eyes and squealed as his hand brushed Jigsaw's velvety nose.

"Look this way, Nin!" my mother yelled, lifting her camera. Jigsaw shook his head to dislodge the big, red bow that my father had tied around his neck. Monty turned at my mother's command, and she snapped a photo of the joy on his face as Jigsaw's fuzzy nose nuzzled Monty's cheek. She didn't have time to advance the film to catch the next scene: Jigsaw's lips receding to reveal a set of clownishly large teeth, and his ears pinning themselves back as he chomped down on my younger brother's shoulder. A second later Monty, shocked and in pain, turned toward his new toy, made a fist, and punched Jigsaw as hard as he could in the mouth, causing him to snort in surprise and scramble to the back of the stall. Monty, without saying a word, turned his back on the barn and marched home.

I watched him walk away, recognizing for the first time how fundamentally different my younger brother was from me. I would have yelped and run to my mother, then spent the next couple of days feeling hurt that the pony bit me. I would have given his stall a wide berth. In contrast, Monty would now walk by Jigsaw's stall confidently, as the small horse retreated to the back of it in fear of him.

MY MOTHER LOST THE SPARK that had placed her at the pinnacle of my parents' New York social set. My father told us many years later that upon being introduced to a few of the women who passed for high society in Clinton, my mother had alienated them by insulting each one to the others behind their backs. I'm guessing she would not have been surprised that they compared notes one day and realized that my mother didn't like any of them. I presume her contempt for their version of high society (drinks at the comparatively parochial country club, or dinner parties where discussions veered toward small-town gossip) made her societal exclusion an acceptable risk, and perhaps even the preferred outcome.

I didn't adjust to the move well either. I continued to excel academically, but I remember nothing from my two years at the Clinton public elementary school, or of the kids who went there with me. I don't remember if I had friends or was bullied, what I ate for lunch, or anything I was taught. I can only assume now that school was either extremely dull or incredibly traumatizing.

By our second year on the farm, my family had developed a routine. My father always left for the barn early, usually heading out the door before my brothers and I awoke, no matter what day it was. Sometimes we saw my mother in the mornings, but often it was only Cathy who was up and getting us ready for school. When we returned from school in the afternoon, my mother was sitting in front of the television watching soap operas, or "her stories," as she started to call them, using Cathy's word for them. At seven years old, I had begun to notice how my parents co-opted Cathy's language and mannerisms as a joke. Cathy laughed along with them, even when it felt more mocking than funny.

Something fundamental had changed in my mother since the move, but I had no frame of reference to understand what it was. She rarely smiled, and spent much more time in and around the house than she ever had before. She often carried a drink in her hand. She was more uninterested than angry, reserving her energy for biting comments aimed at my father when he returned from the barn. He ignored her taunts, which made her more sullen and unresponsive.

Most afternoons, I would end up down at the barn for lack of anything better to do. I wandered around, probably appearing to the farm's assistant manager, Mellisa, like the spoiled offspring surveying the master's domain. I have no other way to explain why she hated me. Perhaps on some level she resented my father for taking on a business he knew nothing about, and she took her anger out on me because she couldn't take it out on him. Or maybe she was just unhappy. Whatever the case, she would bark at me to fetch supplies, haul feed, or muck out the horses' stalls, making it clear that my presence wasn't welcome otherwise. She slapped me across the face one day because I wouldn't stop talking. I looked at her stunned, but didn't say anything or tell anybody.

MY PARENTS LEFT FOR A EUROPEAN VACATION our second summer in Clinton, the year I turned eight years old. Robin was ten, and Monty was just about to be five.

Ordinarily, Cathy would have taken care of us, but she had left abruptly earlier in the spring. I remember wondering why she would leave us when she seemed so sad about it. I thought that maybe we had done something to make her leave, or she had been taken away from us as punishment. My parents told us it was time for Cathy to go back to "her family."

In Cathy's absence, nineteen-year-old Lola had become our primary babysitter. She and her mother, Barb, came to the farm most afternoons to ride the horses they boarded there. Lola was tall, gregarious, and friendly, in contrast with her mother, who was barely five feet tall, quiet, and slight. My only interaction with Barb was the occasional shy smile as she led her horse through the barn. Robin dubbed Lola "Crisco," which became the way we greeted her every day no matter how much she pleaded for us to stop. Robin explained to me that Crisco was "fat in the can," which didn't shed any light for me on what made Lola so upset.

Lola must have been unavailable to watch us when they went on vacation, because instead, my parents brought in the fifteen-year-old son of their close New York City friends to stay with us. Jamie had fallen into a bad crowd at his home in Westchester, his parents explained to mine, and they thought it would do him some good to get out of the city for part of the summer. My brothers and I idolized Jamie from afar when we'd encountered him during summers at the club in the Adirondacks. He was the good-looking, tall, and exotic older brother of our summer friends. He had barely acknowledged our existence before.

Jamie walked in the door looking taller than I remembered, beaming from ear to ear as he shook my father's hand. I'd never seen him smile before. Whenever we saw him at the club, he looked grumpy and intense. I could tell right away that he was performing for my parents. My mother had likewise drilled this behavior into us from the moment we could talk: look adults in the eye, say "It's nice to meet you," and smile like you mean it.

"Hey guys!" he said, turning to Robin and me. "Are we going to have some fun this summer?"

"Yeah!" Robin said. Robin was a little like Jamie, in that he intuitively knew the benefits of performing enthusiastically for adults. I would have normally been more suspicious of the performance were it not for Jamie smiling at me and shaking my hand as if he was genuinely happy to meet me. When you're starving for something, you don't ask the person who's feeding you why they're doing it.

On our first night with Jamie, after Monty had been put to bed, he brought out some dice and a score pad and asked Robin and me if we wanted to play a golf game. He asked us what players we wanted to be, but I didn't know any, so he said I should be Jack Nicklaus, who, he explained, was the best golfer in the world. I was surprised he chose me, assuming he would want Robin to be Jack Nicklaus. After we rolled the dice, he looked at the pad that told us whether we had hit a good shot or not, because we had no idea. Every time I rolled, he got excited and said that he couldn't believe how good I was at the game. I kept getting "birdies." I never won anything, and I certainly didn't beat other boys at sports, which is what this game felt like. I couldn't believe that Jamie seemed to like me. He still wore the smile that he had used with my parents earlier, and I wondered if it might be real.

The second night that Jamie was with us, I turned from the top of the stairs to walk to my bedroom and saw Monty sitting in the bathtub in the bathroom at the end of the hall. The hallway was dark and quiet, and the bathroom lights were bright, so I could see Monty in the tub with Jamie kneeling beside him and hear the soft rippling of the water. As I walked toward them, Monty turned to me. His eyes were wide, and he looked a little confused, but when he saw that I was walking his way, relief washed over his face. He smiled at me in a way that I can only describe as hopeful. Jamie picked up a wet washcloth and started rubbing Monty's arm; I could see that his other arm was bright red.

"You're not clean until you're *squeaky* clean," Jamie said, digging into Monty's arm. Monty winced and stared straight at me, his mouth twitching while Jamie worked his four-year-old skin as though he were planing wood. He was looking into my eyes to see if having a bath was supposed to hurt, but I didn't know. I had never had a bath like that before. I wondered if squeaking his skin was something that Jamie was doing to make Monty laugh, though all I saw in his face was fear and pain. Jamie didn't look like he was trying to make anyone laugh.

"I can't believe you're squeaking Monty!" I said happily, and sat down beside him. I wanted Monty to be assured that what Jamie was doing was a fun game. But my chest ached with each upward motion of the washcloth and the slight squeak it made. "I wish I could squeak like that!" I said. Monty smiled at me. I knew that he would do anything for me to pay attention to him. I didn't like how easy it was for me to change how he felt.

After two days with us, Jamie was sullen and angry all of the time. We gathered together now only at meals, where he stomped around the kitchen muttering under his breath while throwing pre-prepared plates of food at us. Robin and I started spending more time down at the barn, until Mellisa figured out that without my father there she could order us around with impunity. I didn't like manual labor, Mellisa, or being told what to do, leaving me with few attractive options for how to spend my days. On day three, I left for the barn with Robin soon after breakfast and then snuck back into the house. I entered through the back door, relieved to hear both Jamie and Monty moving around upstairs. I knew that the creaky steps would provide plenty of warning for me to escape into the shadows if either of them descended, so I slouched low on the couch and watched the TV.

All in the Family was playing. It was one of my parents' favorite shows. I didn't like it, but I couldn't change the channel or Jamie would know I was there.

I heard Jamie walk into the upstairs hallway. He knocked on my younger brother's door, at the top of the stairs. "Monty, did you clean up your toys like I asked you to?" he said.

Edith is crying hysterically, sitting on her chair. "Edith, c'mon! Will you stop slobbering there?" Archie exclaims.

I heard Monty's muffled voice from behind his door. "Yes," he said tentatively. His voice was higher than usual, as if he was about to cry.

"It ain't your fault," Archie says, "it's the world, Edith." He's tapping her hand gently.

"What do you mean?" she asks.

"I mean that the world just ain't ready for you."

"Are you sure you're telling me the truth?" Jamie asked softly.

"Yes," Monty responded, his voice cracking.

There was a pause. I froze on the couch.

"You aren't lying to me, are you?" Jamie's voice was muffled, as if his head were leaning against the door. I heard him jiggling Monty's doorknob.

35

"I don't understand," Edith says.

"I just mean that you ain't never hurt nobody, never told a lie to nobody, and I know damn sure you ain't never stolen anything before," Archie replies.

"I'm not lying!" Monty cried. His voice was frantic. I didn't understand why he sounded so scared, and Jamie so serious. I never picked up my toys. Didn't Monty know just to shove them into the back of the closet like everyone else?

"Open the door," Jamie said evenly.

"Do you really think so?" Edith asks.

"Well, certainly!" Archie replies. "The only thing somebody can pin on you, which as far as I know ain't no crime, is being a dingbat."

"All you need to do is to tell me the truth, Monty," Jamie warned. "That's all."

"I am!" Monty pleaded. He started to make a strange sound, like our dog when it wanted to come inside.

"Open the door, Monty," Jamie said, a hint of warning in his voice. "I promise nothing is going to happen to you. It's okay. But you need to open the door, or I'm going to get angry."

"Oh, thank you, Archie!"

I heard the door opening slowly, and the sounds of Monty's muffled whimpering. Then I heard Jamie move more deeply into Monty's room. "You lied to me," he said.

"Nooo!" Monty cried, his voice receding as he backed up. "I didn't lie—please don't!"

I heard Jamie walk toward him, and the sound of the door creaking on its hinges. My mother had been asking my father to do something about the creaking for weeks, afraid that the sound would wake Monty up when she checked on him at night.

"I didn't mean it," Monty cried. "I'll pick them up now! Please don't!"

I heard a loud crack, like the sound of a baseball bat—crisp and clean and violent. There was an eerie silence, and then another new sound.

I knew all of Monty's cries: the whiny fake one, the one he used right before bed, the one for when he was angry, and the one when he got hurt, like the time his finger was slammed into the car door. The hurt cry started out the same as this one, with a four-second delay as his lungs filled with enough air to adequately express his pain. But that cry was still human. This new cry was of an alien pitch, louder and higher and without pretense, equal parts horror and pain. Jamie was introducing Monty to something new. He was introducing both of us.

The blows fell. *Crack! Crack! Crack!*

"Are you going to lie to me again?"

"Noooo!"

Crack! Crack! Crack!

"Are you going to LIE to me again?"

"Noooooo!"

I looked at a pair of birds in the tree outside of our picture window. One of them was hopping around the other, using its beak and wings to get the other bird to play. The annoyed bird moved its head back and forth as the playful one hopped from one side of the branch to the other. It reminded me of when Monty sat in front of the TV watching a cartoon and I stood behind his chair and flicked his ear. By the time he would turn to look for me, brushing at his ear, I was already on the other side of the chair, flicking his other ear. Four-year-olds were so easy to tease. He never picked up on the pattern—just kept turning to one side and then the other. "Cock, STOP!" he would eventually cry.

I slithered from the couch and tiptoed toward the kitchen. The steps of the stairs started creaking; Monty's whimpering grew fainter. I reached the refrigerator as Jamie walked into the living room. I angled my body so that it looked like I had come from the other side of the house.

"Did you just get here?" Jamie asked me.

"Yes," I said.

"What are you doing?"

"Nothing," I said.

"Are you hungry?" he asked.

"No," I said, "I was just going back down to the barn."

Later that night, Jamie asked Robin and me if we wanted to see something. He took us upstairs, where Monty was lying on his stomach in bed, sound asleep. Jamie switched on a flashlight and rolled down Monty's pajama bottoms to reveal a patchwork of blue and purple splotches. He laughed and said, "My God, do you see that?" Robin laughed nervously and said, "Whoa." "Wow," I said. I looked at Jamie's face, his smile lit up like he was telling a ghost story around a camp-fire. Robin's mouth was smiling, but his eyes were scared. I looked from one to the other, trying to figure out what my eyes and mouth should be doing. I felt something inside of me collapsing, and the reordering of what was now possible. I didn't know if what Jamie did was wrong simply because it felt that way. Kids sometimes got spanked when they lied or didn't clean up their rooms, didn't they? Surely our parents wouldn't have left us with somebody who would hurt us without a good reason?

The next day I was sitting under a large tack table in the main horse ring, leaning against the barn wall. My eyes were looking straight ahead as Jamie punched my shoulder over and over again with one knuckle. It didn't hurt, even though he kept hitting the same spot.

"You aren't going to tell anyone what you saw last night, are you?" he asked.

"No," I said.

"Are you?" he asked.

"No," I said.

I waited for something worse to happen. I hoped if I kept looking straight ahead and didn't move he might leave. He stopped hitting my arm and got up. *I'm so glad I'm not Monty*, I thought to myself.

It was morning, and my brothers and I were all still in our pajamas, when my parents returned from their trip. My mother ran straight to Monty, picked him up in her arms, and dropped into a brown armchair to hug him and rock him back and forth. I'd never seen my mother so excited. It was the longest she had ever been away from him, maybe any of us. "How is my baby?" she cried. "Oh, I missed you so much!" My father walked straight to Jamie and shook his hand. "How did it go, champ?" he asked.

Monty squirmed in my mother's arms, climbed up her body, and squeezed her neck. His pajama bottoms fell down a little so that I could see the top of his bruised backside. My skin grew cold. My mother kept saying how much she missed him as she held him tight, while he grasped more firmly onto her neck. She patted his fanny and he squirmed more, trying to escape her hand. She sensed something was wrong. "Why are you squirming so much?" she asked him, lifting him away from her neck and looking at his face. I saw his terrified expression. I backed up toward the open living room door. She scanned his body up and down and noticed the discoloration at the top of his backside. Frantically, she pulled his pajama bottoms down.

"What the . . . ?" Her face looked confused. "What the hell happened to you?!" She looked toward my father. "Bobby, come here! What the hell HAPPENED TO YOU?!" she screamed. I looked at Robin and moved back against the wall. Robin turned away from me. Jamie was on the other side of the room. My father walked over to the chair, saw Monty, and turned back toward Jamie. Monty was crying.

The rest happened in slow motion. My father shook as he asked Jamie what he had done. Jamie said that he was sorry, and started backing up toward the door.

"Get the hell out of my house!" my father screamed.

Jamie said "Yes, sir," and disappeared out the door.

I was with my mother in her dressing room a few nights after Jamie left, watching her clip on a lion-headed gold earring as she looked at herself in the mirror. I told her everything that had happened while Jamie was in our house, and how scared I was. I had expected her to look sad, but her face didn't change as I told her my story. I waited for her to turn and hug me. I waited for her to be as upset as she had been a few days before, but she looked straight ahead into the mirror with a steely expression. "I don't want to talk about it anymore," she said.

This was the first moment I understood that there were limits to what my mother could fix, or what anybody could. I also wondered if she was judging me as harshly as I was judging myself for not having stopped what was happening, or telling anyone. She was clearly angry, but her anger had disappeared inside of her to a place unavailable to me.

We didn't see Jamie again until he returned to our Adirondack Club for the first time after fifteen years—an absence that was never explained. Perhaps my parents told his parents that he couldn't come back while we were still children. Maybe he was embarrassed, or scared, and so stayed away. He told somebody that he wanted to see us, and that he would be waiting on the club diving platform one early morning should we want to see him. He smiled as we approached, the same smile that I remembered from fifteen years earlier. Robin and Monty smiled back and shook hands as if they were greeting an old friend. I held out my hand but didn't look at him. He seemed sheepish, perhaps remorseful, but then he tried to joke about our time together as if we were all just young and foolish kids. Robin and Monty laughed along with him. I kept my eyes down. Another ten years passed before the three of us talked about that summer for the first time. Monty was thirty years old. For twenty-five years I had assumed that we had shared the same experience, and that the memories were so painful and vivid that we couldn't talk about them. But when I recounted the bath, the spankings, and Jamie with the flashlight, neither Robin nor Monty remembered any of it, even though they knew something bad had happened. Monty started shaking and crying, and said he knew there was always something wrong with him. "Why didn't you stop him?" he pleaded.

"I don't remember it," Robin said.

"We were there, looking in the crib," I replied, dumbfounded.

"I had no idea," he said.

SIX MONTHS AFTER my parents ejected Jamie from the house, Robin and I were running around when they called us into the family room. My parents sat on the couch holding hands. I knew that something was wrong. Robin didn't seem to think anything was strange, and it took them a few minutes to get his attention. I couldn't stop looking at their hands.

"Your father and I are getting a divorce," my mother said. "We love you both very much."

I felt nothing, just a strange curiosity that they seemed more together than they had in years. Robin cried and ran out of the room.

"Are we staying here?" I asked.

"Your father is staying here," my mother said. "We're going to Bermuda. You like Bermuda, don't you?"

"I guess so," I said. My father looked so sad that I didn't want to say how excited I was to go. I didn't want him to know that I didn't care that we were leaving here, or leaving him. I felt loved when he called me by my nickname, "Cuzzy," the only word he said to me that landed softly in my ears. But I also knew that he loved Robin more. I was my mother's son. There was a whole world swirling behind her eyes that wasn't revealed by the words coming out of her mouth. I felt that way every day too.

The Jamie incident, combined with other factors that I only learned about many years later, woke up something in my mother. Looking back now, she must have known that her having checked out as a parent had contributed to what happened to Monty. But even though she couldn't admit her own guilt, she found no difficulty in admitting my father's. She felt he had cheated her out of her glamorous life in Cedarhurst, and perhaps, if that was all he had taken from her, she could have learned to be content as the wife of a horse farmer. But now that former life had come back in hideous form, revealing a toxic by-product of the carefree privilege that had made them all feel so superior and untouchable. Perhaps she thought that returning to the golf courses and pink sandy beaches of Bermuda would help her reclaim what had been lost.

Part II

Chapter 4

We landed in Bermuda on Valentine's Day, 1977, a month before my ninth birthday. My mother had planned our arrival well ahead of time, laying out the clothes that we would be wearing when we started school the following morning. I felt like I was in a dream, following a path of nonsensical events—a character dressed in winter clothes and trudging through two feet of snow one day, and an English schoolboy dressed in gray wool trousers, a white shirt, and a blue-and-red-striped tie on a remote Atlantic island the next. I had no idea where the dream would take me, so I surrendered to it, floating through those first few days in a trance.

We lived on a hill overlooking a road that led to the north shore of the island. An old cedar sign read "Savannah" as you turned into the driveway that we shared with the family who owned a compound of two houses at the back edge of our property. I imagine the name was influenced by the small plot of farming land that hugged our driveway, owned and harvested by one of the many Portuguese families who grew most of the island's fresh produce. Or perhaps by the citrus orchard bordering our driveway, hidden behind a row of casuarina and oleander trees.

Our house was furnished and came with a car—the remnants of a life abandoned by a middle-aged English couple who had sold their possessions to buy a boat and sail around the world. Like all houses on the island, ours was constructed from Bermuda stone—a mixture of limestone and concrete designed to withstand hurricane-force winds, since evacuation was not an option. The house was white, with light blue shutters, which my mother painted navy after we arrived, to match the palette favored by the Bermudian elite. The living room looked like an early seventies love den, with a deep orange shag carpet with flecks of black, bordered by a bright white wraparound couch that faced a glass-enclosed fireplace. From dead trees in the expansive backwoods that bordered our property my brothers and I collected old Bermuda cedar to feed the fire when the temperature dipped below sixty degrees, which it did for most of the winter. Each log looked like a sculpted piece of art, ghostly white and twisted into a dramatic shape, like the silhouette of a calcified corpse. It was the kind of wood that you displayed next to your fireplace for decoration. We couldn't afford not to burn it.

Although we lived in a nice house and went to a private all-boys school, I came to understand that my father paid cash for the house and covered our tuition, but financial responsibility for our basic necessities was an unresolved matter. We overheard our mother on the phone with her lawyer talking about our "trust funds," supposedly set up by my father's father when we were born. My mother believed that, as our primary guardian, she should have control over that money; my father held that it was his family's money to do with as he saw fit.

According to the scenarios that my mother weaved on the phone with her lawyer, my father's true intention was to drain our trust funds to maintain his own lifestyle. The family had taken a significant hit after the deaths of his parents and the subsequent failure of my great-grandfather's engineering company, the yearly stock dividend of which provided the lion's share of my father's income. Child-support checks arrived here and there, but only after my mother made a flurry of phone calls, angry ones to her lawyer and desperate ones to my father. She would start out defiant and finish defeated and crying, reduced to playing on pity and love for his children. On the calls that I could listen in on, my father's voice never changed. He sighed every now and then, the way an exasperated parent might when talking to an inconsolable child.

I was aware that my mother wanted us to hear what was going on, so I took every opportunity to listen, and determined that my father either didn't seem concerned about how we were living or didn't believe what she was telling him. Robin stormed off to our shared bedroom so he couldn't hear anything. I believed everything my mother said was true, and I never understood why Robin didn't want to hear firsthand what was going on so he could align his loyalties accordingly.

We frequented a local grocery store run by two Portuguese brothers and their wives. I would move to the back of the store when it was time to check out, and look at the wide array of cereals that we couldn't afford, while my mother asked our bill to be placed on credit. I didn't like the way my mother looked down at her purse when she asked, or the slight hesitation in the voice of one of the wives before she said "of course," so I dreamed of the day when we could choose the Lucky Charms or Trix over the "family-sized" boxes of Corn Flakes and Rice Krispies. There were times when my mother made a point of holding me or one of my brothers close to her when she checked out, and instead of looking at her purse, her bright green eyes held the storekeeper's wife's gaze, until the cashier looked down, smiled at one of us sadly, and asked my mother to pay when she could.

Milk and water were the most precious commodities in our household. My mother bought a half gallon of reconstituted milk each week (it was cheaper than real milk, given the paucity of available land for grazing cows in Bermuda), and she allowed us to pour just enough to wet our Corn Flakes at breakfast every morning. Under no circumstances would she permit us an actual glass of milk during the day; just powdered Kool-Aid or frozen orange juice, as long as they both lasted. We picked fresh grapefruits and oranges when in season. We always had a bunch of bananas hanging from a wire in the garage, which my mother or older brother had cut down by machete from one of our ten banana bushes. As the bananas yellowed and then browned, my mother turned them into endless loaves of banana bread that she stored in the garage deep freezer and pulled out for breakfast when the milk for our cereal ran out.

We caught drinking and bathing water on the roof and stored it in an underground tank. We turned off the water while we soaped up or shampooed. We wet the toothpaste on the brush, and only turned the water on again to rinse. My mother grew visibly upset when she lifted the heavy metal lid of our tank and heard the echo of her voice reverberate through an empty chamber. Extended periods of cloudless skies were mixed blessings for Bermudians—particularly those of us who couldn't afford to buy water when it ran out. Even now, the sound of rain on a roof relaxes me.

As spring approached that year, our school uniforms switched from gray wool to khaki shorts and short-sleeved shirts, necessitating a trip to a school-sponsored thrift store set up in the basement of one of the school buildings. Three women volunteers, mothers of other students, smiled sweetly as we browsed, before one of them asked my mother if we needed any help. "We are fine, thank you," my mother replied tersely, which elicited the same sad smile I had seen from the woman at the grocery store. My mother grabbed shorts that she thought would fit and demanded that we try them on behind a makeshift curtain at the back of the room. She paid, and ushered us out the door as quickly as possible, muttering venomous insults as we got back into the car. "God, her dress was hideous," she said. "Who put the rat nest on that lady's head?" I didn't answer, not understanding why she hated ladies who were nice to her.

WHEN WE FIRST MOVED, Robin and I shared a bedroom at the end of a long and narrow faux-marble hallway on one end of the house. Monty's room was on the left down the same hallway. The previous owners had left us matching sets of polyester drapes, bedspreads, sheets, and towels, decorated with large red roses on bright white backdrops. It felt like the décor was trying too hard to be joyful, as if it had been chosen to cover up sorrow and regret. My mother couldn't afford to redecorate, so we lived with the roses for years, until mildew started dulling the white with green and black streaks. We got rid of them just as they started to feel comforting.

In spite of our straitened circumstances, Bermuda felt gentle compared to upstate New York. People smiled and greeted one another on the street instead of lowering their eyes and speeding up. The air was welcoming. The soft breeze blowing off the ocean tousled your hair. The sea—which was never far, no matter where you were—smelled of fresh fish and sand filtered through cedar trees. There was color everywhere, from the hundreds of shades of blue in the ocean—dark navy on the horizon to a translucent aqua as the sea hit the shoreline—to the houses that peppered the landscape in pink, blue, white, green, and orange pastels.

We had an obstructed, distant view of the ocean from our living room window, which reminded me of sailing on my grandfather's yacht when my parents were still together. We lived among people of more modest means now, in a neighborhood where you could see flames rising from the local Piggly Wiggly as it was set ablaze during the racially tinged riots of 1977 that started just a few months after we arrived. We listened to the crackle of exploding canned goods mixed with the angry shouts of young men. It seemed to come closer and then retreat again, as if somebody were fiddling with a tuner. I looked to my mother, unfazed in her brown armchair, sewing a button onto one of Monty's school shirts.

"Do you think they're coming this way?" I asked. I had seen enough movies about the French Revolution to know what angry mobs could do.

"No," she answered decisively, without looking up. She seemed bored by the question, as if the shirt she was fixing was more worthy of my curiosity. I relaxed, assuming that she knew the rhythms and habits of Bermudian mobs better than I did. It's easy now to imagine how terrified she must have been, and how good she was at hiding it from us. I assume it went into the same secret compartment where she stored most of her fears.

I was old enough to understand that there were racial tensions in the world, and that those tensions were based in inequality, but young enough to believe that those conflicts had nothing to do with me. My mother talked about the rioters as if they were born criminals, and the only remedy was to round them up and put them away. I could identify with anger sparked by unfairness, and the hopelessness that came from feeling like there would never be any justice to quench it. What if Cathy wasn't as easygoing as she appeared? What if the people who waited on us at our club in Cedarhurst had ambitions beyond what I could see? What if my father made jokes about blacks, Polacks, gays, and Jews because he was afraid of them, or because it was only in belittling them that he could justify why we deserved more? At the same time it was terrifying to understand that I was part of the group on the receiving end of the rioters' anger. These questions didn't seem to trouble my mother. I didn't know it at the time, but she was focused solely on elevating herself and us beyond our current means.

This new world took its psychic toll on each of us. When it was warm outside, we left the windows and curtains open, and I spent the first hour after we turned out the light trying to determine whether I was hearing the breeze through the trees or the rustling of an angry black man outside my window. Robin was more concerned about people *not* being able to get into our room to save us, and spent the five minutes before bed each night turning the bedroom doorknob to release the door lock. (He was afraid that we would burn to death if firemen couldn't open the door during an all-consuming blaze.) No matter how many times I pointed out that it only took one turn of the knob to release the lock, he continued—*click, click, click*—pushing in the button and releasing it as if in a trance. More often than not he rose from bed a second time to make sure that the knob hadn't magically relocked itself. All that soothed us was the sound of the television in the distance, evidence that my mother was still awake and keeping watch. Years later I realized she might have been staying awake because nobody was keeping watch for her.

The Bermuda nighttime introduced us to a soundtrack of whistling frogs, screeching cicadas, and the omnipresence of terrifying new creatures that only came out at night. Enormous brown banana spiders, at least three inches in diameter, hovering on the ceiling or crawling between creases in the drapes, greeted us at bedtime. I refused to turn out the light until we had hunted down and killed them. More insidious were the two-inch cockroaches that appeared on walls or in bathroom sinks and flew haphazardly around the room, bumping into light fixtures, bedposts, and bodies. They too needed to be crushed and flushed before lights-out.

* * *

OUR NEW ENGLISH PRIVATE SCHOOL was as foreign to my brothers and me as the rest of our new life on the island. On my first day, I met my new principal, Miss Hawkins. Uninterested in any display of nonsense or warmth, she greeted me with a clipped "Well, hello there, young man; let's get you to class, shall we?" I entered the fourth form, the English equivalent of second grade, and was fortunate to have Miss Jones as my teacher, the only English adult I had encountered up until that point who smiled more than she scowled.

Much was made of appearances at my new school. A student's hair was never allowed to grow below the collar, and every week or so a teacher lined us up at the doorway to morning assembly to make sure that our fingernails were clean and cut to the proper length. There was no way to be a nine-year-old boy and not have dirty nails, so as we lined up you saw a twitch of boys chewing and scraping at their nails to get them clean enough to avoid detention. The first time I went through the line, my nails were filthy, and my anxiety grew as I approached Mr. Harris, the seventh-form teacher doing the inspection. I could see him berating certain boys ahead of me and issuing detentions, punctuated by the occasional swat to the side of the head.

When I got to the front, Mr. Harris's gaze traveled up from my trembling hands to meet my eyes. His initial look of disgust turned first to confusion and then a form of resignation as he jerked his head for me to move along. I noticed over time that he gave preference to the better-looking boys. Although never a standout in that department, I was growing into my looks as I got taller and thinner. When I joined his class, a few years later, he would stand behind several of us during work assignments and rub up and down the sides of our bodies while whispering encouragement in our ears. I knew what he was doing was odd, and yet it felt good. He singled out one boy in my class for special attention, moving his hand from the side of the boy's body to his backside, digging into his pants while nestling his nose into his neck. We never talked to one another about it.

I didn't have many friends before moving to Bermuda, and didn't make many after I arrived. Bermudians talked quickly, laughed easily, and had a shorthand with each other to which I never adapted. The formality of the English expat students felt just as alienating. I ended up gravitating toward the smarter kids in my class, though they weren't the kind of friends I hung around with outside of school. The only place I felt like myself was at home with my mother.

We moved to Bermuda to be closer to my mother's parents but spent little time with them except for church on Sundays, where I assume my mother and grandmother prayed condescendingly for each other, before we went to my grandparents' house for lunch. Robin and my grandfather spent their time before we ate chipping away at a small opening in the backyard that my grandfather said could be the entrance of a massive subterranean cave, while my mother, Monty, and I drank a sour concoction my grandmother made from lemon oil, and ate McVitie's digestives imported from England. After lunch, my mother left to run errands, and the three of us played Yahtzee with my grandmother on her carpeted living room floor with the blinds closed, even if the sun was shining and it was cool outside. I don't know if the perpetual darkness of her childhood home was why my mother didn't like to be there, but her mood would deteriorate throughout lunch, and she was always antsy to leave. My grandmother was noticeably hurt when she hurried out the door, but stopped trying to get her to stay after the first few Sundays, perhaps having learned far earlier than we did that my mother's stubbornness solidified in direct proportion to being asked to do something she didn't want to. I never figured out what my grandmother was doing to upset my mother so much, having not yet understood that the damage might have been done long ago.

ONE SUNDAY AFTERNOON during our first late-spring weekend on the island, we loaded up the car with towels, bathing suits, and pool gear and headed to the Castle Harbor Hotel to have lunch and swim in the pool. Eating lunch out was one of the few luxuries my mother insisted on maintaining, even when we didn't have money for anything else.

To use the pool at Castle Harbor, one had either to be a member (which we weren't) or accompany somebody who was (which we never did). Although my father's family had once been primary investors in the hotel, our interest had dwindled over the years to the point that we had long ago become minority shareholders, the kind who received fifty-dollar dividends in the mail every quarter.

When my mother pulled up to the roundabout at the entrance of the hotel, we assumed she was going to drop us off and return to the parking lot a hundred feet back down the hotel road. Instead, she pulled into one of the two temporary spaces reserved for taxis and VIP guests and turned off the engine.

"What are you doing?" Robin asked.

"Grab your stuff, boys," my mother said.

"You can't park here," Robin said.

"Kirkland, hold your brother's hand." My mother got out of the car and lowered her sunglasses onto her nose. I grabbed Monty's hand.

"You're not allowed to park here!" Robin yelled.

"Of course we are," my mother replied.

A look of panic crossed Robin's face. He turned to me as I opened the back door, pulling Monty along behind me. "What do we do?!" he asked frantically.

I shrugged, unconcerned. Since moving to Bermuda, my mother had unleashed a part of her personality that I hadn't seen before, and I liked it. Without my father around, she had transformed from somebody who muttered under her breath and looked unhappy all the time into somebody who expressed herself without reservation. I felt safe with this new version of my mother, and excited by what she might do next. In contrast, Robin now chewed on his top lip in a state of constant anxiety, perpetually on the lookout for ways in which she wasn't sub-scribing to parental norms. Every time she went off-script, he felt compelled to rein her back in.

The doorman at the front of the hotel walked up to my mother as she placed a floppy cotton hat on her head, the one she had once worn while sipping Bloody Marys on the bow of my grandfather's yacht. She had on a purple one-piece bathing suit with a flared tennis skirt. Her toenails, polished in a pink that matched her fingernails, stuck out of the flip-flops she'd worn almost everywhere since we'd been on the island. Robin lowered his head and covered his eyes as the man approached.

"Good day, ma'am," he said in a polite English accent. He was tall and thin and wore white safari garb. He tipped his hat to my mother.

"Good day," my mother said cordially.

"I'm terribly sorry, ma'am, but you will not be able to leave your car here," he said.

"And why not?" she asked, rifling through her bag. She didn't meet his gaze.

"These are private spaces, ma'am."

"I'm well aware of that," my mother said, lifting her eyes to look at him directly while applying the lipstick she had found in her bag. She moved around the doorman and walked toward the entrance. "Come on boys, let's go."

Robin had wandered off and was pretending to look up and down the cliff wall that bordered the hotel. I pulled Monty forward, following my mother.

"I am happy to assist in moving your car if you would prefer," the doorman called after us, his voice wavering.

My mother paused and looked back. "I do not *prefer* anything but to leave my car exactly where it is." She turned her body toward his, leveling her eyes and sighing as if annoyed that she had to spend any time explaining herself. "Do you have any idea who I am?" she asked.

The doorman's face dropped, his body tensed, and his eyes widened like those of a child who had been caught stealing.

Robin's head whipped around toward my mother, his expression furious. "My children happen to *own* this hotel," she said, turning back toward the entrance, "and my car will be staying *exactly* where I put it."

The doorman stood in place.

"Put a nickel in it, boys; I don't have all day," she called to us as she sashayed through the glass doors and disappeared into the hotel.

Later, as we sat by the pool, Robin confronted my mother, demanding to know why she had said we owned the hotel.

"Because you do," my mother said simply.

"We do not!" my brother yelled back.

"*Well*," my mother said, exasperated, "you *might* have, if your father hadn't been so stupid."

"It's not the same!"

"Oh, calm yourself," she said. "I don't know why you get so worked up." She shooed him away, leaned back in her chair, and put on her sunglasses. "Kirkland, do your mother a favor and tell that nice bartender over there to make me a Planter's Punch." She let out a long, contented sigh. "Tell him to put it on my tab."

MY FATHER CALLED US EVERY WEEK. I knew it was him when my mother's phone greeting changed from her usual singsongy "Helloooo" to a deadpan "Oh . . . hi," followed by the sound of the receiver being dropped onto the glass table in the hallway. She would then yell, "Your father's on the phone!" to nobody in particular, while moving away as if to avoid contagion. Robin usually ran to the phone. When it was my turn to talk to him, I made sure to sound as uninterested as possible while answering his questions, aware that my mother was lingering out of sight nearby, listening. It made her sad when he called. She would ask me what we talked about, looking for clues about his life, even though the smallest details that we passed on only made her sadder.

On Christmas Day, ten months after we had left New York, my brothers and I were in the living room, surrounded by ripped paper, dismantled boxes, and opened gifts. They were mostly clothes, plus one extravagant gift for each of us that my mother splurged on, something I knew she couldn't afford. She had asked each of us what we wanted a few months before Christmas, and I told her I didn't want anything. A new sweater represented a half gallon of milk we wouldn't be able to buy. A pair of pants was the fingernail that my mother would chew down to the nub. The stereo system my brother received that year meant several nights in a row of my mother staring into the distance, drinking her glass of scotch, while we tiptoed around her and went to bed without saying good night.

When the phone rang that morning, my mother picked it up in the hallway, her clipped "Hi" triggering Robin to stand up to wish my father a merry Christmas. But instead of tossing the receiver down, she asked Robin to hang it up after she had picked up the line in her bedroom. We knew a closed-door conversation meant that my mother would emerge altered, either by anger or by sorrow. Most of her private conversations with my father revolved around the mysterious trust funds, and usually ended with my mother storming out of the bedroom or with the sound of her muffled weeping into her pillow. This time, there was an eerie silence when my mother opened her door and summoned us to her room.

"Talk to your father," she said quietly. Instead of leaving, as she usually did, she moved down the bed so we could sit next to her. I got on the phone first.

"Hi," I said.

"Merry Christmas, Cuzzy," he replied. "Did you get the stuffed animal I sent you?"

"Yup," I said. "Thank you." He had sent me the small, fuzzy gray elephant that I had asked for. I didn't want a stuffed animal. I didn't want anything, but I wanted him to feel like he was giving me what I wanted.

"I've got some exciting news for you," he continued. "I got *married* last week." He emphasized the word "married" as if he wasn't sure I knew what it meant.

I looked to my mother with eyes that must have communicated that I really *didn't* understand what he was saying. Was it legal to get married again so quickly? My mother smiled slyly, lowering her chin and looking up at me with an expression that said, *Can you believe that?*

"You did what?" I said.

"I got married! To Barb, from the farm—do you remember her?"

I did. She was the short, quiet mother of our babysitter Lola. Now my father had married her, which didn't make any sense, unless I misunderstood the reasons that people got married. It was too soon. Didn't you need to know somebody for a long time? And wouldn't you marry somebody who was somewhat like the person you had married before? Barb looked a lot older than my father; she was short and sporty rather than glamorous, and showed little interest in being noticed, unlike my mother, who commanded attention wherever she went. I handed the phone to Robin. Robin listened to my father's news, looking surprised at first. But then he smiled and offered his enthusiastic congratulations, aware that my mother was watching him.

"I can't believe he's married!" I said to my mother afterward. Unlike Robin, I wasn't going to be sure how I felt about the whole thing until I saw her reaction.

She turned her head, looked out the window, and chuckled. Then she sighed, her enigmatic smile lingering.

"I wonder what that daughter thinks about the whole thing," she said eventually. "What I wouldn't give to be a fly on the wall for that conversation."

At the end of the following June, Robin and I left Bermuda to spend the summer with my father and his new wife at Rough House, the name of our family camp (a compound of rustic buildings and individual sleeping quarters) that sat on the fifty-three-thousand-acre preserve of a private hunting and fishing club in the Adirondack Mountains. Monty stayed in Bermuda, I'm assuming because my mother didn't trust my father to keep him safe after what had happened the last time she left him.

It was the second time Robin and I had seen my father and Barb since they announced their marriage, the first being when we visited them in Clinton during our spring break a few months earlier. I spent that entire two-week vacation in bed, writhing in pain from a stomachache. When the pain didn't subside after a few days, and with no other symptoms to suggest anything was wrong with me, I was left to wrestle my demons alone. My father and Barb seemed to take my condition personally.

Returning to the Adirondacks after our first year in Bermuda felt like coming back home from an exotic exile. Summer nights in the woods offered a different symphony of sounds from Bermuda, especially when the wind blew through the canopy of trees that surrounded our camp. Almost all camps had electricity, connected by a series of wires that slapped against the outsides of the cabins. Buoys moored two Sunfish sailboats, and as the waves got bigger, you could hear the metal clasps banging against their bows. Tree limbs knocked against the roof and sides of our sleeping quarters, each species creating its own signature sound—the heavy oak branches banging as if they were demanding entry and the softer fir trees brushing and sliding as if they were trying to sneak in.

By the beginning of that summer, my stomachaches had gone away, though they had lingered in some form or another for a month after we returned to Bermuda from spring break. Once a doctor determined that there was nothing wrong with me physically, my mother seemed to take them as personally as my father and stepmother. "Mind over matter," she told me, on a day when I was doubled over and moaning in the back seat of our car.

Robin and I didn't know what to expect that first summer. I remembered Barb as sweet and quiet at the farm, but I was old enough to understand that there were often two versions of adults, one that could be known from afar and another visible only up close. I felt confident that Robin and I could team up to combat anybody who exerted too much influence over my father. He had grown up with few boundaries, and I expected he would back our claim to the same freedom.

Fortunately, Barb showed no interest in parenting us. She moved around the camp like a shadow, watering plants and tending to her two new Cavalier King Charles spaniels while Robin and I ran in and out of the house to change or grab something from the refrigerator. She smiled as we moved past and around her, and turned away to let us know she didn't need us to smile back. She passed along information to my father about where we were going, responding to us with benign phrases such as "That sounds like fun" instead of ever suggesting that we take an extra sweater or return earlier than we had planned. She was neutral without seeming uncaring, the only balance that would have worked given my hair-trigger intent to defend any incursion on my mother's territory. It never occurred to me that she might be as wary of us as we were of her.

One rainy day a month into the summer, I was playing an Olivia Newton-John record on my father's old turntable, performing "Have You Never Been Mellow" in front of the living room mirror. I engaged in this type of performance often when I was alone, certain that one day I would be performing in front of huge audiences. There was nobody else home, allowing me to articulate a full musical vision from beginning to end. In those days there were no music videos, just prerecorded performances shown on various variety shows, and even though I had seen Olivia perform multiple times, I never felt she expressed the range of emotion that the lyrics demanded. I placed the needle on the record and stood back with my head down and my eyes closed, hands by my side. As the song began, I lifted my head and started singing in a whisper, letting the tinkling piano keys of the opening lift my eyelids as if being gradually pulled out of a trance. My voice gained power with each note. I waited for the lyric "I was like *you*" before opening my eyes fully and staring into the imaginary camera in front of me, feeling the emotional impact of my connection with the audience. My arms rose up from my sides, reaching for my public, imploring them to find comfort inside themselves. I had placed a decorative squash just to my left so that, as my right arm swept in front of my body, I could grab it like a microphone and pull it toward me, gripping it with the passion that Olivia never seemed to access and lowering my head again to prepare for the next verse.

As I waited for the second verse to begin, I kept two hands on the squash and opened my stance to ground myself. I wanted to show my audience that they didn't have to carry the weight of the world, that they could let somebody else be strong. I looked to the left and tilted my head as the opening chords of the second verse started with the soft tinkling of piano keys. As the words "Running around as you do" left my lips and my eyes opened, I saw Barb standing in the doorway, paralyzed, looking like one of the deer that we regularly passed on the club roads at night.

"You have a beautiful voice, Kirkland," she said.

I was sure that I sounded just like Olivia, so I wasn't surprised at her reaction, even as a bolt of humiliation ran up my spine and flooded my face. "Thank you," I said.

Barb placed the handful of ferns that she was holding on the entry table and walked toward her bedroom. "I have some pictures of you and your brothers that your dad just developed. Do you want to see them?" she asked.

"Sure," I said, dropping my gourd. The spell I had cast over my imaginary audience had been broken, and Barb and I had stumbled into a state of intimacy before we had even had a full conversation. I followed her down the long hallway that separated the master bedroom from the rest of the camp. She grabbed a stack of photos from the bedside table, handed them to me, and moved to my side so we could look at them together.

The first few pictures were staged shots of my brother and me in the living room, swimming in the lake, and at the club picnic the weekend before. A few pictures into the stack, there was one of me alone. I was smiling into the camera with my hip jutting out and my pants hiked up. My alligator shirt was tucked in tightly. I immediately noticed the conspicuous outline of my package camel-toed to one side of my pants and placed my thumb over it.

"I can't believe how white my hair is! I look like a freak!" I said. I pushed hard on the print, subconsciously attempting to flatten the front of my pants and pull focus toward my other conspicuous physical trait, hoping she'd hand me the next photo.

"I think you're a very handsome young man," she said, placing her hand gently over mine and moving my thumb off of the print. She smiled at me. "You should be proud of that."

I wasn't. I didn't want to be a girl, but I knew I wasn't performing "boy" correctly. My two brothers roamed the earth figuratively lifting their legs on everything around them and trotting off in new directions without feeling the slightest sense of shame. They screamed when they were angry or hurt, laughed when something funny happened, and tapped, slapped, and egged each other on in pursuit of the most inane ends. In contrast, I placed events in an internal queue to be sorted, analyzed, and processed before reacting. I knew that my mother loved me, but she often made me feel like there was something about me that needed fixing. In that moment, Barb made me feel like I might be okay just the way I was.

BARB PROVED HERSELF SIMILARLY ADROIT in dealing with the rest of my father's family, a feat my mother never accomplished. My father had two living sisters, Nancy and Joan, who came to visit the last two weeks of that first summer. Robin and I hadn't seen either of them in a while. My mother thought my aunt Nancy was a flake and my aunt Joan an adulterous slut. The only sibling of my father's my mother liked was their oldest sister, Kit, who had died of breast cancer not long after both of my grandparents. "God takes the good ones young," my mother said about Kit, "so those other two will outlive us all."

Joan and her husband Bob visited first, in mid-August. Joan was the more conventional of the two living sisters, having settled into a life of waking up to views of the ninth hole of one exclusive golf course or another, lunching at the club on beef-tongue sandwiches, and mixing up the first cocktail at noon—what my uncle Bob called his "noon balloon." She and Bob had determined a secret code should either of them end up in the hospital unable to communicate with the other; one blink meant "Get me gin," and two blinks "Kill me." Uncle Bob wore the same outfit every day, a white Lacoste golf shirt, yellow Bermuda shorts, and loafers with no socks. Aunt Joan wore polyester white shorts and a printed top. Her hair was white/gray and always the same shape, sitting atop her head like a centurion helmet. Joan never moved fast enough for him. Throughout the day he consistently summoned her with the phrase "Goddammit Joan," which she ignored. He was a small man, and spooked easily, like a cat, as if he wasn't expecting to see you even when you were standing right in front of him. It made his gruff persona more comic than intimidating. He was the least likable of all of my relatives, yet somehow one of the most endearing.

When my parents were first together, Joan was still married to her first husband, Monty. My mother loved him for his gruff, masculine energy that she compared to her father's. By contrast, my mother called Joan a "walking mattress" in front of us, well before we understood what she was implying. Joan had had numerous suitors before she married Monty, and then apparently one or two afterward, the last being my new uncle Bob, which led to her divorce. Instead of distancing herself from my uncle Monty along with the rest of the family after Joan's divorce, my mother named my younger brother after him. My mother had a zero-tolerance policy on infidelity, and no doubt she was aware that her living memorial to my aunt's first husband would also be a walking reminder of Joan's perceived low moral character. "You didn't know him,

Wendy," Joan would say to my mother. "He was an abusive drunk." My mother dismissed these characterizations, and though she never said it out loud, I'm guessing she held firm to a belief that if my uncle Monty had been abusive toward my aunt, she had probably brought it upon herself.

Bob was a renowned Hearts player, and taught Robin and me how to play one rainy afternoon. When Robin unexpectedly took a heart when Uncle Bob was trying to shoot the moon, Bob glared at him with his blue eyes and hissed, "That's not how you play the game!"

"If you got all the hearts you would win though, right?" Robin replied.

"Goddammit!" he yelled, throwing his remaining cards on the table.

"We're supposed to stop you when you're hunting the moon, aren't we?" I asked.

"Shooting. It's *shooting* the goddam moon," he said.

"Sorry," I said.

"Jesus *Christ*."

I lifted my cards up to my face and tried not to laugh.

"You passed me your . . . and you had the *jack*?" he said, glaring at Robin.

"I guess," Robin said, shrugging his shoulders.

"This is . . . I can't . . . ," he said, shaking his head and getting up from the table.

"Sorry, Uncle Bob!" Robin yelled. We heard the heavy door of the ice maker open and the angry sound of ice being thrown into a glass.

"I think you popped his noon balloon," I said to Robin.

Many years later, when my brothers and I hit drinking age, Uncle Bob started hosting a lavish annual lunchtime celebration for all family and friends in camp at the time. The camp slept up to eighteen people, so there were years when we took up an entire section of whatever upstate New York saloon we ended up patronizing. Uncle Bob would sit at the head of the table, motion for the server to come over as soon as we were seated, and say, "We may need some extra help here. And I hope you have plenty of booze and mayonnaise."

My friends Lee and Ruth visited late one summer. They had already heard many stories about my family, but I warned them that this particular event had its own energy—more Roman gladiator battle than pleasant afternoon outing. When we arrived at the restaurant, Uncle Bob summoned the server and said that we were ready to order the first round of drinks.

One by one, each family member ordered straight gin—some on the rocks, some straight up, some with olives, some with cocktail onions. As the orders continued, I watched as my friends on the other side of the table looked more anxious, whispering to each other, gesturing subtly, strategizing what to do. Ruth had already announced to the group that she was unable to drink because she had a physical allergy, an excuse that my family accepted reluctantly as it fell into the medical exemption category. Lee had no such protection.

When the server got to him, Lee, visibly flustered and unsure of how to proceed, paused for a moment before saying "Gin and tonic, please."

Uncle Bob whipped his head in Lee's direction, his eyes widening, his head cocked quizzically to the side. The rest of the table fell silent. The collective family organism, sensing a foreign entity, went into full defensive mode as if the host body had been attacked by a cancerous cell. I looked over at Lee and shrugged helplessly. Simultaneously, the family erupted:

Brother Robin: "BOO! HISS!"

Aunt Joan: "What did Kirk's friend just say?"

Stepsister Lola: "Oh, that's not going to work."

Father: "Kirkland, where did you find these people?"

Brother Monty: "Pussy!"

Stepmother Barb: "He seemed like such a nice boy."

Ruth looked shocked, then a slight smile crossed her face as she realized that it was one thing to have heard my stories over the years, it was another thing entirely to be living in one of them. She turned to Lee and said, "I don't think that's going to fly here, bud."

Lee changed his order to gin on the rocks, the first of four. An uproarious celebration swept across the table as the family started chanting Lee's name. Robin, my stepsiblings, and I beat the table with our fists; Monty started doing a "churn the butter" dance, and my stepmother and aunt Joan waved their hands above their heads like they were doing elder aerobics. My father stood up, raised his water glass, and turned to Lee. "Welcome to the family, darlin'," he said. "I think we're all going to get along just fine."

Nancy and her husband, John, came to visit the week after Joan and Bob left, the last week of the summer. Nancy was the middle of my father's three older sisters, a craggy woman who trilled when she spoke. She was tall and willowy and always wore a long jean skirt and a loose cotton top that registered every spastic movement of her uncoordinated limbs. She was a seismograph after an earthquake hit. Her facial expressions were equally jarring and out of synch with the content of what she was saying, registering emotions well before the words that accompanied them came to her lips. "Your uncle John had a cancer scare (*smile—long pause*) but it turns out he's okay."

My aunt and uncle had started their family life firmly rooted on the path my grandfather had imagined for them. Uncle John was a senior CIA director in charge of intelligence for the Iron Curtain countries during the Cold War, and Aunt Nancy was a stay-at-home mom and wife who always had a martini waiting for him when he returned to their home in McLean, Virginia, at 6 p.m. After a few years in the job, the pressure of Uncle John's position started to register with his superiors, and he was ordered to take a sabbatical to recharge his batteries. John took his family to India for the summer, discovered an alternative community called the Golden Temple, and returned to his office in an Indian-print shirt and sandals to inform the CIA director that he was never coming back to work. By the time I knew them, my aunt Nancy had become "Ana," and my uncle John had traded in his black power suit and cropped hair for a long white robe, a wispy beard, and a turban that contained his waist-length hair. He smelled like garlic and cocoa butter.

They usually pulled up around cocktail hour, which was the time my brothers and I were expected home. My father had few rules, but one of them was that we dress for dinner in semi-formal attire and nice shoes—ones that would be acceptable for wear on a teak-decked yacht, like topsiders, were fine, but we were not allowed to wear sneakers or flip-flops.

Every year, John and Ana brought a rope of fresh garlic from their Charlottesville farm and a reusable grocery bag of various cheeses. Their life philosophy meant that they never traveled over fifty-five miles per hour, and stopped often at roadside fruit stands and other shops to browse, even though they rarely bought anything. They were never in a rush, to the point where it seemed to me that they spent a great deal of energy restraining an instinct to move faster in order to maintain their aura of serenity.

I don't remember them ever visiting when my parents were married, and I learned later that Ana didn't like my mother, so I assume they weren't welcome or didn't want to come. "The first time I saw your mother, I thought she was an angel. I had never seen anyone so beautiful," my aunt once said to me, as if she was describing something unpleasant.

When my aunt and uncle arrived that first summer, they greeted Robin and me as if they were a visiting delegation from another country. Uncle John grabbed my outstretched right hand in both of his, looked deeply into my eyes, and said, "It's so nice to see you again, Kirkland," in a way that made me feel like either he was really happy to see me, or he was really happy with the way he was acting when he saw me. In all my years of knowing him, I never came to a conclusion as to which was the truth. John walked into the living room and up to the large picture window that looked out onto the lake. He smiled knowingly and said nothing for two minutes as my father, Robin, and I shared looks. I imagine we were all concerned that disturbing him might violate a meditative ritual and assumed that he would give us the signal when it was time to engage. My uncle wasn't one for making others feel comfortable, however, so after three minutes, my father interrupted him.

"How are things, Johnny?"

"It's so very lovely this time of year; thank you for asking, Bobby," John replied. He was one of those people who always answered the question that he would have preferred to be asked.

"It's been marvelous all week," my stepmother said, reappearing with a scotch. During John's three-minute nature interlude, she had shown Ana to the back bedroom and fixed herself a drink. "It's so peaceful here." Barb had introduced us to the word "marvelous" that summer, her go-to superlative from the first day we met her.

"And Priscilla and Katherine are doing well?" my father continued.

"Glorious," said John. "Priscilla and Taran Tarn have just started an alternative school nearby. And Maha A'kal is working at a grocery store. She just loves it."

Taran Tarn, born Andy Friedberg from Long Island, married my cousin Priscilla. Maha A'Kal was their oldest daughter, originally named Katherine, after my grandmother.

"Oh, how *interesting*," Barb said. "Would anyone like some cheese and crackers?"

"Oh, good heavens, Barb, let me get it. We bought some wonderful cheese from a stand in Charlottesville on our way here," Ana said.

"So, Bobby, tell me," Uncle John began, "how *are* things going with the club? Everything doing well?"

My father had become manager of our lake community that summer, the first time they had hired a member for the job. He replaced the longtime married couple who "retired" after it was discovered they had embezzled club funds. The job entailed a lot of socializing, which he enjoyed, and an open bar tab, which he loved.

"Everything is just fine," my father replied. "We've had a really busy summer, and it's just getting to the point where—"

Uncle John farted loudly, stopping my father midsentence. Uncle John didn't seem to notice, though, and remained focused on my father's words, an earnest expression on his face. Barb and I caught each other's eye and looked away. She took a big swig of her scotch. I sank deeper in my chair and placed my hand over my mouth. Robin looked behind him as if someone had just come to the door.

"—where we're almost at full capacity," my father continued, shifting in his seat. "Labor Day is our busiest time."

"Oh, that's such good news," Uncle John said. "It really is a special place."

"I have some cheese," Ana interjected as she returned to the living room. "We found some wonderful ones in Charlottesville, but nothing can beat the cheddar from New York."

"We have great cheese," said Barb. "And syrup. We have marvelous syrup in this part of the country too."

"The syrup's really good," I said. "I really like pancakes."

"He ate forty of them in one sitting," Robin chimed in. "We couldn't believe it."

"Well, you are a growing boy," Uncle John said. "You'll probably be as tall as our son John. He's six-foot-five now."

"How is John doing?" my father asked. "Last I heard he was—"

Uncle John leaned to one side of his chair and let rip another bellowing fart, followed by a short grunt. His eyes never left my father, who once again paused before continuing. "—um, not working at the farm anymore, is that correct?"

Barb hopped up out of her seat as if the sound had been an alarm signaling that something needed to come out of the oven. "I'm going to get started on dinner," she said. "I'll be right back."

"I'll help," I said.

"Me too," said Robin.

"Yes," Uncle John replied as we exited, "John's on his own path. We are very proud of him."

"I bet you are," I heard my father say from the other room. There was a long pause before he continued. "You'll be happy to know that we're using the garlic that you gave us for the chicken tonight. If I'm not mistaken, you must have had quite a bit of garlic for lunch, so I hope that's okay."

"Divine," Uncle John replied.

OUR SUMMER ENDED FOR ALL OF US the Monday of Labor Day. I gave Barb a hug that morning while my father loaded our duffel bags into the back of the car for the long drive to New York City to catch our afternoon plane back to Bermuda. She smiled at me and said, "We loved it," in a way that made me feel as though she might mean it. I imagined what my mother would think if she could witness this scene, and made a mental note not to talk about Barb at all.

At the airport, my father said goodbye to us the way that he always did, with a peck on the cheek and an "I love you." I thought back to earlier in the summer, after we had first arrived, when I had tried to sit in his lap. I don't know why I had done it; perhaps it was an innate desire to make some connection with him, or force him to accept my presence in his life. Maybe I just needed affection from somebody, and he was my closest option. But as I tried to fit my larger-than-average nine-year-old body onto his, I noticed annoyance on his face, as if he were being forced to contend with an unruly Great Dane that wasn't allowed on the furniture. I abandoned the attempt quickly, and he got up and walked into the kitchen. I was embarrassed, and angry, and once again frightened of the part of me that felt unlovable.

My mother greeted us at the Bermuda airport, waving frantically, as if she had been standing in the same spot since she dropped us off two months before. Monty stood beside her, smiling. I realized as we walked toward them that I hadn't missed them, and I felt a twinge of guilt, followed by the anxiety of returning to a place that I hadn't yet figured out how to live in.

Chapter 5

During the first few years in Bermuda, our lives shrank to school during the week, the beach on the weekends, and whatever we could find on Bermuda's two television stations for entertainment at night. Robin became a star athlete, and I rose to the top of my class academically. Monty went to the feeder preparatory school at a different location, so I didn't see him during the day and didn't pay much attention to him otherwise.

On a typical morning, my mother would burst into the bedroom that I shared with Robin, a long, flowing polyester robe trailing behind her. "Wake up, you filthy beasts!" she would scream. "It's time to face the beauty of a brand-new day!"

She would then walk back down the hall and tap on Monty's door. "Ninny No Zoney—time to get up, sweetheart. I have your favorite lih lih [Monty's word for 'cereal' then] ready for you on the counter." She would make a second visit to my room after Robin was up and showering. "Get your skinny white ass up," she would command, "chop chop."

We spent many of our weekends at the beach, my mother tanning in her large fold-up lounge chair while my brothers and

I bodysurfed and buried one another in the sand. We always packed sandwiches, and a large green thermos of powdered lemonade filled with ice that bounced on the inside as we carried it from the car. My mother would fit Monty with his earplugs and put on his water wings and warn him that he couldn't get water in his ears (Robin and I never understood the exact nature of his ear problems), and then sit on the edge of her seat worrying that a big wave would take him out. At least once every beach visit he would grow tired of playing it safe, a large wave would knock out his earplug, and my mother would leap from her seat, pick him up, and frantically dry out his ear as she yelled at Robin and me to find the plug. Monty would cry, and she would tell him he was going to be fine, even though we didn't know if he was going to be fine because we had been told over and over that he couldn't get any water in his ear or something bad would happen. In the face of what she feared, my mother shifted from anxiety to calm, which made us feel like everything was going to be okay because we didn't know she was acting.

We set up a decathlon course around our house, including a long-jump pit, a high-jump bar, and a place to throw shot puts, which were grapefruits that had fallen from the trees in our orchard. My mother sat in her lawn chair and acted as the referee, since we needed her to watch what we were doing and tell us how good we were and how proud she was at how far we could jump or fast we could run. As the final event, Robin and I would run around the house until one of us gave up. Even though Robin won most of the other events, I would usually win the marathon, and my mother would praise my perseverance and grit as if they were traits that she and I shared.

At Robin's basketball games, my mother stood up and cheered loudly for Robin and berated the refs for bad calls while the other mothers sat silently—disinterested, perhaps, or afraid of making themselves too conspicuous. I covered my face with my hands when she erupted out of her seat on fast breaks, but noticed how my brother's friends smiled up at my mother in the stands, perhaps wishing their mothers were yelling as loud.

Yet after dinner every night, my homework done, I would park in front of the TV and wait for the moment when my mother would get up from her chocolate-brown chair and head into the kitchen. I listened for the first soft *clink* as she removed a bottle from the cupboard, carefully as if she didn't want to wake a baby, and placed it gingerly on the counter. The gentle sloshing of the liquid in the bottle made my body tense. In the background, Robin was usually playing the set of drums that he had purchased with money from his two part-time jobs, banging away to Molly Hatchet and Lynyrd Skynyrd songs, the beating becoming more frantic and furious as the evening progressed.

Then my mother would walk to the other side of the kitchen, five steps, the soft *thwap* of slippers smacking her heels. She would open the cupboard that held the glasses (another soft *clink*), turn around, and walk three steps to the freezer—*thwap, thwap, thwap*—where she would pull out an ice tray and twist until there was a sharp, violent pop.

My mother would return to her chocolate-brown chair with glass in hand as a sadder and quieter version of herself, even before she took the first sip. At first, I thought I could keep her with us by draping myself over her body in an extended hug. I could hear the beating of her heart. She would pick up the glass, ice tinkling like a wind chime, and swallow. It sounded like the rush of sewage through pipes in a thin wall.

My mother rarely went out at night, even on the weekends, so after we were sent to bed, she turned off the lights in the living room, sat in her brown armchair, and watched TV while sipping a glass of wine (liquor was for before dinner, wine was to accompany dinner) and eating her evening meal, which was almost always just half of an avocado from the tree outside or an acorn squash, with a puddle of Italian dressing in the middle. I don't know why she didn't go out like she used to when she and my father were together and happy. I asked her about it once, and she answered that her life was about us now.

"What would you do if we weren't here?" I asked.

"Take a swim in the ocean and just keep going," she said.

I NEVER THOUGHT ABOUT MONEY while my parents were still together, but in Bermuda the lack of it was a constant presence. We attended the most expensive private school on the island but couldn't afford to replace our secondhand uniforms when a shirt lost a button or pants came unhemmed. Robin worried more about appearances than I did, so when he couldn't shame my mother into fixing his clothes, he learned how to do it himself. I just got better at hiding the rips and missing buttons. Every now and then, a family friend of my parents' visited the island and invited us to join them for lunch at the Coral Beach Club or Mid Ocean Club. My mother approached these invitations with a mixture of anticipation and dread, excited to once again feel a part of the world that we had left, yet resentful that we were now the recipients of what she viewed as charity. It apparently never occurred to her that these former friends might want to see her, or us. Or perhaps she couldn't bear the reminder of what she had lost, or the pity of those who still had it. In any case, they mostly stopped calling after the first couple of years. But whenever an old friend did reach out, my mother ordered us to dress in our finest clothes and drilled us on our "pleases" and "thank-yous." The underlying message was clear: *Don't embarrass me.*

Nonetheless, the year that I turned eleven, two years after arriving on the island, my mother was noticeably excited about an overnight package that arrived at our door. She opened it and began shuffling through the pages of a black book with bright orange writing on the cover. The *New York Social Register* listed the addresses and phone numbers of the New York City elite, not that I knew that at the time. I had noticed earlier versions of the book lying around the house but had never given it much thought.

"Why do you still get that book if we don't live in New York anymore?" I asked her as she scanned the pages for our names.

"Why wouldn't I?" she replied.

She found the page that she was looking for and handed the book to me so that I could see our names listed under hers: Robert Lyon Hamill III—13 years, Kirkland Knight Hamill—11 years, and Montgomery Crawford Hamill—8 years. I noticed the names of familiar-sounding Hamills peppered on our page. I flipped through the book and saw my aunt listed under her married name, as well as the names of my parents' friends from Cedarhurst, several godparents, and Adirondack people whom we saw every year. We were not the only people with a Bermuda address, but for everyone else it was a second or third address, their primary home being in New York City or one of the surrounding suburbs—Rye, Tarrytown, or Greenwich. The register identified where offspring went to boarding school and college, almost all in the Northeast and Ivy League. I didn't see my father's name.

"How come Daddy isn't in here?" I asked.

"Because he married the Jew," my mother said.

This book, which had seemed silly the second before, took on a dark and menacing complexion. I felt protective of Barb.

"Well, you can take me out of it too," I said.

She looked surprised, and annoyed. "You'll regret that," she said.

"No, I won't."

"Yes, you will."

"I don't understand why it matters that we're in there. You don't even talk to the people who are in there."

"Kirkland," my mother said, sighing (she only called me "Kirkland" when I was in trouble or she wanted me to pay close attention), "you were born into a world that everyone wishes they were born into. You don't understand what that means right now, but you will one day."

"I don't think I will," I said.

She smiled her all-knowing, sad smile, the one that let my brothers and me know when we had waded into an area of life that we were too young to understand. I came to hate that smile as I wrestled with whether the world I didn't yet understand was meaner than I thought it was or whether my mother's interpretation of it revealed something about her that I didn't like.

"Well, as long as you're living under my roof, you're staying in the book," she said.

PUBERTY FELT LIKE A PUNISHMENT. I had grown attached to my smooth body and velvety voice, and the onslaught of wiry, black hairs protruding from my nipples and the strangled chicken noises coming out of my throat felt as if I had been infected with a virus. I kept a pair of scissors in the bathroom to clip the hairs, only to find that another one showed up the next day with a buddy in tow. My pubic hair came in a bright auburn, meaning I was blond up top, dark in the middle, and red below.

We never talked about sex in our house. There was no moment when one of my parents sat any of us down to discuss what was happening to our bodies, what parts of the body went where when people had sex, or what could happen as a result. Our family's theory of change, which extended to changing bodies, was to mock that change until the person enduring it had no choice but to accept what was happening or hide it better to avoid ridicule. During the late spring months, as the weather in Bermuda got hotter, my brothers and I spent most nights sleeping on the floor of my mother's bedroom, the only room with an air-conditioning unit. In the mornings I waited until my brothers got up, and my mother rolled over so her head was facing away from the bedroom door, before I hunched over and scurried out of the room, juggling my stubborn morning erection like a parade leader fumbling with his baton. I realized I wasn't fooling anyone when my mother got up one morning and walked through the living room doing an exact imitation of my morning routine. "And you, juggling your goodies every morning like a retarded circus clown," she said, laughing. "Priceless!"

I had my first orgasm the summer of my thirteenth year, accidentally. I pretended I was the convicted murderer, and my pillow was the female security guard, in the R-rated movie *Penitentiary* that I had watched the evening before. My mother allowed us to rent these movies from a young age, and I wonder now if they were her shortcut for teaching us what happened between men and women. Discussing it with us was never her plan. Rubbing against the pillow felt good enough that I kept doing it, even though I didn't understand the point until my penis transformed into a magical vessel, igniting my body and depositing an unusual, sticky substance on my pillow.

I may not have had an orgasm until thirteen, but I had been having wet dreams since I was young. I didn't know that's what they were. They happened when I was half-asleep and restless, and at a point in my life when I was still wetting the bed, so the pleasure I felt was conflated with the shame of waking up with pajama bottoms plastered to my front and the pungent smell of urine in the air. It all stopped sometime after I walked into my bedroom at five years old and saw a diaper draped across my bed. Was my father smiling when he told me that only babies wet the bed, and babies wore diapers? He seemed proud of himself for using humiliation to fix the problem efficiently, a plumber plugging his leaky kid.

Monty had a large stuffed Winnie the Pooh doll that my mother brought back from a trip the two of them took to Disney World when Robin and I were in the Adirondacks. Even when seated, Winnie stood about four feet high and took up the whole corner of the bedroom that Monty and I now shared. Robin had lobbied my mother for his own space, his pitch being that as the oldest he deserved it. I never quite figured out what my argument for special treatment could be. There was no "est" associated with being in the middle, so I never leveled one.

Winnie was nearly as wide as he was tall and sat with his arms and legs open, inviting a barrel of honey to be placed in front of him. I walked past him every morning on my way to the bathroom without giving him much thought, until one day I wasn't looking where I was going and tripped over one of his huge paws, landing on top of his soft fur. Winnie and I started fucking in secret after that, at least three times a day, in every feasible position. I was on top, then he was on top; I took him from behind and the front. By the end of our first week together I was exhausted, and it was difficult to find patches of his fur that weren't matted down and crunchy. Our relationship ended when Monty walked in on us one morning. He exclaimed in horror, "What are you doing to my stuffed animal?"

"We're just hugging!" I screamed.

"Without any clothes on?!"

I jumped to my feet, grabbed my underwear, and ran into the bathroom. Monty followed right behind me, laughing, as I slammed and locked the door. *Does he know what he saw?* I wondered, frantic to prevent him from telling Robin.

I could hear Monty chuckling outside the door. I decided that the only way to distract him was to do something unexpected. I asked him how he was doing.

"You looked a little upset yesterday. Is everything okay at school?"

Monty's laughter stopped. There was a pause. Eventually he said, "Yeah, it's okay."

"Are you sure?" I asked. "You can talk to me about it if you want." I squinted my eyes closed and held my breath.

"I'm okay. Math's a little hard, I guess."

"I can help you with that," I said, straightening. He didn't answer right away, but I could hear him slump down to the ground and lean against the bathroom door.

"Okay," he said. There was another pause. "How's school going for you?" he asked.

"Great. Everything's fine," I said.

I paused, shivering on the lip of the bathtub. Monty sat on the other side of the door, waiting for the conversation to continue. It was the first time I had ever asked him anything about his life.

"Hey, Monty," I said. "Why do you toss and turn so much when you're going to sleep?"

"I don't know—it just helps, I guess."

"It's kinda weird," I said.

"Yeah," he replied. There was another pause as I heard him get up. The silence of new intimacies replaced his laughter.

"Robin is not going to believe what I just saw," he said, running off down the hall.

*   *   *

MY MOTHER'S SELF-IMPOSED EXILE extended to her love life, which was nonexistent for our first few years on the island. She had gained weight, and her arms had ballooned out of proportion to the rest of her body due to a "hormone imbalance" that she never explained and said couldn't be fixed. But she was still more beautiful than our friends' mothers and attracted creepy come-ons from men everywhere she went, which were dismissed by her withering glares. We frequented a small hotel restaurant near our house on the occasional Sunday, when we were often the only people seated in the small bar area. One day a drunk man sat down at our table and propositioned my mother. She turned her head, pretending that he didn't exist, while my brothers and I looked between the two of them, wondering why she wasn't saying anything. The man intimidated me, and I didn't understand why my usually fierce mother seemed smaller in his presence. After the waiter shooed him away, she turned to Robin and me and asked, "Why did you let him talk to me that way?" I once again felt like I'd failed a manhood test whose rules were never explained.

Before my stepfather entered the picture, there was only one man my mother dated for any noticeable amount of time. Even then, their liaisons happened largely when we were away for the summer with my father. He was a short, stocky, motorcycle-driving Welshman who played rugby weekend afternoons and then drank with his mates until they were swaying back and forth, arms over each other's shoulders, singing rowdy pub songs. He visited my mother after we had gone to bed. Robin saw him speeding away on his motorcycle early one Sunday morning and confronted my mother when she came out of her room.

"Did Mr. Lyle spend the night last night?" my brother wailed.

"I don't know what you're talking about," my mother replied.

"I just saw him leave on the bike!" Robin screamed.

"Maybe he just fell asleep on the couch?" I said. "He's usually pretty drunk by the time he gets here."

"What if Monty had seen you? What would you have *said* to him?" Robin loved the "what about the children" angle when it came to these battles with my mother, which grew more frequent as he advanced in his teen years.

"This is none of your business," my mother said.

"BUT HE'S MY MATH TEACHER!"

"What, do you expect me to spend the rest of my life looking after you children?" my mother said, exasperated. "How come I don't get to have any fun?"

"I HAVE A TEST ON MONDAY!"

"I'm sure you'll do just fine, darling," my mother said to Robin. "He seems like a good teacher." She winked at me, a naughty smile on her face.

Robin stormed back to his bedroom and banged on his drum set as if it were my mother's head.

I followed my mother as she retreated to her bedroom. "I have a test next week," I said, "in geography. You haven't met Mr. Smith, have you?"

She laughed. "You're on your own there, I'm afraid. I'm much better at math."

*   *   *

ALTHOUGH MY MOTHER'S GLAMOROUS LIFE as a New York City socialite disintegrated after the move to Clinton, and disappeared altogether once she became a single mother raising three boys in Bermuda, her rich inner world and penchant for denial allowed her to maintain the illusion that she was still perched firmly atop the social pecking order. She viewed her exile as temporary, like Jesus wandering the desert for forty days. As such, she insisted on maintaining the rituals of a cultured life, which meant having a formal sit-down dinner every Sunday night and speaking French whenever possible.

Unfortunately, my mother didn't speak French, and so the few words that she had picked up over the years were used repeatedly, in mangled Franglish phrases. My mother begrudgingly invited her mother to dinner one Sunday, since we didn't see her that much anymore. My mother had stopped insisting that we go to church. My grandfather never joined us for dinner. We didn't know why.

As we sat down to dinner, my mother gestured to a bottle of red wine. "Kirkland, would you pour *le vahh* for your grandmother, *see vous play*?"

"Le what?"

"*Vahh* is French for wine."

"Oh. Yeah. I mean, *wee*." I stood up and reached for the bottle.

"I want some," Robin said.

"And you may pour *un putt-ey purr* for yourself and your older brother," she said.

We had had our first sip of wine when we were young. My mother wanted us to be "raised like the French" when it came to alcohol consumption. What she didn't realize was that, on this night, I'd been drinking like an American as I set the table, taking swigs from the open two-liter bottle of red wine by her place mat. I concentrated on maintaining my balance as I filled my grandmother's glass.

"I think Kirkland's had more than a *perty pur*," Robin said.

I filled my mother's glass and poured a little for Robin and for me before returning to my seat. "*Fair may la boosh*," I said to Robin, throwing my hand up at him as I assumed a French person might.

"Wendy, what on earth are these children doing drinking wine?" my grandmother gasped. "Kirkland's twelve years old!"

My mother turned away from my grandmother, lifted her glass, and motioned for us to follow. "*Bon appettee*," she said. Robin and I took small sips from our wineglasses. I reached for the platter of beef in the center of the table.

"We will not eat until we have said grace," my grandmother said, grabbing my wrist and placing it on my lap.

"The French allow their children to have wine at dinner every night," my mother continued, "so they learn how to drink when they're younger and don't become raging alcoholics later. It's very civilized."

"Well, your 'civilized' middle child just poured wine down his front," my grandmother said.

"*Vive le France!*" I said, raising my glass. "*Encore de vahh!*" My glass was now empty.

"You're wasted," Robin said.

My mother looked over at me, trying hard to seem appalled. Her formal veneer never lasted under direct confrontation, especially in front of the mother she herself was not done rebelling against. I could see the sides of her mouth suppressing a smile. "That's more than enough *vahh* for you, young man," she said. "You may excuse yourself from dinner until you can act like a gentleman. And go change your shirt."

I swooned as I got up, making it as far as the carpeted hallway before lying down on the floor to watch the ceiling spin. From the other room, I could hear my grandmother lecturing my mother about my behavior, suggesting that it might be time for us to come back to church.

"Well, he's just drowned himself in the blood of Christ, Mother," she replied, "why don't we give that a shot first?"

I remember my grandmother now, I realize, mostly through the filter of the disdain my mother had for her. It never occurred to me to try to see her in any other way, and I wonder now what I might have missed. I had always assumed that my mother's contempt signaled an injury perpetrated against her in childhood, a transgression so severe that the bonds between them were severed permanently, leaving only the uneasy peace of family held together by blood alone. It's more frightening to think that perhaps there was no falling-out, just a moving away from the stench of middle-class life that my mother despised, a prison that she had escaped from only to find herself incarcerated once more. I don't know if my grandparents left Bermuda for Australia two years after we arrived for a new adventure, to be closer to my aunt Gail, or just to flee the relentless onslaught of my mother's judgment.

*   *   *

FOR ALL OF THE CHANGES that I noticed in myself during my twelfth and thirteenth years, the changes in my mother stood out most. I pieced together a pattern that played out most evenings, beginning as she poured her first glass of scotch. Robin and I would share a sideways glance on the couch, wondering how her drinking would progress from there. On this particular night, she was sitting on her brown chair staring blankly at the television when I drew her attention to a strange smell in the kitchen.

"What are you talking about, darling?" she slurred.

"I think dinner's ready," I replied. "It smells like it's burning."

"Then take it out of the oven, sweetie."

"But I don't know what to do with it," I said.

"I'll get it," Robin said, cutting his eyes at my mother, who kept her blank gaze straight ahead. She seemed to be looking through the television at something else.

On nights like these, each of us tried to reach her in our own ways, like kittens nuzzling the corpse of their unresponsive mother, unaware that she has already left them. I had always been able to make her laugh, and attempted to snap her out of her haze by telling funny stories from multiple angles, hoping that one of them could navigate through the fog and trigger a reaction. She would occasionally look in my direction and give me a sad smile, which I interpreted as a silent plea to stop.

Robin attempted to reach her through anger, his energy level rising as hers dropped, until he would erupt. On this night, he confronted her after we had eaten the burnt roast that he had salvaged from the oven and he had put Monty to bed. She was walking out of the kitchen with a full glass of wine in her hand.

"Are you going grocery shopping tomorrow?" he demanded. "We don't have any food in this house."

She stared at him, her body swaying.

"What is wrong with you?" he screamed. "Why are you drinking all the time?"

"I do not . . . drink all the time," she said meekly.

"Yes, you do! That's like your third glass of wine in the last hour! You've got to stop!" Robin reddened as he stepped toward her.

In these confrontations, as Robin brought to life my mother's anger, I internalized her sadness. We were opposite sides of the same coin, channeling and acting out her various emotions as she denied all of them. "Robin, leave her alone," I said, keeping my voice low.

"But what the fuck is Monty supposed to eat tomorrow?" he yelled at me. "There's no fucking food in this house!"

"She'll go tomorrow, right?" I looked at my mother, pleading with her to say something that would make him stop, even if she didn't mean it.

"I don't know, Kirkland," she said. "If your father would send us the money he—"

Robin grabbed the wine from my mother's hand and slammed it against the wall, shattering the glass and spraying wine like blood splatter at a violent crime scene. He started to cry. "Shut up! I'm so fucking tired of hearing you say that. Just shut the fuck up!" By this point in their relationship, Robin and my mother were routinely engaged in all-out warfare, punctuated by weekly battles in which he demanded items she couldn't provide, and she called him selfish and leveled the "you're just like your father" accusation.

But even Robin could only manage to take a stand against her for so long. The next morning, I woke up to a house that had been sanitized of any lingering evidence that there had been a confrontation. Robin had cleaned up after the wreckage, run the dishwasher, wiped down the counters, and fluffed the pillows in the living room. My mother awoke restored to her former self and summoned us to breakfast. Robin turned to me as I walked into the kitchen.

"What's with your hair?" he said cheerfully. "You look like a Muppet."

"Shut up about my hair," I said. I looked at my mother, who was busy stacking dishes on the counter, and back at Robin, who was whistling as he tied a knot in the garbage bag beneath the counter. They both raised their eyebrows back at me, registering the confused look on my face.

"God, you're grumpy in the morning," my mother said.

"Don't forget afternoon and evening," Robin added.

"Hey, Mommy, where's the cereal?" Monty asked.

"Are we out?" she said. "We'll go by the store and get some after school today."

I tried to catch Robin's eye as he hefted the garbage bag out of the can. He never looked up.

"Have your brother cut you up an orange, and I'll make you some toast," my mother said.

Chapter 6

My mother's increased stress coincided with the deterioration of our financial situation, which evolved from tenuous to desperate. She held a couple of jobs in those first few years, but neither of them lasted long. She never explained why she was employed one day and then not the next; I just assumed she was the kind of woman who wasn't meant to work. Defeated sobs replaced her screaming fights with my father, all evidence of her early defiance having given way to raw appeals meant to trigger a paternal concern for our welfare, which never yielded the desired effect. Robin couldn't stand the sound of my mother crying, and so he would retreat into his room and pound on his drums. I often stood alone, looking out our living room window, bracketed by the sounds of despair and anger, mesmerized by the tranquil scenes of large sailboats on the far-off horizon. I began to notice that there were other stories being told in other places that might be happier than mine, and to think that one day I might be able to sail into another story.

We celebrated Monty's ninth birthday in June (even though he was born in August), before leaving for the Adirondacks to be with my father for the summer. Our birthdays were the one night of the year that my mother insisted we go out for dinner, even when we didn't have enough money to cover the weekly grocery tab. She seemed to view these birthday indulgences as the one compromise she refused to make in the midst of all of the others thrust upon her, her Alamo, even though Robin and I had convinced her that we would rather celebrate our birthdays at home.

When my mother asked Monty where he wanted to go for his birthday dinner, he said, "Henry the Eighth!"

My heart sank. "I don't think we should go there this year, Monty. It's really expensive," I said.

"We will go wherever my lovah wants to go. Right, lovah?" my mother said to Monty. Her voice was thick and wet. "Come give your mother a hug."

"Are you sure it's okay?" Robin asked.

"Of course it is! It's not every day your lovah turns nine years old, is it?!" My mother held her arms wide open for Monty, an exaggerated smile on her face. Monty fell into them happily, not yet having learned to register the despair in my mother's enthusiasm.

"Okay," Robin said.

I looked at him and shook my head in disbelief. My mother had stopped going to church, but her faith that great reward would follow great hardship had only increased the more dire our situation became. I had gotten a glimpse of this earlier in the month when she arrived triumphantly home, waving a twenty-dollar bill in my face, saying that she had found it at the bottom of the driveway. "I didn't know how I was going to pay for groceries this week," she told me, a certainty in her voice, "but then I found this."

By the time we returned from Monty's birthday dinner, my mother's steel core had been hollowed out and filled with a bottle of cheap wine. She had put on a sad, desperate charade for Monty, each phony attempt at enthusiasm pushing her closer to the tears pooling behind her eyes. Robin and I ordered the cheapest options we could and played along, but over the course of the evening Robin's frustration grew as my concern deepened. I reserved my anger for my father. I had called him "selfish" and "cruel" on the phone the week before, and he dismissed the accusation, saying that I was just mimicking my mother, who received hell from him on the phone afterward. I learned to communicate my anger through one-word answers and tone from then on, not wanting to make my mother's difficult situation worse.

When we got home, Robin locked himself in his bedroom, and Monty went straight to bed, seemingly oblivious to the awkwardness of the evening. My mother sat in her brown chair, pulled out the cash from her purse, and started counting singles to the light of a single lamp.

I went to my room, retrieved $45 that I had saved to buy a new boom box, and begged her to take it. In my mind, subtracting $45 of despair from my mother's emotional bank account was more important than having to ask Robin for permission to use his stereo.

"No, darling," she said, "that's your money."

"I don't want it!" The bills were shaking in my hand.

"But you're saving for your radio," she said.

"I don't need a radio. I can use Robin's," I said.

She laughed unexpectedly. "Good luck with that," she said.

Her laughter lifted my mood. I wasn't aware until much later in my life how tethered I was to her reactions.

"I'm not going to take your money, darling," she said.

I hugged her and cried, grateful that she was still able to make me feel better by pretending.

She rubbed my back as I rested my head on her chest, soothed by her heartbeat. "It's going to be okay," she said. I had stopped believing that a long time ago.

AFTER THE FLING with Robin's math teacher died out, there were no other men in my mother's life until John showed up sometime during my thirteenth year.

The first time I met him, I opened the door to see a man standing with a bouquet of flowers in his hand and a large, nervous grin on his face. He was short and fat, and wore bright yellow shorts that met his sheer white stockings at the knee and were held to his bulk with a white belt. His patterned Hawaiian shirt was buttoned only halfway up a protruding belly, revealing a braided gold chain nestled amid a tuft of graying chest hair. His face looked like a sack of small potatoes had been papier-mâché'd and painted a splotchy red. He had heavily lidded, toad-like eyes, one of them drifting off to the side, that were framed by a pair of thick, black-rimmed glasses.

"Hello!" he said cheerfully. "Is your mother home?"

"Hold on," I said, chuckling. I closed the door, peering around the frame at the creature before me as long as I could.

I knew I would never see him again. His smile didn't fade as he brought a white handkerchief out of his pocket to wipe away the sweat collecting on his brow. "There's someone at the door!" I yelled toward my mother's room. It seemed cruel to use the word "date," since I couldn't imagine my mother making it past the first course at whatever Japanese Kabuki bar he would be likely to take her.

Weeks later, he was picking her up for their eighth date. Each time, he showed up at the door with a different bouquet of flowers, in a gaudy outfit, with the same goofy grin on his face. His name was John, but my brothers and I dubbed him "Froggy," an epithet that my mother not only sanctioned but also used within the confines of our house. She seemed as surprised as the rest of us that she was still going out with him.

At first, the only way my brothers and I got to know Froggy was through the dramatic transformation that my mother went through after she met him. Her wardrobe—which had previously consisted of polyester shorts and T-shirts—shifted toward ornate silk tops, muumuus, and long, flowing parachute pants. Her chipped nails were now a manicured pink. She had always worn sunglasses, like a sixties starlet prepared for an assault by the paparazzi, but now refused to take them off whether she was inside or out. She kept a collection of them on the hallway table in different colors, from yellow to blush and various styles of brown and black, but her favorite pair was tinted blue. Each week now also saw the unveiling of a new piece of jewelry, the most prominent of which, a six-carat diamond ring, never left her finger. There were nights she left our house draped in emeralds, rubies, and sapphires, looking like she was running off to join a harem. My brothers and I never teased her, no matter how cartoonish she looked. We realized Froggy had thrown her a lifeline just as she was about to go under.

MY MOTHER INTRODUCED US to John's world after they had been dating for a few months. She warned us that we wouldn't be seeing him often, though. "John's been married before and has his own children," she explained, "and he doesn't want any more."

His older child, Jimmy, was a well-known Bermudian conservationist and bluebird expert. He designed and built bluebird houses without an entrance perch because bluebirds had the ability to fly directly into the opening of the house, whereas other birds needed a perch. According to a story my mother told us, and who knows if it's true, his career had been cut short at twenty-five years old, when he fell a hundred feet off of a rocky cliff after an all-night cocaine binge. The fall paralyzed him from the chest down, leaving him dependent on his father to cover his hospital and caretaking expenses. The nurse he met and married in the rehabilitation facility, a woman my mother referred to as "the gold digger," took care of his other needs.

We met John's younger son, Louis, at one of John's all-night cocktail parties. Upon arriving, my mother told us to go "play" outside, where we encountered a muscle-bound, younger version of John swinging a pit bull around his head.

"How ya' doin', mates?" he said, releasing the animal, which helicoptered gracefully to the ground. He smiled and held out his hand. He had a thick, masculine Bermudian accent similar to John's, the kind of voice you would expect to hear from a salty captain who had spent most of his life at sea. I held out my skinny arm, self-conscious of my monogrammed shirt and penny loafers.

Louis used an old bath towel to aggravate another pit bull until it clamped down on the end of it, whereupon he spun around in a tight circle until the dog was airborne. Once the animal was in the air, he twirled it around his head like he was launching a shot put. "It's how I exercise," Louis explained as he released the second dog. He flexed his bicep, which looked like a surgically implanted grapefruit. "You should give it a shot, mate," he said, slapping me on the shoulder. At thirteen, I was already close to six feet tall and barely 150 pounds. I took the towel, more frightened of being perceived as weak than of the snarling animals circling us.

Luckily, one of the smaller dogs latched on to the end of the towel, and I lifted him easily into the air. We twirled like ice dancers rather than shot put and tosser, and after a few seconds I released him, feeling once again that I had successfully approximated what I imagined boys would enjoy doing.

John and my mother introduced us to his social set that first holiday season they were together. This coming out into Bermudian society felt jarring, as if we had been sequestered from the rest of the country and were seeing it for the first time. John's friends shared a multigenerational Bermudian heritage, a toxic racism toward their black fellow countrymen, and a severe drinking problem. Two of the most colorful, and infamous, were the Terry twins, women in their early sixties who looked much older. They lived together in an old cedar house inherited from their father; one was a widow and the other had never married. They entertained constantly and lavishly, and with an open-door policy that encouraged people to drop by anytime, day or night, whether they were invited or not.

The twins had invited us for Christmas dinner. One of them, Gillian, greeted us at the door. She was visibly shaking and smiling, as if she had just heard tragic news. She had applied a full hair-and-makeup regimen that looked out of place, as if somebody had painted a burlap sack and tried to comb the fibers down.

"Wendy, it is so *bloody* good to see you! These must be your boys!" Gillian sounded angry, looked like she was having a stroke, and yet the words suggested she was thrilled we had finally arrived. She ushered us into an old Bermudian living room, drenched in cedar-smelling history. Every time I walked into a house like theirs, I felt the emptiness of ours, the sterility of our oddly bright curtains, the lack of old portraits of bygone relatives, our bare floors uncovered by old rugs with frayed edges. There was heft here, something permanent and grounded, immovable.

Gillian led us into the kitchen, and my mother once again told us to "go play," as if she hadn't yet discovered the correct verb to use with teenagers. Robin was uninterested in hanging out with me, so he waited to see where I was going and went in the other direction, no doubt wanting to be judged on his own social skills without having to account for my lack of them.

I wandered around the living room, looking at old photographs and paintings. I was tall, and the ceilings were low, making it difficult for me to blend in. I had been to enough of these Bermudian cocktail parties now to know it was only a matter of time before some well-meaning drunk would register my reserve and try to coax me out of my shell, so whenever an adult stared at me and smiled, I smiled back and moved away before he or she approached. It was eight o'clock, and we had yet to hear about dinner. My head hurt, and the few appetizers available were in the kitchen, where the increasingly rowdy adults were gathered, already in the bag. I kept my head low and entered, walking straight to my mother, hoping I could grab something to eat, get an aspirin, and leave undetected.

"Hello, *darling*," my mother slurred. She noticed my face and placed her vodka on the counter. "What's wrong, baby?" she asked, as if I was bleeding from an axe wound. The room grew quiet.

"I have a headache," I said.

One of the adults started to chuckle and said to another, "Ahh, poor thing. He's so *big*."

"Mind over matter, sweetheart," my mother said. The more my mother drank, the more she solidified her position that anything could be overcome by thinking differently about it, or not thinking about it at all.

The Terry twins, though, had been paying close attention to our conversation and shared a knowing look before one of them grabbed my hand. "The white light, Hattie," Gillian said.

The twins led me to a back bedroom, told me to sit on the bed, and took up positions on either side of me. They closed their eyes in an intense squint, and started circling their hands in unison above my head. They tilted their heads back and spoke to the ceiling. "Oh, white light," Hattie chanted, "come heal this boy from his pain. Flow throoouuugghhh his body with your healing light and take away his paaaaain."

I closed my eyes and tried to envision what the white light might feel like and how long it would take to work. It apparently was supposed to happen quickly.

"Is your headache gone?" Hattie asked after thirty seconds had passed.

My headache had gotten worse. "I think it's getting a little better," I said.

Hattie looked at me like I had struck her in the face. "What do you mean? It's *not* gone?"

"It might be," I said tentatively.

Gillian turned violently toward her sister. "You didn't bloody well summon the light, Hattie, for Christ's sake! This boy is in pain! JESUS FUCKING CHRIST!" she said.

"I'm okay. I think it's working now. I feel much better," I said.

"Are you sure it's gone?" Gillian asked, a childlike wonder in her eyes.

"Yes, it's all gone now," I lied.

Gillian and Hattie looked at each other and smiled. I envied them in that moment, wishing I believed in magic. I wondered how often this scene had played out before, each sister switching between victim and accuser. Their smiles disappeared, and they again looked like they might cry. I had noticed the same distraught expression on my mother's face when she drank too much. As they left the room, my head started to pound harder, and I lay down on the bed and closed my eyes. After a few minutes, I got up and found a bathroom, where there was some aspirin in the medicine cabinet. I realized that I was increasingly living in a world in which I had no choice but to heal myself.

TWO YEARS AFTER SHE STARTED DATING JOHN, the year I turned fourteen, our mother had become a ghost in our lives, spending almost every weekend at his house. Robin took more and more responsibility for Monty during the week, ensuring that he had enough to eat and made it to and from school. On the rare weeknights that she didn't have dinner with John, our mother sat drinking her glass of scotch, looking blankly at the television, while my brothers and I did our homework, found something to eat, and went to bed, sometimes without saying a word to her.

When she was home, I thought that if I could make her remember how we used to be, it would transform her back to the mother we had known before. We were always the most connected as a family in the mornings, so on one of the few Saturdays she was home I asked her if she would drive me into town, even though she was already well into her second scotch and it wasn't yet noon. She agreed and carried her drink with her to the car. At the end of the driveway, she wasn't sure which way to turn, so I snapped at her to take a right and asked why she was biting her fingernails. "I'm not, darling," she said, as she chewed on her cuticle.

Halfway into town, she still hadn't looked at me or said a word, but half of the scotch was gone.

"Lola sent me a birthday card, just got it yesterday," I said. "That was nice of her, don't you think?" I looked at my mother, knowing the mention of Lola's name would elicit a reaction. "It had one of those cute little Boynton hippos on the front, and it said 'I mithed your birthday,' and when you opened it up, it said 'oh thit'—I thought that was funny."

She scoffed and shook her head. "She forgot your birthday, did she?"

"Why do you hate her so much? I can sort of understand why you might not like Barb, but what did Lola ever do to you?"

She sighed and tapped her finger on the steering wheel, looked out to the left and forward again, before looking back at me and saying, "Why do you think your father and I got divorced?"

"I don't know," I said after a few moments, confused as to why she asked the question. "I mean, I thought it might have been because of what happened to Monty."

"I caught him red-handed. He didn't think I'd be awake," my mother's jaw tightened and her fingers gripped the steering wheel, "or knowing your father, maybe he did and didn't care."

"*Caught* him?"

"The goddam babysitter," she said as if she was talking to herself, "cliché even by your father's standards. And then he goes and marries the mother."

For the first time during that car ride, my mother looked at me and smiled. My brain, still wrestling with the revelation that my father cheated on my mother, shuffled its molecules around once more until I could focus on the reality that he did so with Barb's daughter, and our babysitter, Lola. I flashed back to the day we heard my father had remarried, my mother's enigmatic smile, and her musing about being a fly on the wall when Barb told Lola about it.

"How . . . ?" I let the unfinished question linger, not knowing what I wanted to ask. I felt like an anaconda that had just swallowed a deer.

"Now you know," she said. She went on to tell me that she had caught them kissing on a couch in the Adirondacks on one of the weekends when we had traveled there as a family, with Lola as our babysitter. They had tried therapy for a while, but my father wasn't interested in making the marriage work. "He told me he didn't love me anymore," she said. "You're old enough to know this now."

I didn't ask for any more details, not wanting to learn anything that would further strain the already frayed parental connections. I knew that my mother had been distant and was drinking heavily for much of our time in Clinton. I had always assumed that it was because she was unhappy, which made my father unhappy, which contributed to their divorce, but now I wondered which came first. Did my father's affair lead to her drinking, or did her drinking lead to my father's affair?

Looking back, I'm guessing she didn't want to be alone in her pain anymore, and had chosen me as more sympathetic than Robin to her perspective. Or maybe she didn't like that I liked Barb, which made my time with my father easier, and wanted to reclaim the territory she'd lost to the two of them. Once the shock and anger I felt on my mother's behalf wore off, I started worrying about Barb. I assumed she knew about it, because I had come to understand that my father would more likely lay bare his character flaws than work on them. Nor did I think Lola, big-hearted and open, would be able to keep it from her mother. My mother's confession helped solidify my evolving awareness that my father operated with total impunity in the world, while the women around him were left to accept, forget, or reopen their wounds over and over again in a futile effort to heal them.

THE FIRST TIME MY MOTHER CALLED ME "faggity fag" was a day like any other, except my effeminacy must have been flaming up more than usual, like seasonal allergies. Usually her go-to behavior modifier of choice was to call me "overly sensitive" when my feelings were hurt, which was often. My feelings could be hurt by a lot: a teacher scolding me, an eye-roll at something I said, or any of a number of comments about my appearance.

I wasn't sure I had heard her correctly the first time, because as with my previous nickname, "Lulu," meant to critique the way I tripped over everything around me with my oversized feet (and also, of course, to imply "sissy"), she said it in a singsong voice with no hint of malice. But I didn't miss her point. I had been teased enough about my sensitive nature to know that it was noticeable, and less than ideal, but the words "faggity fag" pierced deeper. Like the diaper on the bed, she was warning me that I was leaking out and needed to be contained. When I asked her not to call me that, she once again told me "not to be so sensitive"—a phrase that not only criticized how I was acting but also provided the remedy to change her behavior. At the time I considered it a small victory that I could eventually get my mother to drop the nickname with my stoic approach to her taunts, not realizing that it was my behavior that was being modified.

It was around this time that I saw the movie *Making Love* on video, the story of a married man (Michael Ontkean) who falls in love with another man (Harry Hamlin), eventually leading to the end of his marriage. When the men have sex for the first time, the camera pans around and in closer until you can see the two actors kissing the way men kissed women in R-rated movies. I said "Ewww" out loud as the camera held on the two men, to register to Robin that I was grossed out by what I was seeing. But my body was tingling and I could feel myself getting an erection.

The movie established a clear battle line between how my body was reacting to stimuli around me and how my brain chose to interpret what was happening. I related to Michael Ontkean's character, but found enough loopholes to make the case that I wasn't like him. Harry Hamlin was beautiful, but something about the hair on his upper arm didn't turn me on. If I fixated on that hair long enough, my desire dwindled to the point where the gay feelings were undetectable. I also thought I could neutralize any unwelcome feelings by giving in to them, so I started masturbating by shoving the handle of a broom up my ass and interpreted the feelings of disgust that I felt over the next hour as proof that the "real me" wanted something else. I found over time that I could keep the gay from leaking out into the open as long as I could manufacture an intellectual escape hatch for every unwelcome feeling that I had. I couldn't be gay because I didn't want to dress like a girl. I couldn't be gay because I didn't lisp. I couldn't be gay because I had hairy legs. I couldn't be gay because my shoes were scuffed, and my pants were baggy, and my room was a mess. I couldn't be gay because, at the height of arousal, I could replace Parker Stevenson's face with Farrah Fawcett's and come just as hard.

ONE NIGHT MY MOTHER WAS SITTING by herself in the living room drinking a glass of scotch and I asked if she would rub my back. When my brothers and I were younger, we would lean against her chocolate chair, and she would draw designs on our backs and see if we could decipher what they were. I thought that maybe if she could remember how life used to be when we first moved here, she would be happy again.

"I don't really feel like it, darling. I'm tired."

"Please?" I sat down before she could say no and took off my T-shirt.

I heard the ice cubes tinkle in her glass as she lifted the scotch to her lips. She placed her free hand on the top of my back, where it met my neck. I leaned back a little farther. At first her hand didn't move, but then it started to travel along my collarbone. Her touch was light, grazing my skin as it reached the top of my shoulder. Her fingernails traced the contour of my shoulder until she reached the gap where my shoulder met my arm. Two of her fingers reached under and found the long, fine hairs that had formed a small thicket in my underarm, pulling them gently from the root. She stroked them tenderly, like she was placing a piece of hair behind her ear. My body tensed, and an electric, nauseous feeling shot down my throat and into my gut. I kept still, thinking that the feeling would evolve into something else. I didn't know if she was so drunk that she didn't realize who she was touching anymore, or she didn't think there was anything wrong with the way she was touching me. Could this be her way of showing me how women could please men, thinking it might trigger an interest in girls that I had yet to demonstrate? Or was this her way of telling me I was too old to have my back rubbed by my mother? Or perhaps I was overreacting?

She reached back up to the root of the hair and gently pulled again, while her thumb continued to trace the contour of my shoulder. When she leaned over to take a sip of her drink, and for a second lifted her hand off of my body, I stood up and walked out of the room, stopping as soon as I was out of sight to rub my underarms roughly, desperately trying to replace the lingering feel of her touch with my own. *I hope she's too drunk to remember this tomorrow*, I thought to myself.

JOHN, MY MOTHER'S NEW BOYFRIEND, lived on the most exclusive part of the island, in a house near the water called "Swan Cove." He also had homes in London, Paris, and Boca Raton, Florida—and owned a one-hundred-foot motor yacht named *Beluga* (caviar not whale) that he kept moored in Miami. In the few times that my brothers and I went to Swan Cove, John would welcome us at the door, point us to the living room, and disappear into the bar. "What would you boys like to drink?" he'd call from the other room, before spending the next ten minutes delivering refreshments, one by one, before refilling his own. He would monitor our glasses like a golden retriever fixated on a ball, and when they were close to empty he would hop up to refill them without asking. If for some reason too much time elapsed before there was a drink to fetch, he'd down his own and disappear into the bar. I came to believe over the years that John survived by staying in motion, as if the sins he was escaping wafted in his wake.

All we knew about John was how difficult it was to be him. My mother told us how his first wife had died of cancer, and his children were a burden. She talked about how "devastated" he was going to be when his ninety-year-old mother died (she wasn't ill). The boat needed constant maintenance, performed sloppily by lazy immigrants. Everyone took advantage of his generosity. "I wouldn't wish what John is going through on my worst enemy" was a common refrain, as if his troubles had no expiration date. Meanwhile she reminded us how fortunate we were, even though I still walked around with holes in my socks because I didn't feel comfortable asking for new ones.

When John wasn't in residence in one of his homes, he was on the boat or traveling through Europe. As Robin turned seventeen, I turned fifteen, and Monty approached his twelfth birthday, my mother accompanied him more frequently, unless he designated the trip as "business," in which case she wasn't invited. This annoyed her, even more so when he suggested it was a good opportunity to "spend time with your kids." My mother didn't take kindly to subtle judgments about her parenting, and didn't seem to grasp the irony of complaining to us about it.

With my mother less present, my brothers and I formed a little family of our own. I rode to school with Robin on the back of his motorcycle every morning. The mother of one of Monty's friends picked him up, and often took him to her house to spend the night when school was done. We cooked Steak-umms, and hot dogs, and made chef's salads with cut-up ham, turkey slices, and American cheese, drenched in Italian dressing. We continued shopping at the grocery store where we had once placed food on credit, but now Robin did the shopping and my mother paid the charge account on time. I did my homework at the kitchen counter, and called my friend Liam to talk about the latest episode of *General Hospital* before retiring to my room to listen to Stevie Nicks songs. I dissected her lyrics, certain that I knew what she meant when she invited somebody to walk gently through her shadow, or why the gypsy was dancing away, and how she was only a wish anyway. She sang about poets, white-winged doves, beauties, and beasts. She was forever in love and heartbroken. Too ethereal to hold on to, too needy to satisfy. Most important she was resilient. I read every magazine article I could find about her, cut out her pictures, and pasted them on the wall by my bed.

Our house started falling apart, the pristinely decorated façade left by the previous owners devolving into a jumble of worn carpets, ripped curtains, and stained surfaces. The chandelier, consisting of eight tulip lights, hung crookedly, and one of the broken stems dangled over the scratched dining room table by a thin wire. My mother had once had a collection of crystal and ivory figurines arranged on the glass étagères, each now broken by the throw of a stray football or basketball. My mother no longer commented on our disintegrating house, having invested in a brighter future with John. She downgraded us from starring roles in her life to occasional guest appearances. In my more generous moments, I wonder if she was protecting us from her alcoholism, having realized that she was powerless against it. It's more likely that she was relieved to have been saved from the poverty that never suited her, and the day-to-day realities of raising children.

When John was away on business, my mother returned to the house and acted like a fourth sibling. Ours had become the default party house for our friends—a development my mother sanctioned, positing that it was better for us to get drunk at home than drive around the island at night. Up to fifty kids showed up on Saturdays for our *Animal House*-inspired "toga" parties. On the rare nights that she was home, our mother would come out of her bedroom in her own toga, bum a cigarette from one of Robin's friends, and dance in the living room with a glass of wine in hand.

"Look at your mama," she would say to me as she put her hands in the air and shook her hips, "she's still got it. I'm one *sexy* lady! Come on, Kirkland, show us what you got!" I would be embarrassed for her, as the ill-fitting toga revealed that she wasn't as beautiful as she once was. Her face had gotten puffy, and she moved like an old lady trying to be sexy. But I also sensed that she knew how she looked now and danced anyway. It was once again the admiring looks on my brother's friends' faces, their unspoken wish that their parents could be as fun, that overcame any mortification I felt and compelled me to dance with her. It was also one of the few times she looked happy. I wanted to help her hold on to that feeling as long as she could.

As the toga parties wound down, in the wee hours of the morning, a group of us, my mother included, would sit in a sharing circle in the living room. My brother's friends would tell her about their lives while my mother puffed on a cigarette and nodded understandingly. I was proudest of her during these moments, as I listened to these closed teenage boys open up while she listened. It seems she was able to act like a mother only when it wasn't expected, which is the only way I was able to access her—the recipient of reflected rather than direct light.

As I STARTED MY SOPHOMORE YEAR of school, I knew it was time to leave Bermuda. Robin was leaving for college the next year, and I didn't want to be left abandoned in our crumbling home with Monty. I had outgrown the island, and our school. I never hummed on the Bermudian frequency the way Robin and Monty had learned to do, mastering the combination of island ease and polite formality. I was unhappy and getting more so, and I didn't know why. I was constantly scared of being exposed, or being rejected, or perhaps making a connection and then feeling stuck, so on the weekends, I stayed in the house, while Robin and Monty developed rich social lives. The as yet unidentified feelings trapped inside me had no safe outlet if I remained.

One of my Adirondack friends had just spent her first year at Phillips Academy in Andover, Massachusetts, and talked about the freedom she felt there, and the myriad of choices that had opened up for her. That was enough for me to decide that's where I wanted to go.

When I told my mother, she simply said, "Okay."

"But I don't know if I can get in," I said.

"Of course you will."

"But how are we going to pay for it?"

"Don't worry about that."

"But we don't have any money."

My mother got that twenty-dollar-bill-at-the-base-of-the-driveway look in her eye. "If you get into Andover, I will figure out a way to pay for it," she said. I wondered if she was going to ask John to foot the bill, but I didn't ask.

Part III

Chapter 7

I didn't connect my mother's descent into alcoholism with my decision to leave Bermuda, but by the time I departed for boarding school my mother's transformation from butterfly back to caterpillar was complete. She had folded up her wings and enveloped herself in anger and self-pity, each drop of booze helping to spin a new layer around her self-imposed cocoon. She re-emerged with her beauty stripped away, replaced by a dull, prickly shell and no colorful wings to camouflage or fly her to safer ground.

My mother accompanied me from Bermuda to Boston in early September of 1984 to start my upper year at Andover, which was the equivalent of junior year in a regular American high school. On the day of enrollment, my mother and a family friend dropped me off a quarter of a mile from my dorm room because the moving trucks of other students were blocking our car's path. I took my one duffel bag, slung it over my shoulder, and kissed her goodbye. As I walked away, I turned back to see her clutching the arm of my friend with a forced smile on her face and a tear falling from beneath her sunglasses. When I turned back toward my dorm, I was overcome with a feeling of relief. I thought I had escaped, still unaware of the extent of my internal injuries. As I climbed the steps to my dorm room, the feeling of freedom receded into a familiar sense of anxiety and doom. I noticed my new dorm mates laughing with each other, while their parents carried boxes and talked with other parents about the classes their kids were taking. I smiled and kept my head down, and they smiled back, seemingly without a care in the world.

MY ROOMMATE WAS ALREADY in the room when I arrived, sitting on the floor and staring out the window.

"Hi, I'm Kirk," I said.

I looked at him and waited. He sat still for a few seconds, then turned his head in my direction, like an owl, and looked at me with the brightest, roundest blue eyes I had ever seen. "Hi," he said, and turned his head back toward the window. He said nothing else, so I walked past him into the unoccupied bedroom. I sat on the bed and closed the door, feeling safe in the tiny space.

My roommate was Yuri, from Yugoslavia, although I'm not sure if he told me or I learned it from the "facebook" that all incoming students received, which provided a head shot of everyone in the student body and basic biographical information. (These types of books, prevalent at schools like Andover and Harvard, would become the inspiration for Mark Zuckerberg's Facebook.) The facebook didn't explain that Yuri was high twenty-four hours a day and lived in a constant philosophical haze where basic communication was a multi-dimensional exercise.

"Hey Yuri, I'm heading to Commons. Do you want to go get something to eat?"

Slow head turn. Eyes locked on mine. Slow blink.

"Or maybe you ate already?"

Blink. Slight head tilt. Slower blink.

"Okay, then; I'll see you later."

I spoke to Yuri with as much enthusiasm as I could muster, wrongly assuming that he could be elevated into semiconsciousness if I lent him some energy. My attempts seemed to push him farther away. He attracted other people to our room, I can only assume telepathically, and soon developed a group of friends who shared his economy with words and lack of interest in my existence. I spent most of my time alone in the room with the door closed, listening to Top 40 radio.

One of the benefits of having a stoned roommate was that you could sing "Careless Whisper" at the top of your lungs and feel confident that he wasn't paying any attention to you, or if he was, he didn't care what you were doing or forgot soon thereafter. Mine was an unpopular music choice for boarding school attendees, an indication that I lacked taste and sophistication. Those who listened to the Grateful Dead were the most admired; close behind were B-52s punk lovers or aficionados who dissected the meaning of deep cuts from less commercially successful Rolling Stones albums. There were a few charismatic individuals who could get away with a genuine appreciation for R&B Commodores ballads or an ironic love of fifties barbershop quartets. What was never acceptable, under any circumstances, was pop music. But I sang it anyway, even when the door to the main hallway was open and I knew Yuri, his stoner friends, and the preppie next-door neighbor could hear me. Without being aware of it at the time, I was committing to my innate feeling of being "other" and leaning into it, having found no other pathway forward. I started to wonder if this made me more like my mother than I had previously thought.

I had trouble making friends. I was under the impression that the more wounded and unapproachable I was, the more likely somebody would want to crack through the veneer to discover the complicated, interesting person underneath, as I had been taught by John Hughes movies. But the Molly Ringwald in me was disappointed and confused that the script never quite wrote itself. Andover was not a small-town microcosm of misfits who had no choice but to interact with one another, but a larger society of individuals who had already begun the process of understanding their place in the world. Their self-discovery seemed to happen through the nurturing of seeds already planted.

My mother didn't visit, and only called occasionally on the upstairs phone shared by the entire dorm. I never spoke to her for long, as she only wanted to hear that I was doing okay, without my going into detail. Her questions led me to the answers that she wanted, providing me the pathway to ensure that she had the information necessary to check me off her list of worries: "You're happy there, aren't you? Your teachers are better than the ones in Bermuda, aren't they? You're getting enough to eat? You've made some good friends?" My mother's voice had taken on a permanent slur and a weepy quality that left me feeling that any indication of my unhappiness would only sink her more.

"Did I tell you that John traded *Beluga* for a larger yacht?" A long, exasperated sigh followed the question.

"No, I didn't hear that."

"Well, I told him not to. What do we need a hundred-and-twenty-foot yacht for? Was a hundred feet not enough?"

"Seems like it would be."

"It means we need another crew member," she said, "like I don't have enough Cubans rifling through my knickers."

"I'm no expert, but it seems like a one-Cuban job."

"You laugh. You have no idea what it's like living with strangers."

I looked down the hall at the familiar faces gathered outside of a dorm mate's room, realizing that after eight months I still didn't know any of their names. Maybe one of them was Jessie? "Perhaps you could introduce yourself to the people working on the boat?"

"You think it's funny." She laughed a short, piglike chortle.

"Just a thought."

She went silent on the end of the line, my cue to hang up before she said something that reminded me how sad she was.

"I'm glad you called. I have to go now. People are waiting for the phone."

"Okay, darling. I love you very much, sweetie."

"I know. I love you too."

MY MOTHER CALLED THE MONTH BEFORE my graduation to let me know that she wasn't going to be able to attend. She was having a hard time figuring out her schedule.

"Can't get the time off of work?" I joked.

She wasn't in the mood. She sounded defiant, which I intuited had to do with the fact that my father and stepmother were planning on attending, albeit reluctantly. I had spent the past several months pitching the possibility of graduation attendance to both of my parents, to a tepid reception. My father had blinked first, presumably because it was becoming embarrassing that neither one of them had committed yet. My father's and Barb's attendance was the best outcome for everyone. They would be easier for me to manage, my father would feel like a good parent, and my mother would be handed another building block for her fortress of self-pity.

In my mother's mind, my father should have never been extended an invitation to my graduation from the school that she had made possible and paid for. This justification weakened some years later, when I received my first bill from Andover for payment on the multiple loans that had been taken out in my name. When I asked my mother why she had taken out these loans without telling me, and suggested that I shouldn't be responsible for paying them, she became combative on the phone and ended our conversation by saying, "I gave you a good education so that you wouldn't need handouts," before hanging up on me.

My parents assumed that I would go to college, even though my father hadn't gone at all and my mother only went for two years, but neither one talked to me about it. I had done well enough to graduate in the middle of my class—which, when you went to Andover, meant that you could only hope to get into second-tier schools. My college counselor pushed Tulane

University, in New Orleans, a place I knew nothing about in a part of the country to which I had never been. I liked the idea, because once again it offered a change of venue at a time when I still believed that there was a geographic cure for my unhappiness. And the drinking age was nineteen. My father and stepmother agreed that the lower drinking age would "make things more fun." Whenever I had visited them in the past two years, my stepmother got on the phone and asked beforehand, "So, is this going to be another one of your 'find myself' visits, or are you going to join your old step-monster for a martini?" I applied to Tulane, got in, and decided to go without visiting the campus. I was on a quest to find a place that fit, having spent my life up to this point feeling like an observer of other people's lives. I had already determined that the carefree privilege of Cedarhurst, the stoic simplicity of Clinton, the sophisticated quirkiness of Bermuda, and the intellectual quaintness of Andover weren't it, so why not head south?

I WASN'T PREPARED FOR COLLEGE. I didn't even know where I was physically going. A couple of weeks before I was scheduled to show up at Tulane, I looked at a map to figure out how to get there. I had assumed it was somewhere south of Pennsylvania, and that I could grab a ride with one of my friends from the Adirondacks who might be heading back to school in that direction. When I didn't see New Orleans listed anywhere on the Eastern Seaboard, I scanned farther south and then looked left, shocked to discover it was halfway across the country, nestled between Texas and Mississippi.

"Did you know this?" I asked my father, explaining what I had just learned.

"What do you mean, did I know it?"

"Did you know that New Orleans was that far away?"

"You didn't know that?"

"Fuck no. I wouldn't have gone to college that far away."

"I thought you were the smart one." He laughed.

"You know I'm not good at directions."

"I don't think this counts."

"And you forget I grew up in Bermuda. It's not like I studied American geography."

"I know where you grew up. I can even point it out on a map."

"Shit."

"Barb!" my father called to my stepmother as he walked out of the living room. "You won't believe what Kirkland just told me!"

I entered college hoping that I would find something that would help me make sense of who I was, since I had been disappearing gradually. I didn't even have enough perspective to know whether there actually was a "me" who had disappeared; maybe I had never been there to begin with. I landed at the New Orleans airport having arranged for my new roommate, Eric, to pick me up. He was from Jackson, Mississippi, but he might as well have been from a Soviet republic or a northern Canadian province. I had never met a person from Mississippi, and held a caricature in my head of a slow-talking, racist, beer-bellied smirker in a Chevy pickup. In contrast, Eric was slight and nerdy, with pressed khakis and round, yellow-rimmed glasses. He looked like John Lennon before John Lennon had discovered drugs.

We shared a room in a dorm overlooking a large field, adjacent to the main campus, where freshman boys played pick-up games of touch football in the afternoon before classes started for the semester. I watched them from my dorm window, wondering how the game had begun, unable to imagine either starting it or accepting an invitation to play. Yet there everyone was, some of them fit and gifted, some of them less so, enjoying themselves as if it was actually only a game and not a test or a ritual. I was afraid to walk out of my dorm, thinking they might try to draft me into playing, so when I left the building I wore a large coat that hid my emaciated frame and moved away.

I met Ethan, who lived down the hall from me, the first week of school. Our friendship grew gradually, and at his convenience. He attended one fraternity function after another, unsure where he would fit in best. In contrast, my social life revolved around a small pack of guys on my hall who had decided against the fraternity system, which is what one tells oneself when that system has decided against you.

During the introductory phase of our friendship, I peppered my biography with details of my blue-blooded pedigree. I understood that Ethan had an innate fascination with old money, and the access he assumed came with it. After a party where he was treated dismissively by one of the snooty Deke brothers, he asked why people "like me" were such dicks.

"WASPs sting," I said.

"You did not just say that."

"Buzzzzz."

"So clever. Do all of you think you're better than the rest of us?"

"Don't snap at me. You're the one trying to be friends with these people, not me," I replied. "I've already realized how stupid it is to separate yourself in the pursuit of feeling superior."

"That's bullshit," he said. "You sit here alone in your room, acting like you're above it all, and then lecture me on how stupid it is to be above it all?"

"Not as stupid as aspiring to be a part of a group that thinks it's better than you because you were born Jewish, or didn't have the right address growing up. You think there's some great revelation to be had by 'breaking through' to the other side. There's nothing new over there—it's just the same people wearing different costumes."

Our conversations were exhilarating. I had never met somebody who hummed on my same frequency so effortlessly.

"So, let me get this straight," Ethan said to me one day while we were hanging out in my room. "You were born into money, but now your family doesn't have any, but you're going to one of the most expensive schools in the country. How does that work?" He was sitting on my roommate Eric's bed, strumming a guitar that his parents had given him. Our hall mate was an accomplished guitar player, and Ethan had spent hours with him learning the basics of chord progression. He spent every down moment practicing.

"My father's paying for it," I said.

"I thought you said he didn't have any money left."

"Well, he's kind of paying for it. I think I'm paying for it too. I'm not really sure," I said.

"What do you mean, you're paying for it?"

"I have loans. But I also think he controls my trust fund. And if he does, I want to make sure that he at least spends it on me and not on something else," I said. The summer before, I'd had a conversation with my father in which he suggested I go to a community college. I was offended, and disheartened. I felt like a financial problem to be neutralized rather than a possibility to be invested in.

ETHAN ROWED CREW IN THE MORNINGS, returning to the dorm at about 9 a.m. I'd hear him burst through the hall door while I was still in bed, yelling, "I do more before nine a.m. than you do all day!" My heart would quicken as he got closer to my door. Sometimes he would find somebody to talk to before he got to me, and his voice would fade as he retreated into another room. But every morning, I would lie still under the covers with my eyes closed, trying to calm my heart, hoping that he would pick me, even though I knew we were all just mirrors that he used to admire himself.

"Get up, brahhh," he yelled one morning. I winced the first time he addressed me with this white, southern version of "brother."

I lay still. I had calibrated my reaction over the past few weeks, angling to hook him for an extended visit. If I moved too quickly, he spooked and moved on to the next door. If I moved too slowly, he grew bored and left. After a few seconds of him lurking in the doorway, I moaned and said, "Get out of my room," a phrase I knew would ensure he stayed.

"Man, we must have rowed thirty mahles today," he said, moving into the room. I loved how he said "miles." Southern people always left their sentences open, as if they welcomed a response. In the Northeast, communication was a competition where the person who had the last word won.

On the mornings when I did my job well, Ethan would end up launching himself onto Eric's bed (Eric always left for class early). I'd roll over to face him. He would tell me about rowing practice, or the fraternity party he was going to that night, while I nodded and threw out supportive, world-weary responses. I think he viewed my lack of interest in the Tulane social scene as evidence of sophistication, when I was just protecting myself from almost certain rejection.

As we chatted, he would get up off the bed and circle the room, rooting through Eric's belongings. He would flip through Eric's extensive, alphabetized album collection (filled with punk and alternative bands like the Jam and the Cocteau Twins and a new band called 10,000 Maniacs), remove a single album from its assigned spot and place it in a different section. I looked forward to the moment when Eric would come home, examine his albums, and lose his shit as he placed them back in order.

Ethan was everybody's annoying, bullying big brother. He liked to wrestle. I was mortified the few times he tackled me, simultaneously repulsed and excited by the intimacy of his body pressed against mine, and the sound of his labored breathing close to my ear.

Ethan's parents lived in Mobile and came to visit him often, usually bearing bags of food and clothing. If they couldn't come for a few weeks, his mother would send him care packages filled with new shirts, still wrapped in their original packaging. Ethan would open each shirt, decide which ones he wanted, and toss the others aside until the next visit, when his mother would gather the rejects to return them. The only clothes I had were the ones I had arrived with. I couldn't afford to buy anything else, and my parents didn't know what a care package was, so Ethan gave me his old clothes. He chuckled as he handed me the blue flannel shirt that would become my favorite item of winter clothing. "You are the poorest rich person I know," he said.

Ethan and I didn't go out socially together. Our friendship existed in the bubble that we created during long conversations in my dorm room, where he quizzed me on my childhood and tried to make sense of the world that I was describing to him.

"You had a butler?" he asked me one night.

"We didn't have a butler. My great-grandfather had a butler, Eugene, who then became my great-aunt's butler."

"Oh, I'm sorry. The *family* had a butler. My mistake."

"Noted."

"I'm surprised they didn't give you your own, considering what a slob you are."

"I need one. And I'm not saying I don't deserve one."

"Clearly."

"Eugene used to escort my father from his bedroom to the dining room and announce him for breakfast."

"Come *on*."

Ethan shook his head in disbelief, lowered his head, and smiled.

"I'd feel sorry for the guy if I wasn't so mad at him," I continued.

"You're mad at the *butler*?"

"I'm mad at my father."

Our conversations evolved from playful to serious. When I spoke to him about my life, I not only held his attention, but also fascinated him. I could see him struggling to find a way to relate to my family situation when his was so normal: He had a younger brother, a younger sister, a cardiologist father, and a stay-at-home mom. When he spoke to his father on the phone every week, he answered questions about his physical-fitness regimen and study habits with "Yes, sir."

He didn't want to be like me, or the people that I knew. But he wanted to live without constraints, and he viewed the world that I came from as conquerable if he could gather enough intelligence from an inside source to navigate it. He didn't realize yet that the people I had grown up around built a system whereby they could recognize their own through the subtle clues that only generations of conditioning could create, a corner of a shirt unself-consciously untucked, a frayed belt, laughter at an inappropriate time. There was no way to dress, act, or play the part.

Ethan was conflicted about his Jewish heritage. For my part, the Jewish people on my hall showed me what families could be like, and I gravitated toward them. Tulane was 40 percent Jewish, which I hadn't known before I decided to come. I still held in the back of my mind the derisive tone my father used when talking about Jews, and battled my own reaction every now and then. As a group they were louder, and wore bright clothing. The girls wore their hair high, and some of them chewed gum loudly and with their mouths wide open. The Jewish boys on my hall were cornier than they were clever, and when we went out together they would always want to split the bill, triggering the most damning of the slights I had heard leveled at Jewish people. (The people I grew up with always fought to pick up the bill, even the ones who didn't have any money.) But they were kinder and less aloof, and they seemed to genuinely care about me in ways that my childhood friends might have felt but rarely expressed openly.

"I don't think ZBT is going to rush Caleb," I told Ethan one night. Caleb lived at the end of our hall.

"Aww, that's too bad, man," Ethan said. "I know his parents really wanted him to get in."

"He may do that other Jewish fraternity—with the Pi sign in it."

"Don't act like you don't know the name," he said, annoyed.

I DON'T REMEMBER HOW I MET Avery my freshman year, but I was drawn to her kindness and openness. She had curly blond hair like Shirley Temple and radiated an infectious energy. Her voice was her most distinctive feature: whiskey-thick, husky, and twanged with a cartoonlike North Carolina mountain drawl. She sounded like she was recovering from laryngitis.

I spent the first part of the year nursing a huge crush on her, watching from afar as the Greek world absorbed her. She and Ethan ran in the same social circles, and when I asked about her, he would say she was "cute" in a way that let me know she wasn't his type (meaning—in his estimation—she wasn't hot enough for him) but that she might be fine for me. His lukewarm response to her may have been the only reason I was eventually brave enough to ask her out on a date.

She said yes, which I didn't expect. Ethan helped me pick out the restaurant, a place to have a drink afterward, and, should I be able to run both of those gauntlets, a place to go dancing. I don't remember the details of the date except for the end of the night, when we ended up slow-dancing at a hotel bar. I hadn't expected to get this far. I sensed rejection was just around the corner, and my defenses were readied to absorb the sting once it came. I was surprised when Avery gave no sign that she wanted to go home.

I kissed her. It wasn't passionate, but it was as real a kiss as I had ever had. And she kissed me back.

I took Avery home and kissed her again before watching her walk up to her apartment with a casual "I'll call you soon. I had a nice time."

"I did too," she said. I believed her.

I left a message on her machine the next day, reiterating how nice it was to spend time with her and that I hoped we could do something again soon. When I didn't hear back after a few days, I called again. This time Avery's roommate answered the phone.

"Is Avery there?" I asked, heart in my throat. "It's Kirk."

There was a long pause. "Um, she's not here right now."

"Do you know when she'll be home?"

"No, I don't."

"Can I leave a message?"

Another long pause. "What's your number?"

She wrote it down and hung up, and I waited a few more days before I called again. After I'd invested in the hope that somebody I liked might like me back, it was surprisingly hard to accept that I was wrong.

Her answering machine picked up again. "Hi Avery, it's Kirk," I said. "I haven't heard back from you and I'm assuming I won't, which is okay. I just wanted you to know that I had a really good time with you and maybe I'll see you around."

I SANK BACK INTO MY OLD ROUTINES. One day after class I wandered down the hall to see if Ethan was in his room. His door was slightly ajar, so I peeked in to find him facedown on his bed with his shirt off and his eyes closed.

"Hey man, what's up?" he asked groggily, opening the one eye not smashed into his pillow.

"You don't look so good," I said.

"I'm just exhausted, man. This crew shit is killing me. What are you doing?"

"Nothing. I talked to my mother this morning."

"Yeah? How's drunk mommy?"

"Woozy."

Ethan laughed. When it came to my mother, he wanted me to laugh with him at the absurdity of it all, because he hadn't figured out yet how to fix my sadness about it. Of course, I hadn't either.

"Did she know it was you, or did she just pick up the phone hoping that she got lucky and at least dialed one of her children?"

"She calls all of us 'darling'—that way she's covered."

"It's not like she knows anything about your life anyway, does she?"

"How's school, darling?" I used my hand as a fake receiver and mimicked my mother on the phone.

"Great, Mom!" Ethan continued, playing my role. "It's hot here in *New Orleans.*"

"How's your weather, darling?" I said, slurring.

"Still hot, Mom!" Ethan said perkily.

"You still in Boston?"

"That's Robin, Mom. He's at Babson."

"Okay, sweetie. Bundle up so you don't catch a cold. Boston's freezing this time of year."

"*New Orleans*, Mom."

"Don't you swear at me, young man!"

"I'm a drag queen now, Mom. And I'm dating a black Jew named 'Dreamcatcher.'"

"Okay, sweetie. Take care, now."

"Love you, Mommy!"

By the time we were done with our fake conversation, Ethan was rolling back and forth on the bed, grabbing his stomach and laughing. "Oh my God, that hurts," he said, lying back down on his stomach. His laughter died, and he let out a long sigh. "I could sleep for days." His eyes closed again.

"Do you want me to rub your back?"

The question escaped before I could think about it. I said it casually, like I was a trainer taking care of an athlete.

Ethan opened one eye and looked at me. "Sure," he said. His voice was low. He turned his head around and looked at the wall.

I sat on his bed.

"Close the door," he said.

"Okay."

I placed both of my hands on Ethan's shoulders. He had come to Tulane muscled, but the weeks of rowing crew had filled out his shoulders. They were rock hard beneath my fingers. He lifted his arms above his head.

"That feels good," he said contentedly. "Man, I need this."

After kneading the tops of his shoulders for a minute, I started to run down the middle of his perfectly smooth back where the muscles met the spine. My body warmed all over, starting from the top of my head, into my torso, my groin, and down into my legs. I felt the front of my pants fill slightly. *It's just the touch of skin on skin*, I said to myself. *It's perfectly normal.*

I swallowed hard. "I don't think my mother is going to get better," I said. There was something about the added intimacy of rubbing his back, as if we had crossed a line into uncharted territory. I wasn't sure if I had never considered the possibility that my mother might not recover or if I had just never admitted it to anyone else.

"Aw, man, it just sucks," Ethan said.

My thumbs were now working into the grooves of his spine, moving toward the small of his back.

"She was so strong after she left my father. And she loved us so fiercely, almost to the point of anger. I always had this sense that she was waiting for somebody to hurt us so that she could pounce." I thought, for the first time in a long time, of what Jamie had done to Monty.

I reached the waistband of his shorts. I was careful not to touch them. I fanned out to the side of his body and started working my way back up.

"But there was always this part of her that wasn't there, and now it feels as though she's permanently left. Does that make any sense?"

One of the muscles on his back twitched, like electric charges were running under his skin.

"The bar," he said.

"Huh?"

"I think she left you to go to the bar," he said.

I laughed.

"It's called Froggy's. All the locals hang out there."

"You're a dick."

I massaged the back of his neck and felt the softness of his hair tickling my fingers.

"You love it," he said, sighing. "Man, that feels good."

There was a knock on the door. Ethan leapt from the bed like somebody had burned him with a cattle brand and opened his door.

"Hey, Gil, what's up, man?" he said casually to his childhood friend. "Kirk and I were just hanging out and talking."

Gil looked at me like a shocked girlfriend might if she caught her man with another woman. I was used to this look from many of Ethan's friends and fraternity brothers, who seemed to feel they shared a special bond with him that nobody else could understand; it didn't occur to me until much later that I may have been under the same illusion.

I felt Gil's hunger for Ethan's attention, but I didn't connect it with my own. I was pretty sure Gil was gay, and that he had a crush on Ethan.

"I was just stopping by to say hah," Gil said, cutting his eyes away from me and looking at Ethan, like Scarlett O'Hara in pressed khakis and a button-down shirt.

"What's been up, man?" Ethan asked.

"Just schoolwork—the usual," Gil replied. "You heading home for spring break this year?"

"Nah, man—probably sticking around here." Ethan stretched and looked at me nervously. I knew he wanted me to join the conversation, to make it less awkward, but I had no interest in speaking with Gil, whose effeminacy I viewed with contempt. My feelings for Ethan couldn't be sexual, I felt, because I didn't look and act like Gil.

Gil was interrupting my time with Ethan, and I wanted him to leave. I leveled my gaze back at Ethan, cocked my head, and stared. I had seen women do this when they wanted to send an unspoken message to their men, and my message was broadcasting loud and clear: *Get rid of him.*

After Gil left, Ethan announced that he had to get ready for class and that he would see me later. I got up from the side of the bed and looked at him. But his eyes darted away from mine as he turned toward his dresser.

* * *

A FEW NIGHTS LATER I was lying in bed when my heart stopped beating. I bolted upright and grabbed my chest. In my nineteen years, my heart had kept a steady rhythm, and I had never thought of it unless I ran fast or felt nervous. It resumed beating a split second later with an unfamiliar urgency, as if it had been squeezed into submission and then released.

I got out of bed and walked out into the hallway holding my chest, thinking that if I was going to die of a heart attack, I wanted to make sure somebody in the hallway would find me. I stumbled toward Ethan's room, gripping the wall as I went, and knocked on his door. "I need to go to the hospital," I said when he opened it.

"What's wrong?" Ethan asked. He grabbed my arms, and I slumped a little against him.

"I think I'm having a heart attack," I replied.

Ethan deposited me at my door a few hours later with a look of disgust on his face. We had spent a few hours in the school's emergency room only to be told that I had suffered an anxiety attack. The diagnosis sounded suspicious, like I wasn't any different from the drama-queen mother I had spent the majority of my freshman year caricaturing. "But my heart physically *stopped*," I protested to myself.

I spent the rest of the night wide awake, my heart now estranged from the rest of my body, wondering when it would finally cease beating. My only consolation was that my death would confirm that I was nothing like my mother.

During the next few months, I slipped into an emotional coma. I had entered college hoping that I would find a conduit to help propel me out of my fog so I could once again see where

I was going. But the person I had chosen as this conduit, Ethan, was adding a new layer of haze. I adjusted my schedule to be in my room at times when I thought Ethan might be between classes, but his visits to my room decreased as his social life took off. I stayed in at night, sometimes sitting under my desk in the dark, hoping to find a place small enough to make me feel safe.

When I saw Ethan, he asked me how I was feeling. His tone sounded concerned but with a resolute *you'll be fine* undercurrent to it that sounded like my mother. He visited me only when he was feeling reflective and needed an antidote to the constant adrenaline drip of college life. My misery served as a mellowing balm to his frenetic world.

"What if I'm gay?" I said to him one afternoon. It was the first time I had articulated this fear out loud. I was talking to Ethan about it in a fit of bravery, and to test his reaction, figuring that I was losing him one way or the other.

"What?" he replied.

"How can you say for sure that I'm not?" I asked.

He stopped strumming the guitar and sat up on the bed.

"Don't say that," he said.

"I'm not saying that I am. I don't know what I am."

"You're not gay," he said, getting annoyed. "Where is this coming from, Kirk?"

"I don't know." I shook my head. "I hear you guys talking about girls and what you've done with them and what you want to do with them and it's . . . just pathetic, you know? I just don't get it."

"What don't you get?"

"You all talk about girls like they are a collection of body parts one minute, fawn over them the next, brag about fucking them, yet can't even talk to them without sounding like morons," I said.

Ethan had picked up the guitar again during my diatribe, his hard expression changing back to amusement.

"That's how guys are," he said. "You're just different, Kirk." He always sounded proud when he told me that I was different.

"Well, it's just stupid," I finished.

He strummed the opening chords of "Stairway to Heaven," stopping when he got to the part that he hadn't learned yet. He lifted his head and looked at me across the room. "Have you ever been with a girl?"

"I've been with girls," I said. I didn't elaborate on what I meant, but I could tell from the way Ethan's head dipped that he knew what I wasn't saying.

"Did you enjoy it?" he asked.

"It was okay," I said, thinking back to the awkward wet hump of a girl's thigh the summer before college started. Her name was Camille and she was tall and I whispered an ashamed "Sorry" in her ear when it was over, but other than that, I couldn't remember her or the night we spent together.

"The first time's never great," Ethan said. "The next time will be better."

"That's just it," I said, my voice rising with the truth of what I was trying to tell him. "I don't know why I'm not more excited about the next time."

"You just haven't met the right girl yet, Kirk," Ethan said. "She's out there, man. You're a great guy."

"Or there's always the gay option," I said, laughing.

"Don't say that, Kirk."

"I'm just saying, there are options!" I teased.

"Don't even joke about that—I'm serious." Usually our philosophical musings were conversational, like a dance, but this tone had no rhythm to it. He turned his head toward the window and strummed the opening chords of "House of the Rising Sun."

"I love you, Kirk, and you're my best friend in the world, but if you turned out to be gay, we couldn't be friends anymore." He looked sad, and the dark melody of the song he was playing added weight to his words. They would stay with me for decades to come. "It would kill me, man, but I would never speak to you again."

Chapter 8

I left Tulane after freshman year. I had coasted through my first semester on the momentum from Andover but stalled in the second, barely achieving a 2.0 grade average. I started skipping classes so that nobody could see how miserable I was.

One night, I found myself alone at Fat Harry's bar, a late-night hangout for Tulane students. I watched people laughing and drinking and waited for a break in their conversation, at which point I would focus and try to catch somebody's gaze as their eyes scanned the room. When their eyes passed over me, I felt like a part of me was disappearing, like they were erasing me out of existence. I moved outside to the curb to get some air. Two girls stood by the curb next to me, laughing and smoking a cigarette. I turned to one of them and held out my hand. "My name is Kirk," I said, trying to act as confident as Ethan had the first time I met him. One of them stepped back to take a look at me, scowled, and said, "Dude, gain some pounds."

Ethan took me to the airport the last day of freshman year and hugged me for a long time before I walked through security. It was early June in New Orleans, but I was wearing a full-length Belgian military coat because it was too big to fit into my one duffel bag. Anybody who saw us that day would have found it odd that a tall, muscular athlete was leaning against a mop wrapped up in a wool blanket. I never asked Ethan why he held on to me for so long, especially given that we were in a public place. I wanted to believe it was because he loved me and didn't want to let me go.

I don't remember where the plane took me, but I'm guessing I ended up at my father's place in the Adirondacks for part of the summer. Those first few months were a blur. All I know for sure is that I ended up back in Bermuda in early fall. I had nowhere else to go.

My sixteen-year-old brother and his friends had converted our home into a clubhouse. They congregated after school every day, drinking beer purchased by my mother's charge card. Empty bottles and dirty dishes littered tabletops. Foam poked from the ripped seams of the sectional couch. My mother's étagères, once adorned with Beatrix Potter figurines and animals carved in ivory, were now empty, and two of the glass shelves were missing.

My mother stopped by the house every now and then, when John was gone, and walked through the devastation as if she didn't notice it. I witnessed the interactions between my mother and younger brother like I was watching an afterschool special that had yet to announce the moral of the story.

"How was Greece?" my brother asked one afternoon, sipping a beer. My mother had come to grab some clothes to take back to the house she shared with John.

"Oh, it was lovely, darling. I would have preferred that John didn't invite the Smiths, but never mind."

"Did Gerald puke on the boat again?" Monty asked.

"He can't handle his liquor. And his wife is worse," my mother replied. "I don't even know why they want to be on the boat, to be quite honest with you. The poor bastard gets seasick just looking at the ocean from our patio."

Monty finished his beer and got up from the couch to grab another one. My mother waited for him to return from the kitchen, keeping her eyes fixed on the window above my head. It was the only window through which we could claim a water view, no more than glimpses of blue through the thick casuarina trees that dotted the north shore of the island. The house that she shared with John had 270-degree water views, with only a few scattered trees to block the scenes of high-masted yachts sailing into and out of Tucker's Town Cove.

"Hi, darling," she said to me cautiously.

"Hi," I said, not glancing up from my book. Ever since I had come home, my mother and brother avoided talking to me, lest I unleash the rage and horror I felt at how they were living their lives.

"Did John tell you the massage story?" Monty asked my mother, returning with a fresh beer.

"I don't want to hear it."

"It's the one where Gerald was getting a massage from this hot Irish girl—"

"Honestly, Monty . . ."

"—and their friend Stewart came by the house, saw that Gerald was getting a massage in the living room, and then tiptoed in and took over for her? You've heard this one, haven't you?"

"I have no idea what you're talking about," my mother huffed.

"And then he started tickling Gerald's seeds underneath the towel. And Gerald started moaning . . ."

My mother laughed with her mouth closed, like she didn't want to but couldn't help herself. "I'm sure his twitchy little wife hasn't touched those shriveled-up prunes lately," she said.

". . . and he kept moaning louder and squirming and Stewart kept twiddling his balls while his little pecker got hard." Monty laughed and rocked back and forth with his Heineken bottle. I glanced up from my book.

"That fat little thing would break her in two with one pump." My mother thrust her hips out to illustrate the point. "She'd snap like dried twigs!"

"So finally he turns around, planning to see if the lady massaging his balls was ready for more, and sees Stewart sitting there with a big grin on his face. You've never *seen* a fat man jump so high!"

"I can see it." My mother was doing her moaning laugh now. "Oh, I can *see* him jumping!"

"John said they were up all night laughing about it. God, I wish I was there."

"No, you don't," my mother said, wiping tears of laugher from her cheeks. "Stewart and Gerald are filthy old men. You were brought up to be a gentleman."

"Yeah, right," I said.

"You were too," my mother said.

"It speaks!" Monty said.

I dropped the book on my lap and stared up at my mother. "Does it not bother you that Gerald's 'twitchy little wife'—your supposed friend—is being cheated on by her husband?"

"Gerald did not *cheat* on anyone," she replied.

"He would have," I said, "if things progressed as he thought they would."

"Why did you come back here if all you're going to do is sit on your ass and judge the rest of us?" my mother said. "Your brother and I were doing just fine without you."

I chuckled. "Yeah, looks like you're doing great." I gestured around the room at the moldy curtains, the half-broken figurines on dusty shelves, and the stained couch.

"You left," Monty said, slamming his beer on the coffee table, his hands shaking. "You and Robin both fucking LEFT."

Monty erupted from the couch, grabbed another beer from the kitchen, and stormed out of the house, the screen door slamming behind him.

"Now look what you've done," my mother said.

I laughed. "Yeah, what *I've* done."

"For years I spent EVERY WAKING MOMENT doing EVERYTHING for you children. It's MY time now. I won't be made to feel guilty about that!" My mother's voice cracked as she turned away and headed into her bedroom to retrieve her clothes. She didn't look at me when she came back out. She fumbled for the keys in her purse.

"Are you coming back tomorrow?" I asked.

"I don't think so, Kirkland. I don't know why I came here today. I woke up feeling good," she said.

"It's just that you went through the same thing as your friend," I said.

"I have no idea what you're talking about," she said, pulling the keys from her purse and heading toward the door. "And tell

Monty to mow the lawn this afternoon. The yard looks like a bunch of goddam inbreds live here."

"When Daddy cheated on you—with Lola. You know what that feels like."

My mother stopped walking and grabbed for a dining room chair to steady herself. She sighed and dropped her head. It seemed my words never brought us closer, just triggered a pain that didn't go away.

"Monty and I will be fine," I said. "Go back to John. Tell him I said hi."

My mother left, and I went to my bedroom and closed the door. I didn't want to talk to Monty when he came back. Robin and I had left him to save ourselves, just as we had all of those years ago with Jamie. When I saw him the next day, we pretended that nothing had happened.

THE FIRST THREE WEEKS of living back in Bermuda, I stayed awake late at night with my door open, waiting for the phone to ring. I had called Ethan upon landing and had tried him once a week from then on, keeping my messages light and easy. "Hey, it's Kirk. No need to get back to me if you don't want to, I know you must be busy at school. Call me when you can." I practiced this message, fighting the urge to tell him how desperate I was to talk to him. Each night that went by without him calling back felt like I was falling deeper into a hole. I had few friends left on the island, so my weekend nights were spent with my door closed, trying to drown out the sound of Monty and his drunk friends blasting reggae from huge speakers throughout the house.

Monty had adopted Rastafarian culture, preaching "one love" and sporting red, yellow, and green tie-dyed bracelets and T-shirts while strutting around the house like a stoned cockatoo. But his mellow demeanor disintegrated whenever I was near, replaced with a biting disregard that let me know he no longer subscribed to the brotherly pecking order. I didn't fight back. I knew that I was partly responsible for making him this way. He had crafted a life from the ruins I left him in.

Ethan called after the third week, at 11 p.m. on a weeknight. I erupted out of bed. I ran down the marble hallway in my socks, slid my body into the wall to stop my momentum, and grabbed the receiver. I held my palm over the receiver for a split second, took a deep breath, and said "Hello" as casually as I could.

"Hey, man, it's Ethan."

Those four words lifted me out of despair. We spoke for an hour, about school and his family, and my time in Bermuda. I felt my haze dissipate and a renewed energy take hold.

"Well, I better get going, class tomorrow," he said.

"Thanks, Ethan. I can't tell you how much I needed to speak with you," I said.

"No problem, man. I love talking to you."

"I love talking to you too. I miss you."

"Man, I miss you too." He paused for a second. "Hey, man, I forgot to tell you the biggest change that's happened. Can't believe we haven't talked about it. I really need to talk to someone."

"What is it?" I said, concerned and excited. I had always been the one who needed Ethan.

"I've really got to go, but I'm going to call you back tomor-row. I need your advice."

"You know you can call me anytime."

"Good, because this is all brand-new for me and I don't know what to do. I'm a mess. I met a girl, man. Her name is Paisley. I think I'm in love, Kirk."

IT TOOK ETHAN ANOTHER FEW WEEKS to call me back. We launched into his relationship with Paisley, even though I had already filled in the story in my head. I knew she had to be a pretty sorority girl, and popular. On those counts I was correct. I hadn't anticipated that she came from an old-money southern family with an alcoholic father.

"She reminds me of you, Kirk," Ethan said.

They had started going out in the summer, both having stayed in New Orleans after the end of freshman year. Ethan recounted their sexual exploration in detail over the phone, describing every grope and tickle that stopped before inter-course. She wanted to go all the way, but he believed that he shouldn't have sex with the woman he was going to marry.

I listened and asked follow-up questions. I was flattered that he was telling me what I assumed he didn't share with anyone else, yet the intimacy of what he was sharing was excruciating to hear. I decided I needed to have sex with someone.

I had no interest in going out, but sex required a second participant. So when a friend of mine from school invited me to join them at the downtown bars full of U.S. college students on spring break, I said yes. By the end of the evening we were swimming in my friend's pool with some girls from a small Ohio university. When one of the girls lingered next to me by the side of the pool, I acted as if I were interested. An hour later I was driving her to my house on the back of a moped, hoping I was sober enough not to kill us, and drunk enough to go through with what would come next.

She wanted to cuddle and spend the night, and I wanted her out of my bed and out of my house as soon as possible. The look in her eyes, hurt and confused, as I rushed her to get dressed, saying I needed to get up early the next day, confirmed that I had done something wrong, to her and for me. Yet underneath the shame, and the craving that hadn't eased, there was the baseline relief that I was no longer a virgin.

"I NEED HELP to get my mother to stop drinking."

The counselor sat a few feet away from me. I expected her expression to change, but her blue eyes held steady as she looked back at me without pity. For years I had become accustomed to people scrunching up their eyes in sadness and tilting their heads when I referred to my mother's problem. This woman didn't flinch. *What a heartless bitch*, I thought. And then, almost in the same moment, *Her parents must have been drunks too.*

She had short brown hair that looked like it had been curled and permanently set, every strand perfectly placed in its hierarchy, either through intimidation or loyalty to its host. Her composure seemed linked to her hairdo somehow, as if one defecting hair could trigger a follicular mutiny.

"Why do you think she needs your help?" she asked. I wasn't used to this question. Up until now, every person I had spoken with had assumed from my concern that there was something to be concerned about.

"Because she drinks too much. She's drunk all of the time. She never takes her sunglasses off . . ." I stopped and turned my head, feeling the words ushering in the despair that I otherwise managed to hold at bay.

"Let me ask you," she said, looking down at the clipboard in front of her, "what do you think normal drinking is?"

Is she reading her questions off of the clipboard?

I shuffled in my seat. "I don't know—a couple of drinks at lunch, a couple at night, maybe some wine with dinner." I was thinking about how my father and stepmother drank. They were always a little tipsy after dinner, but they might have three drinks before we sat down and then a nightcap afterward. I knew my mother was a drunk, but I assumed that my father and stepmother were still within the range of what was considered normal consumption.

"Do you drink?" she asked.

"I drink socially, I guess."

"What's 'socially'?" she asked.

Usually, saying that you "drank socially" was a euphemism for drinking heavily with other people who were also drinking heavily but who could still function the next day. Everybody accepted that.

"I have a few drinks when I go out with my friends, like most people my age. I have a little too much every now and then—normal college stuff."

"When you say your mother is drinking all of the time, what do you mean?" she asked.

"I mean that every time I see her, she has a drink in her hand. It doesn't matter if it's day or night. It doesn't matter if she's in the car, at a party, or in her bedroom. There is always a drink in her hand."

The counselor looked down at the clipboard again and flipped through the pages as if she were looking for the part that addressed "drinks whenever awake" on the diagnostic continuum of alcohol abuse. I now understood why the ad in the yellow pages said "Alcoholism—free counseling," since she clearly hadn't been doing this long enough to get paid for it. She flipped the first few pages all the way over and wedged them between the clipboard and her aqua-blue polyester pants.

Her face softened as she leaned forward in her chair and lifted a hand to her ear as if to brush back an imaginary strand of hair with her manicured red fingernails. "First of all, Kirk, I want to thank you for coming here today. You're in the right place." I pictured that line on the top of her page, with a blank space for my name. "You should know that for adults, normal drinking is one or two drinks per week, not every night. This might go up if people are socializing occasionally, but even then, most people have one drink, maybe two. What you're describing is way past what is considered normal."

I flashed through images of my childhood, to every party that I had witnessed with my parents' friends, where the host filled drinks as soon as they were empty, and how normal everyone had seemed to me. Happy, even. I thought about the first time I got drunk on beer, when I was fourteen years old, and my father handed me a cigar and encouraged me to smoke it, without telling me not to inhale. After I had stumbled away and thrown up, I stood and faced the mirror, slapping my cheeks with cold water, and then stumbled back to the party to tell my father that I was just fine. He laughed and nudged the guy next to him, a circle of smoke from his own cigar hovering like a cloud over both of their heads, and said to me, "Gentlemen hold their liquor, Kirkland." The next morning, when I asked him why he had given me the cigar, he said, "I figured if you got sick, you would think twice about drinking so much." I decided then that when I got drunk, I would never let anybody know it, that I would get better at it.

"One or two drinks per *week*?" I asked. "Are you sure? Do you mean for everyone?"

"What do you mean?" she asked.

"I mean . . . are there certain groups of people who drink more than others?" I was trying to ascertain if there might be a special category that existed outside of this rule. My own non-scientific study of my people suggested that this must be the case, or else everyone I had ever known was a raging alcoholic.

"Certain groups are more susceptible to alcoholism than others, but we don't know what causes it. We do know that alcoholics tend to like being around other alcoholics, if that's what you're getting at." She stated this matter-of-factly, an edge of anger in her voice. She was unlike most of the counselors I had seen on TV, who spoke with their patients in soft tones and handed them tissues while they cried. "Let's talk about your mother. What you told me is very disturbing."

No shit.

"If your mother is drinking the way that you tell me she's drinking, it is very likely that her organs are going to start shutting down within a few years and she will die." She flipped to the back of the clipboard and pulled out a pamphlet and handed it to me. "Furthermore, you should know the likelihood of her getting better is slim. There's a ten to fifteen percent recovery rate for alcoholics who are as bad as your mother." She tapped the pamphlet that I now held in my hands. "I think you should consider going to Al-Anon meetings. Al-Anon is a support group for friends and family of alcoholics. There's a schedule in there. They can help you."

A visual Rolodex of my mother's friends flashed through my head. Some of them were at least twenty years older than her and still alive, though they drank as much as she did. *She's trying to scare me so that I'll take this seriously and help my mother*, I thought, *because it's not too late.*

"You should also know that you didn't cause your mother to drink and you can't cure it."

"I know that," I said.

"You didn't," she repeated.

"Got it." My father had caused my mother's drinking. And her mother. And probably my older brother. I was the one who tried to make her laugh when everyone else was driving her up the wall. If anything, I was slowing down her disintegration.

"Does having an alcoholic mother do anything to the kids?" I asked.

"What about the kids, specifically?"

"I just mean, how I might act. Are the children of alcoholics different than other kids?" I leaned forward, expecting her to step right through the door that I had opened for her.

"Well, they are at a much higher risk for alcoholism themselves," she replied, "and are at greater risk for anxiety and depression. The alcoholic home is a confusing place."

"So, it would be normal for me to be confused about stuff?" I asked.

"I would be surprised if you weren't feeling confused," she said.

"I mean relationships, or friendships," I said.

"Are you confused about a relationship you're having?" she asked, returning to the clipboard.

"I have a friend," I said. "He's been the one I talk to about my mother. He's my best friend, I guess, but sometimes I wonder what that even means. I don't know. It's weird."

I looked down and started squeezing the fingers on my left hand with my right one, a habit I had picked up not long after I had my first anxiety attack. The harder I squeezed them, the less anxious I felt. One of my knuckles cracked audibly. I switched sides and started squeezing my other hand.

When I looked back up, the counselor's eyes were wide and fixed on me with the kind of paralysis that I noticed in people preparing for a conversation outside of their comfort zone. I had nobody else to ask.

"I just sometimes wonder if I might be gay," I said.

Her lip twitched into a scowl that disappeared almost immediately. "You're not gay," she said.

"I don't think I am either," I said. "I'm just wondering if the alcoholism thing is making me confused about that."

She scanned me from head to toe, her eyes narrowing. "I've met gay people, and you don't seem anything like them," she said.

"Okay, good," I said, relieved. If Ethan didn't think I was gay, and this woman didn't think I was either, then maybe I was just confused.

"Is there anything else I can help you with today?" She turned her chair back to the desk.

"I don't think so. I guess I'll check out Al-Anon, then?" I got up from my chair and stretched, feeling much lighter than when I had come.

"Yes, they can help. I promise." She stood up and held out her hand and smiled for the first time, looking relieved that it was over.

"Thanks for your help," I said. I walked out of her office with the Al-Anon pamphlet held against my chest, feeling the first flicker of hope in as long as I could remember. My mother was going to become one of the 10 to 15 percent of people who survived her alcoholism. I was going to help her.

I CALLED JOHN THE NEXT MORNING at his office and asked if I could come speak with him. I didn't know the details of his business, just that he owned real estate in the middle of downtown Hamilton and made most of his money from rental income. Bermuda had evolved from a tourist economy to an international tax haven in the eighties. Offshore businesses paid exorbitant rents, sometimes to house a shell office that did little but satisfy a corporate residency requirement.

"Kirkland! Come in, mate. This is a nice surprise." John held out his arm and gestured toward a leather chair on the other side of his desk. "Can I get you anything? Water? Tea?"

"No, I'm fine. Thanks." I sat down and placed my motorbike helmet next to the chair. John looked down at his feet and shuffled behind the desk, then looked up and toward the receptionist's office. "Are you sure you don't need anything? Sandra can run out and get you something to eat. Are you hungry?" He started walking back toward the door on his way to give Sandra my order.

"I ate this morning." I fixed my eyes on him and waited as he returned to his chair, looking to either side of it before sitting down as if he might have dropped something. He arranged the papers on his desk into small piles and mumbled something about the mess. I sat still, waiting for him to finish. Every nervous gesture of his made me feel calmer. "What can I do for you, mate? Everything okay? Do you need money?"

"No." I chuckled. "I don't need money. I came here to talk about my mother."

"Okay." His voice lowered and his demeanor changed, the nervous twitches replaced with a still focus. I got the sense that he had shifted into business mode. I understood the tactic an adversary might face in a negotiation with my stepfather: disarm and conquer. "What about your mother, mate?" he asked.

"Do you think she drinks too much?" I asked.

He lifted his hand to his glasses and shifted them off of his nose and then back down, a nervous habit I had noticed before. He cleared his throat. "She tips a few," he said, "but we all do."

"I know. I'm just wondering if you've noticed that she drinks more than most."

"That's a high bar, mate," he said, laughing.

"Do you know that she pours a scotch and takes it into the car with her wherever she goes?"

"No," he said.

"She's going to get killed one day. Or kill somebody else. She shakes now, when she's driving."

"I know she takes a little nip every now and then to calm down," he said, fidgeting in his seat.

I'm not explaining this clearly, I thought to myself. I assumed he drove when they went someplace together, so it was possible he'd never seen her drinking in the car.

"I know she's been worried about you boys," he said. "You and Robin seem squared away at school, or at least you were until you took this little break, which is a good thing to do, if you need a break." He cleared his throat again and looked away from me. "Monty is the one she's worried about. She's not sure what to do about him."

This was the first time I'd heard that my mother and John talked about us. I had assumed that she kept our lives sequestered from him, either as a way to protect their relationship from the messiness of her children or because she felt proprietary when it came to us. My mother had always talked about herself as if she were the architect of our lives, and my impression was that she didn't want to share credit for the outcome. *You didn't cause your mother to drink*, the counselor had said. Was John insinuating the opposite?

John leaned back in his chair and drummed his fingers on the desk. I felt the vibration from his foot tapping the floor. Was he uncomfortable or angry? The air between us closed up as if we had both pursed our lips and sucked it back in. I now realized that as much as I may have blamed him for my mother's drinking, he had done the same with us. In his eyes, if she had a drinking problem, it was because she had a children problem.

"Okay, well, thanks for seeing me," I said. I grabbed my helmet, stood up from my chair, and held my ground for a few seconds, staring at John before extending my hand. I felt the need to let him know that I wasn't going anywhere. *We* weren't going anywhere. She had been ours before she was his.

"Thanks for coming in, mate," he said, relieved that I was leaving.

"Don't tell my mother that I came by," I said.

"No worries, mate," he said. "Would love to have you and Monty over to the house soon."

"That sounds like fun," I said.

Chapter 9

Al-Anon meetings were held every Friday night in a basement room of one of the auxiliary buildings next to the hospital. Bermuda had only one hospital, located in the middle of the island. I planned on being a few minutes late, wanting to avoid any personal conversation and hoping to sneak in the back and listen to gather intelligence on what steps I needed to take to get my mother to stop drinking.

I parked my bike and proceeded down the stairs. The stone walls bracketing the staircase were crumbling from the moss and leafy plants poking through cracks. A drip echoed below. Stepping into the building's dimly lit hallway, I heard the faint sound of human voices escaping a half-open door at the end of the hall. As I got closer, there was a pause, followed by a burst of laughter that ignited a chorus from around the rest of the room, followed by another silence. The voice of a middle-aged woman spoke. "Step Twelve—having had a spiritual awakening as the result of these steps, we tried to carry this message to others, and to practice these principles in all our affairs." I reached the doorway just as she finished, and peeked in to find a small room with twenty or so people arranged in a circle, with several empty chairs interspersed among them. The woman who had just finished talking looked up briefly and smiled but made no effort to invite me into the room. I stepped through the doorway onto an old cedar plank, which creaked, prompting a few of the people to look up and look back down or to the speaker.

"Hi, I'm Dorothy," the woman said.

"Hi, Dorothy," the room repeated in unison, like a monastic chant. The movie *Children of the Corn* flashed through my head.

Dorothy went on. "I've been struggling with letting go lately. I have sat in this room every week for over five years now and I still can't get this one quite right." She chuckled and shook her head.

"Last night I got home from playing bridge with a group of friends, and when I got to the front door of the house, I could tell something was wrong. I just *knew* it." Heads nodded around the circle.

"I walked in expecting to see Jim lying facedown on the carpet with an empty bottle of gin by his side. But nobody was home." She smiled slightly to herself. "When Jim was drinking, I used to dream of coming home to an empty house. I used to pray for him to be picked up by the police and thrown into jail just so that I could have *one* night alone without us going through the routine of me yelling at him, him calling me a nagging harpy, and both of us falling into bed exhausted.

"Jim's been sober for over three years now. And here I was, walking into that empty house, and all I could think was that it was so quiet because he started drinking again. So, I called my oldest daughter and asked if she had heard from her father because he was missing."

The group laughed.

"And she said, 'Maybe he's out,' and her voice was so sweet and unconcerned, and I was thinking I've raised a moron—so I was getting increasingly outraged, because she doesn't know her father like I do. And then I remembered—of course she thinks he's fine, because I never told her about the ten thousand times I had to carry him to bed, or how I spent the last hour of almost every night of her childhood cleaning everything to get the smell of liquor out of the goddam upholstery and the floorboards and the windowsills. And then the next morning she and her father would tease me about my late-night cleaning binges, and I would yell at her to get her book bag together, and she would cut her eyes at me and hug her smelly, hungover father and walk right past me as if I didn't exist."

I thought back to those school mornings when my mother and brothers would laugh together as if nothing had happened, while I would be a paralyzed mixture of furious and sad, and they would look at each other behind my back, shrug, and smile that condescending smile that they didn't think I could see.

Dorothy sighed. "Anyway, so I yelled at her that she didn't know what she was talking about, and she hung up on me. And then after an hour of calling the hospital, police stations, and everyone he knows, he walked into the house, perfectly fine, and said, 'Hey, sweetie,' to me, like nothing had happened. And I yelled 'Where the hell have you been?' and he said he had dinner with his AA sponsor and asked 'What's wrong?' and I told him I didn't know where he was and I was SO FUCKING ANGRY and I was yelling about how worried I'd been and I realized how crazy I was acting, but by then it was too late *not* to be crazy, so I stormed out of the room and slammed our bedroom door while he was stammering and looking at me like I'd lost my goddam mind. And I *had*. I *had* lost my damn mind." Dorothy was laughing now, like she had been at the beginning of the meeting, and the rest of the group was laughing with her.

"You'd think I would have apologized to him after all of that." Dorothy shook her head, looking regretful. "But I didn't. I'm not ready. He's been sober for three years, and I'm not ready to apologize to him for anything."

She looked up at the nodding heads around the room. "And the worst part? I could have had one whole hour to myself in my own house. I could have read a book, watched TV, called a friend, or just sat and stared out the window." The group was nodding again and chuckling. How were they finding this story funny?

"We're glad you're here, Dorothy," another middle-aged woman said.

"Keep coming back," said another.

The people around the circle, all women, aged from thirty to seventy, spoke one by one about their struggles, all relating to the theme that Dorothy introduced: the ambiguous topic of "letting go." One woman spoke about how she drove by her boyfriend's house late at night to see if he was cheating on her. Another talked about how her teenage son wasn't speaking to her because she stopped calling the school to say that he was sick when he was really hungover. Almost everyone spoke of a higher power and how they were trying hard to "let go" and "let things be" and "not control outcomes." How was that going to help anyone stop drinking?

I slipped out the back after the meeting started to break up, more confused than when I had arrived. The last thing they said before the end of the meeting was to keep coming back, and that new people should attend at least six meetings before giving up. I assumed this message was directed at me, but besides a random smile here or there, nobody focused on me. I didn't get the feeling that they cared one way or the other if I came back again.

But I did keep going back, the only nineteen-year-old man in a gaggle of disappointed yet inspiring older women. Their laughter was off-putting initially, as each woman told a story more horrifying than the last. But with each anecdote, and the group laughter that followed, the nature of alcoholism changed for me. I started to see myself as separate; I started to identify choices that could be made.

And I started confronting my mother—slowly, at first, and then with more urgency. I had heard these ladies say that I couldn't cure my mother's disease, but I had carved out an exception for myself. I showed her the pamphlets they gave me, which mapped out in detail what was happening to her, and how she could get help if she admitted that she needed it. On the nights when John was away and she was back at the house, I shared my pain with her, and my anxiety, and told her how much I loved her and needed her as she sat in her chocolate-colored chair and sipped from her scotch. I cried on one of those nights, the first time she looked up. I took that as a sign that she might yet still see that there was hope for her, but she only said, "I think you need to talk to somebody, darling." I realized that everything I had been saying had only confirmed for her that there was something wrong with *me*.

At the end of the next meeting, I talked to one of the women about confronting my mother.

"What gives me the right to decide how my husband chooses to live his life?" she said.

"But they're sick," I said.

"So are you."

"It's not the same thing."

"Why not?"

"Because I'm not the alcoholic."

"So?"

I had come to discover that Al-Anon people made a habit of asking obvious questions that didn't have obvious answers.

She continued. "Let's say, for the sake of argument, that you could get your mother to stop drinking tomorrow, which you can't, and let's say she immediately became the mother that you have in your mind that she should be, which she won't. How does that change who *you* are?"

"But doesn't how your husband acts, whether he's drinking or not, have a profound effect on you? That's like saying that somebody who beats his wife is 'living his life the way that he wants to.'"

"His drinking has had a profound effect on all of us, and if he were hitting me or the kids I would be out of there in a heartbeat. Alcoholism is a family disease, and he's the carrier, but we all have it. I am choosing to stay with him, for now, and choosing to address my part of the disease. I know my boundaries. I know what behavior I will accept and what I will not. I have support. I have options. I feel freer than I have ever felt in my life. I know it sounds strange to you now, but I'm telling you that there will come a point when you will look at your mother, with love in your heart, and you will be genuinely at peace with who she is, whether she is drinking or not. You'll see."

It had been so long since I had thought of myself outside of the context of my mother that "who I was" had never been a question that I thought about answering. I stared at the woman, and she smiled in reaction to what I could only imagine was a noticeable shift in my face. I felt like one of those mice in a maze that finally discovers a path to freedom after bumping into the same wall over and over again.

"There it is," she said.

I learned about the National Outdoor Leadership School from the same friend who told me about Andover. I asked my father to pay for me to go on a three-week kayaking trip through the Sea of Cortez in Mexico that coming January. My father hadn't asked me much about my decision to take a year off from school, and I didn't talk to him about it. He had once again floated the idea of community college in a few of our phone calls, like he was looking for a place to park an asset that had lost considerable value, but I would pivot to a different subject.

In the end, my father agreed to pay for the trip after I explained that it wasn't a vacation tour but rather a grueling survival test with the high likelihood of pain, misery, and prolonged discomfort. I played the sissy card, having calculated that the idea of me being transformed from the girly boy he had tolerated into the man that he wanted would be too enticing an opportunity to pass up.

At nineteen, I was among the youngest members of our NOLS group of fifteen, the oldest being two fiftyish men, one a hippie professor and the other a fit Republican businessman. All of us had arrived the night before at a central camping spot not far from the "put in" and had been instructed to pick an area to roll out our sleeping bags and get some sleep before an early start the next morning. The lead instructor, Debbie, was rosy-cheeked and solidly built, with a smile that never left her face. She explained that we would be alone for three weeks, with no communication from the outside world, and each day we would be working together on how we were going to kayak the twelve or so miles a day we would need to cover to meet up with our support team at the end of the trip. We would carry all of our food, with only two restocking opportunities at predetermined stops. If we didn't hit those stops when scheduled, we would have to survive on what we had until we did. The weather was unpredictable, so each day we would need to make the call as to whether we could paddle that day, keeping in mind that if we lost a day of paddling because of weather we would need to make it up on another day. The instructors would not make the decisions for us; as a group we would choose together and live or die on those decisions.

Our days began with a wake-up call at 4 a.m., in preparation to be on the water no later than 5. We had six hours of paddling time. Secluded coves, as identified by the maps, were the ideal stopping points, as they offered protection from the fierce winds that kicked up every morning at 11 a.m. In the afternoons we learned how to spearfish, took hikes in the desert to learn about the local flora and fauna, and practiced our kayaking skills. The instructors taught us how to execute a full roll, as it was always preferable not to dump supplies if your kayak tipped over. Even with Debbie standing beside me, I panicked and evacuated as soon as the kayak went over, unable to relax for the moment it took to position my paddle, twist my body, and come back to the surface. I was one of only two people in our group who never mastered this skill.

Each of us spent one day completely alone, hiking far enough into the coastline desert that camp wasn't visible, but not so far that we couldn't find our way back. I looked forward to this part of the trip, imagining my time as a vision quest during which I would receive new insights. Instead, I ended up finding a small cliff where I could look out onto the ocean, not a single boat or other sign of life besides the occasional gull, and a deep loneliness descended. I started to hyperventilate.

Instead of achieving spiritual enlightenment, I jerked off on a desiccated bush, hoping it would put me to sleep and make the day go by faster. I curled up into a ball and looked out at the sea, curious that I could witness something so beautiful and not be moved. I wondered whether there was something I needed to get out before anything new could come in.

We had one kayak, a single, that was significantly slower than the others. When it was my turn to paddle it, my body reached the limit of where my brain decided it could go, and I slowed down as the pod ahead of me pulled away.

"You need to keep up," Jessie, one of the two male instructors, said as he pulled up next to me.

"I can't," I said.

"Yes, you can," he said.

"Can you slow down a little?"

"No."

I stopped and rested the paddle across my kayak, dropping my head.

"You need to keep going, Kirk," he said, "or you're going to be out here alone."

Jessie caught up to the rest of the pod, each of the kayakers paddling rhythmically, as one, as I sat and watched them go. None of them looked back, and I remembered my first Al-Anon meeting. They weren't going to wait for me. Nobody was coming back to save me. I picked up my paddle and started digging back into the waves, paddling for the first time beyond the limits of what my mind thought possible. As I started making up the distance lost, each stroke took me into new territory.

About halfway through the journey, we visited a small fishing village. The villagers greeted us and offered us lunch of a small portion of freshly cooked fish, which ignited a larger hunger that was our constant companion on the trip. I watched as a couple of people in our party took a second helping, and resisted the urge to do so myself, realizing that we were probably eating into the villagers' allotment for that day. We played a game of volleyball. The villagers laughed at every missed hit. I thought of how my Al-Anon group celebrated the power of simplicity, a concept I had yet to grasp.

A few days before we were scheduled to arrive at our final destination, the instructors sat down with each of us around a small fire to discuss our experience.

"I wish I could go back and do the solo outing again," I said when it was my turn.

Debbie smiled. "You seem more at ease than when we first met," she said.

"I can't stop smiling."

"You did a great job, man," Jessie said.

"I don't want to go back," I said. After three weeks on the water, my body had changed. I had always been skinny, but now my arms were tanned and rippled with the beginnings of muscles I had only seen on people like Ethan. I never realized a defined muscle could help you feel as strong on the inside as you did on the outside.

On our last day on the water, I lingered in my single kayak, waiting for the biggest wave I could find to ride into the beach, no longer satisfied with the safest route to shore.

Chapter 10

In August, I returned to Tulane for my sophomore year. It was hard to return to college life. Al-Anon had outfitted me with new tools, and I was energized from my NOLS experience, but the depth of my losses was only just settling in, and I had yet to realize how permanent they would become. I moved into a one-bedroom apartment a mile and a half from campus, in one of the sketchier parts of uptown New Orleans, my freshman-year friends having established strong social networks and living situations of their own in the year that I was gone. I hadn't had regular contact with anyone besides Ethan.

Ethan didn't seem to want to spend time with me anymore. When he stopped responding to my calls, I called his girlfriend Paisley and asked to see her. I had met her once, and understood that she knew a lot about me from Ethan. I knew that Ethan thought we were alike. But I didn't know her well enough to enlist her help in reconnecting me with her boyfriend. She sounded surprised to hear from me, but agreed to meet at my apartment.

I watched out my window as she pulled up behind my rusted Corolla in a brand-new Accord, got out of the car, and looked around as she walked toward my front door. One of the benefits of having developed a personal old-money narrative was the inoculation it gave me from feeling poor in comparison to others. I was brought up believing that someone who drove a shitty car and looked like a homeless person could be the richest person in the room, while someone who appeared wealthy could be swimming in debt. As Paisley looked for a clean place to sit on the secondhand couch that I had purchased from a thrift store, I saw no indication that she registered my overt poverty as a disguise to hide wealth. She just looked uncomfortable.

"Did you lock your car?" I asked.

"Ethan's truck has been broken into a few times, so he insists I lock my car wherever I go," she said.

"Good idea," I said. I didn't mention that my rusted, ten-year-old Corolla was broken into daily, and I had taken to leaving it unlocked so that the thieves didn't feel the need to break a window. "Thank you for stopping by. Can I get you anything?"

I didn't have anything.

"No, I'm fine. Thank you," she replied.

I wasn't sure what to say to her, so I just took a moment to see her for the first time. She was beautiful in an unconventional way, and had a fragile, soft-spoken quality that I knew Ethan would find appealing, much as my vulnerability attracted him.

She tried hard not to look sad for me as I explained that I was having a hard time getting in touch with him, and did she have any suggestions as to what I might do? "Maybe you just need to give him a call and set up a time to get together," she said. "I know Tuesdays are usually less busy?"

"That's a good idea," I said. "I'll call him and see if we can get together Tuesday. Thanks so much for coming by." I realized she pitied me. I wanted her out of my house.

"I was glad you called. It was good to see you," she said, getting up.

I got on the phone as soon as she was gone and left a message for Ethan. I don't know how long it took for him to get back to me. I assume she told him to call. He greeted me as if he couldn't wait to talk to me and had been dreading it at the same time.

"Kiiirrrrrkkkk. What's going on, *mane*?" I recoiled when he used the term, just as I had when he called me "brah." We made plans to get together the following Tuesday morning. When I pulled up to his apartment, I could see his Sigma Nu brothers scattered outside like extras in an all-white production of *West Side Story*.

Ethan's roommate didn't know where he was or when he would be back. I sat on his couch as guys in backward baseball caps came and went, looking for Ethan, sharing with one another fuzzy memories from the previous night's events. One of his brothers was in the midst of a vomit-themed tale when Ethan came in forty-five minutes late. His face dropped when he saw me.

"I was so surprised to see you here, man. How are you? It's great to see you," Ethan said, walking over.

"You're late," I said.

He sat down beside me and shook his head, letting out a long, exhausted sigh. "I totally forgot, man. I am so sorry. It's the God's honest truth. It just slipped my mind."

"You have a lot of friends waiting on you, so I'm gonna go." I motioned to his fraternity brothers, who were lingering near the door and glancing in our direction every few seconds to see when we would be done. "It's no big deal. We'll just get together another time when you're free." I hated that he knew how hurt I was. I was embarrassed that his world was too full to remember specific plans with me, and my world was so empty that those plans were all I had thought about for days beforehand.

That night I sat in my apartment and tried to cry, but nothing came out. I could feel the sadness stuck inside of me, and no matter how hard I tried to dry-heave it out, it felt fixed.

ABOUT MIDWAY THROUGH MY SOPHOMORE YEAR, I received an unexpected call from Avery, asking me out to dinner. I had not heard from her since our date freshman year. After some awkward small talk at the table, she took a deep breath and apologized for disappearing. "The night after our date, I was attacked in our apartment," she said. "He did things to me that I didn't talk to anybody about for a year. I don't know what would have happened if somebody hadn't come home and scared him off. I'm talking about it now, finally, and I needed to tell you because I really did have a nice time with you, and felt bad that I ignored your calls."

She continued. "On the day that you were leaving, freshman year, I came to say goodbye. Do you remember you called me one last time to tell me that you were leaving school and weren't coming back?" I shook my head no. I couldn't speak. "Well, you called and wanted to say goodbye, and I could tell by the message that you didn't expect that I would come. I was surprised that you called as many times as you did after I never called you back."

"I really liked you," I said meekly. I held her hand across the table.

"I know it sounds like I'm lying, and I've lied a lot this past year, but I saw you get into Ethan's car to go to the airport and I started screaming your name but I guess you didn't hear me. It was so early in the morning, and foggy. The car pulled away before I could get to you. I had run all the way from my house."

"I didn't hear you. I would have stopped."

"I wouldn't have blamed you if you heard me and told Ethan to keep driving."

"I didn't hear you."

"I don't blame myself anymore for what happened to me, but I know I hurt people afterwards."

"I can't imagine how awful this has been for you," I said.

Back then, I thought there were words that could clear the air of things and bring them back to normal. I wanted to let Avery know that none of what happened then mattered now, that I understood all of it. I thought that with each "I understand" and every "I'm sorry" we would be transported back to where we had been two years before. But each consolation landed on a person who lived in a new reality, and as I looked at her, I could feel the words disappear into a deeper part of her that I didn't have access to. I was horrified at what had happened to her, but as much as I tried to focus on that, there was also the nagging part of me that was pissed at how it affected me. *You were supposed to love me.*

*   *   *

AFTER ETHAN LEFT ME, which is how I thought of it at the time, I sought a replacement. I met Leo at Tulane's Entrepreneur Club. I attended meetings for the sole purpose of making new friends, as I didn't know what an entrepreneur was, and once I knew, I didn't want to be one. I arranged to live with Leo and his fraternity brother George my junior year. They were Pikes, which from what I could tell was the fraternity that tried unsuccessfully to emulate the coolest parts of the more popular ones. George was the fraternity president. He talked often about how women were bitches, out to use men for money. He and his girlfriend bickered constantly, and I could hear their angry sex through our shared bedroom wall. I came down from my room one Saturday morning not long after we had moved in together to find George and his best friend passed out on separate couches with their pants down around their knees, sporting hard-ons. George's erection was enormous. I covered him with a blanket after taking a mental picture.

I ended up in a toilet stall on the most deserted floor of the Tulane library one Saturday night. I knew from the offers of blow jobs, phone numbers, and graphic invitations festooning the bathroom stalls—many of which had holes bored into the sides, presumably to fit a standard-sized erect dick—that library bathrooms were the place to find anonymous gay sex. I wouldn't have to see the person; I could just stick my dick through a hole, satisfy myself sexually, and hold on to my idea of who I was. When I walked into the bathroom, I could see that one stall was occupied and I sat in the adjacent one. As the minutes ticked by with neither of us making a sound, I reminded myself that my door was locked, and I could leave at any time, and it was still possible the guy next to me was suffering from constipation.

After fifteen minutes, there was a rustle from the other stall, followed by the heavy thud of a man dropping to his knees and sliding his pelvis beneath the gap in our stalls like Tom Cruise in *Risky Business*. I sat paralyzed as he stroked his erect cock with his right hand and waved his left hand at me like an impatient traffic cop, apparently demanding I drop to my knees too. He breathed like Darth Vader. I wondered if my sitting in the stall for fifteen minutes had entered me into an unspoken agreement that I was now obliged to satisfy. I grabbed his dick and stroked it, knowing that I was performing below expectations, but hoping it was enough to satisfy the sexual energy wheezing on the other side of a thin barrier.

"Come over," I said. I wasn't going to join him on the bathroom floor, there was no hole to stick my dick through, and milking somebody like a cow wasn't turning me on. I unlatched the door, and a short, balding, middle-aged man shuffled in like he was trying to get onto a crowded subway train. "No, no, no," I said and pushed him back out. I sat back down on the toilet, shook my head, and chuckled, reminding myself that it was normal for straight people to experiment sexually in college. This experiment had just gone horribly wrong.

A FEW MONTHS LATER, George and I stumbled back to our house from a bar after getting drunk together for the first time.

Throughout the night he had talked of bonding, as if he were following steps outlined in the douchebag's guide on how to be a bro. As the night went on, I picked up on something flirtatious in the way that he spoke with me, a twinkle in the eye here and a chummy shoulder bump there. Or was this how bonded bros acted?

We arrived at our front door, and George turned and looked at me with a gentle smile that felt like the moment when a couple returned from a date and either kissed or parted ways. I ran down the steps and headed toward my car, saying that I wasn't done for the night and was going back out. George ran after me, grabbed my shoulders, turned me around, and reached into my front pocket to grab the keys to my car. "You can't go," he said. "I'm doing this to help you." He burrowed his hand more deeply, trying to get a grip on my keys as I swayed back and forth. His hand stopped moving, and I felt his wrist nestled against my thigh as we stood looking at each other, my body leaning forward against his. I thought about kissing him. I waited to see if he would kiss me. I didn't trust my instincts when it came to sex, or attraction. One bad move with the wrong guy I knew would destroy my life. After we'd stared at each other for five seconds, I pulled back, and his hand slid from my pocket. He called to me, more quietly this time, as I walked away from the house. He didn't follow.

I MET NICK IN A CLASS that we shared late junior year. Every morning he scanned the room looking for somebody to sit next to he could charm into letting him read his or her notes and copy homework. I was amused by how transparent he was, as if he had no idea that people could read his intentions from the hungry look on his face. One morning his eyes fixed on me. He made a beeline for me and started up a conversation.

Loneliness was my default state, so when Nick introduced himself, I didn't care why he was doing it. It wasn't long before he was asking if I had read the assignment, and did I know what it was about. I knew he was using me, but I was using him too.

Nick was an anomaly at Tulane. He was Latino—not southern or Jewish, nor was he part of the Greek system, even though his persona would have integrated easily into any number of fraternities. I was attracted to people who challenged the status quo while remaining within it—a balancing act I was trying to perfect myself.

Nick was captain of the coed Tulane sailing team. I looked like a sailor, I talked about my sailing ancestors, I spoke of the Royal Bermuda Yacht Club and taking out the sunfish on our Adirondack lake—but I didn't sail with them. I assumed a role that felt familiar and alien at the same time, a cartoon version of a genuine identity.

The team was fun and carefree. They drank a lot, which was comforting, and had sex with one another constantly, which wasn't. Nick telegraphed an almost insatiable desire to have sex, which ensured he had a lot of it. He wasn't tradition- ally handsome. He was on the shorter side, and had a sailor's body—fit but not muscular. He had dark skin and spoke like a California surf bum, using words like "dude" and "gnarly," and laughing with a high-pitched, Spicoli-esque sputter—usually at something he himself had said. He exuded an unexpected confidence, and led the sailing team without hesitation. If for some reason anybody challenged a decision or disagreed with him, he accessed another gear where a thoughtful, calculating side of him emerged.

For my final year of school, I moved in with Nick and two other sailors I didn't know well, a quiet southern boy named Ellery from South Carolina and a short, pot-smoking, brooding fireball named Tom. I went to class enough to graduate and ended up with a degree in international relations, but I can't recall a single academic moment from that year. I know that sometime during the year, Nick and I decided it would be fun to get a dog, a terrier mutt we named "Shithead," in homage to Steve Martin's dog in *The Jerk*. We didn't tell our landlord or our roommates about Shithead. Following Nick's lead, I didn't pay any attention when Ellery told us he was allergic to dogs, and Tom said he didn't want one in the house. I assumed they would fall in line behind Nick, as I had. They didn't. Eventually Shithead was sent to live with Nick's parents.

When I first met Nick, he was dating a small, pretty blond sailor named Eve. Their relationship was like many that I witnessed at college, fueled more by sex than affection. Each dismissed the other to people around them, but they ended up back together at the end of the night, usually after the third or fourth pitcher of beer. Sometime during the year, Catherine replaced Eve. Catherine had no expectation that their relationship was about anything other than sex.

I lived in the room next to Nick, which meant that I could hear everything, provoking the same mixture of unequivocal disgust and unavoidable physical stimulation I'd experienced living next to George. One night about halfway through the year, I was hanging out with Nick and a couple of members of the sailing team in our living room.

"So, you're boning Catherine now?" Joe asked. I met Joe soon after I met Nick. He looked like the quintessential sailor. I could picture him in a yachting catalogue, standing on a dock in a North Face slicker, with one foot propped up on his sailboat and a white-toothed, carefree smile on his face.

"Yeah, and your mom," Nick replied.

"I can hear all of it," I offered. "It sounds like whoever is in there is dying."

"I can smell it," Ellery added. Ellery didn't say much, but when he did it was usually disturbing.

"My mom doesn't date Mexicans," Joe said.

"Who said anything about dating?" Nick asked, laughing. Whenever he laughed, he sucked his teeth in, and a dollop of spittle gathered at the corner of his mouth.

"We need to hook Kirk up," Joe said.

"I would never cheat on your mom," I said.

"Kirk is surrounded by hot sorority girls. I think they braid each other's hair," Nick said.

"I do have beautiful hair," I said.

"He doesn't bring them here. I think he's afraid they're going to succumb to my sexuality, just like Joe's mom did," Nick said.

"My mom thought you were the gardener," Joe replied.

"I did trim her bush," Nick said.

"Seriously, you're not dating anyone, Kirk?" Joe asked.

"Maybe he's gay," Nick said, chuckling.

My head whipped toward Nick, and my eyes widened. I had become masterful at remaining inscrutable when it came to my sex life, but I was surprised by his comment and I didn't realize until too late what my face revealed. Nick's smile disappeared.

"That would explain everything," Joe said.

"Let's drop it, guys," Nick said.

"Drop what?" Joe said.

"I don't want to talk about this anymore," Nick continued. "What are we doing tonight?" Nick stared at me, and I guessed that he knew, and without knowing it he was telegraphing what he knew to everyone else. Joe looked at me, and then Ellery, trying to understand why the conversation had ended. Ellery hadn't noticed that the gay question paralyzed me, but he noticed that Nick noticed that the gay question paralyzed me, and he looked down to the floor.

"I'd vote for Joe's mom," I said, hoping to revive the conversation.

"What just happened?" Joe asked.

I knew that Nick was still looking at me, but I had turned away. "I've got homework to do," Nick said. "Let's meet out later, Joe."

"Okay," he said, looking confused. Nick didn't do homework.

LATER THAT NIGHT, Nick approached me and said, "I'm sorry for the conversation today."

"Why?" I asked.

He held my gaze, his eyes wide and expectant. I knew he was inviting me to talk to him, and I sensed that he might be supportive. But I didn't know how to begin to talk about what I was feeling, and after my experience with Ethan I didn't trust that anyone would keep caring about me if caring about me became too difficult. I said nothing.

"It was just weird, I don't know." He looked away and squinted as if he was trying to figure out what to say next. He shuffled his feet and looked back up at me, waiting for me to say more. I raised my eyebrows and smiled weakly.

"Do you want a beer?" he asked.

"Sure," I said.

My mother came to New Orleans for my graduation. I suspect the guilt of having missed my high school graduation moved her to come, but if that was the case, she never admitted it. All she said was, "Of course I'll come if you want me to, darling,"

"Do you want to come?" I asked.

"I want to do what you want me to do," she said.

The problem with loving an alcoholic is that you never know what iteration of boozebag you'll get on any given day. I didn't know if I was talking to the version that wanted to come but worried I was ashamed of her and was asking only to be nice, or if I was talking to the version who had mentally abandoned her role as parent but felt obliged, so she was going to pack a bottle of vodka and drink her way through it.

"I want you to come if you want to," I said.

Over the past few years, I had started to sell my mother as a character for public consumption, a larger-than-life throwback to another time, a late-era Bette Davis. Her marriage to John ensured that her act was funded, and she threw herself into the role with an unwavering commitment. My friend Sally drove me to the airport to pick her up after I had prepared her.

"I can't promise that she's not going to say something mean," I warned.

"I love it!" she squealed.

My mother came out of the gate in a mink coat and blue sunglasses. One of the airline employees was following, carrying her bag. She had no doubt asked him to carry it for her, without giving a reason why. People often did what my mother asked because she gave them no room to say no.

"Hello, darling," my mother said, kissing me on the cheek. She didn't acknowledge Sally, who was standing next to me with a big smile on her face. "You can leave my bag right here, thank you so much," she said to her unwilling porter. She didn't look at him.

"This is my friend Sally," I said.

Sally held out her hand. "I can't tell you how nice it is to finally meet you."

My mother took a beat and smirked at me before turning Sally's way.

"Hello," she said suspiciously.

"I've heard so much about you," Sally said.

"Well, that can't be good," my mother said.

"Only good things, I promise!" Sally said.

"Kirkland, grab my bag please. I raised you better than that."

I had made a reservation for my mother at the Columns Hotel on St. Charles Avenue, a couple of miles from the Tulane campus. I had chosen the Columns because it was quintes-sentially New Orleans—old, southern, and dark. I wanted my mother to stay somewhere that had as much personality as she did, and that gave her a taste of a city that had become a part of who I was.

"Where's the elevator?" she asked when we arrived.

"I don't know if it has one," I said.

My mother looked around tentatively at the high ceilings, the ornate wall coverings, and the large chandelier that barely lit the foyer, and hesitated. I had never been inside the building before. It reminded me of the Hotel California.

"Isn't it cool?" I said. "I thought you would like something like this."

"It's very nice, darling," my mother replied. Her voice sounded as if she wasn't sure if I had placed her there as pun-ishment for being a shitty mother.

I included Sally during my mother's visit, so that my mother and I didn't have to spend too much time alone. Over the course of my time away from home, my mother and I had moved further away from each other and replaced our short-hand with awkwardness. Each interaction was my attempt to find a vulnerable place in the wall that had developed between us. The attempt was halfhearted, because the thought of trying too hard made me sad. I could catch a small glimmer of who my mother used to be when I made her laugh, which only happened when I stopped looking for the old version of who she was and accepted the new one. It wasn't enough, but it was what I had. There would never be a time, even as events devolved into our own version of southern gothic, that I wouldn't try to save her, but there would come a time when saving myself was all I could do.

I LEFT TULANE after my December graduation and moved to Boston, staying with family friends at a house in Chestnut Hill, an exclusive neighborhood in the suburbs. Joe and I had made plans to move to Seattle together, but he had yet to graduate, and I wanted to attend one of my Adirondack friends' weddings on the east coast in the spring, so this seemed like a sensible short-term move. I secured a serving job at a chain Italian restaurant at the local mall to make money. Any social life I had revolved around my childhood friend Kevin, who lived in the house, along with his mother, and Avery, who had moved to Boston after college.

When I flew into Boston, from New Orleans, Kevin picked me up, and we went straight to dinner with a couple of his friends at a seafood restaurant on the Boston waterfront. I was excited. Kevin brought a six-pack of beer for the short ride to the restaurant, which for a moment made it feel like the party in New Orleans hadn't ended. When the female server asked what I wanted for dinner, I put my hand on her arm and ordered, only to have her pull back and look at me as if I had hit her. The rest of the table went silent. My friend Kevin said, "You can't touch people here." That was the first indication I was someplace new.

Avery was living by herself in a small apartment in the heart of Boston, working at an entry-level job. I remember her telling me that right after the incident in her apartment she had started walking the streets of New Orleans after dark to overcome her fear, to the point where her roommates and parents had intervened and she had removed herself from school for a period of time. The bravery and defiance of a girl from western North Carolina living alone in the heart of Yankee country impressed me.

We spent a lot of time hanging out in her apartment, talking about Pat Conroy books and listening to Tori Amos and Sarah McLachlan. One evening, we sat cross-legged across from each other in her candlelit apartment as Tori sang about rape, and I wondered whether I should kiss her, but I didn't because, I told myself, I didn't know if she wanted to be kissed—even though the way she looked at me suggested she did.

"I don't know why you didn't make a move," Kevin said later, "aside from the fact that the scene you're describing sounds like a lesbian sit-in—which could be hot, but you just make it seem sad."

"I don't know what's going on," I said. "I mean, I really like her, but something's holding me back. Maybe I'm just scared of getting hurt again."

"I would just go for it, dude. She clearly wants you to."

"I don't know. Part of me thinks that she only *thinks* she wants me to. She's been through a lot."

Kevin rolled his eyes, in the way that my male friends had done over the years when my chivalry crossed the line into bullshit. My female friends never reacted this way, assuming they had found a man who cared more about their feelings than their bodies. These same girls dropped me when their body-loving men called, insincerely apologizing for whatever had gotten them into trouble, and I would be left alone, baffled by the capriciousness of love.

A couple of weeks later, I was walking by Kevin's bedroom and I heard him speaking to somebody in a low voice. I asked him who it was when he got off the phone.

"It was Avery, actually," he said. My body went cold.

"What were you talking to her about?"

"Nothing, really," he said.

"I didn't even know you talked to each other."

"I talk to a lot of people," he said defensively.

I shook my head and looked down at the floor. "I can't believe this is happening," I said. I walked toward my bedroom.

"It started a couple of weeks ago," he said, following me, "right after we all went out to dinner. I liked her, so I called her and asked if she wanted to do something. She didn't know anybody."

I kept walking.

"It's not like you were going out," he said.

Kevin's mother was in AA, and she talked often about setting boundaries, which usually evolved into an example of how she was learning to do things even if other people didn't like it. I was living in a family of aggressive boundary setters.

I turned around and looked at him. "I talked to you about her all the time."

"I'm sorry, Kirk. We didn't mean to hurt you. We didn't plan for this to happen."

"Except for when you made plans for it to happen?" *We didn't mean to hurt you.* In one conversation, I had moved from "me and Kevin" and "me and Avery" to being "me and nobody," while they became the "we."

"I'm going to bed. I feel sick," I said.

That night, I called Robin, the only person I could think of to tell what had happened. He was upset for me, if a little confused about what Avery meant to me. I couldn't explain it clearly.

Avery called me that night, and I didn't answer. I'm not sure how long it took me to respond, but we ended up at a pizza place in downtown Boston. She explained that she and Kevin had broken things off right away after I found out, and she didn't know why it had started in the first place.

"He kept calling, and I eventually said yes to going out with him," she said, "and then he was kissing me. It happened so fast."

I could have kissed her.

"I don't know why I didn't tell you," she continued. "I guess I didn't know what was going to happen, so it didn't seem relevant, even though I knew he wanted something to happen, and he was your friend, so I was paralyzed. And then when it started, I didn't want to hurt your feelings, even though I wasn't entirely sure if it would hurt your feelings because you and I weren't together—not that I'm using that as an excuse for anything."

I didn't want to.

"I was so glad that you finally called me back. I am so sorry, Kirkland. The thought of you not being in my life anymore is devastating. Kevin means nothing to me. You mean everything . . . which is why I wanted to see you today."

I was terrified that you wanted me to kiss you.

"I don't know how to tell you what I'm about to tell you, but I need to, because it's important that you know."

195

I don't think we should see each other anymore.
"I love you."

She looked away from me when she said it and swallowed hard. Without meaning to, I smiled, in the way that looks insensitive from the perspective of the one being smiled at after they have revealed something deeply personal. I knew that I didn't love her, and that I never had. I didn't know what to say.

AFTER MY TIME IN BOSTON, Seattle was a welcome distraction. Joe and I found a wood-paneled basement apartment in the city's University District. I don't know what most of the undergrads were studying at the University of Washington, but they must have offered an experimental major in panhandling. Every few feet, a skinny, thin-haired, pasty white kid in his early twenties, in dirty jeans and a T-shirt with the name of an obscure band stenciled on the front, asked me for money or cigarettes. He was usually sitting on the sidewalk next to a skateboard and sometimes a sad-looking dog that reminded me of Shithead.

Joe and I both found temp jobs that paid $8 per hour or so and used whatever small amount of money we had to get to know the city. I didn't realize when we had made this plan back in New Orleans that moving to Seattle with Joe meant moving to Seattle with Joe and his girlfriend, Sue. She had been born and raised in Seattle and embodied its dreary weather. Sue was tall, blond, and humorless. She looked like a Barbie Doll that had been left outside for too long. She didn't live with us, but she spent all of her free time at our apartment, drizzling on the thrift shop furniture we owned while I force-smiled in her direction and Joe laughed too loudly at what Sue thought were dry observations on life, but what were really complaints about how everyone in the world sucked.

After a few months of living together, we were driving the streets of downtown Seattle when I saw a familiar face walking in the other direction. Was she a college friend? An Adirondack friend? A TV personality? Upon realizing it was my friend Mia from boarding school, I called a number I had for her mother, who confirmed that Mia had indeed moved to Seattle. In the span of four hours, my Seattle trajectory changed as I called Mia, who was in the midst of looking for a new place to live. Within weeks, we had decided that we were going to find a house together.

The breakup with Joe was messy but final. He didn't understand my problem with Sue, and I didn't understand his attraction to her. I still lived in the belief that those closest to me would see people the way that I saw them, even if they happened to be dating at the time. Instead, Joe approached me about Sue moving in with us at about the same time that Mia appeared, and I informed him that I would be moving out instead. They apparently needed my half of the rent to make it work, and took my rejection of their couple-hood personally, which ended our friendship.

Mia was the only girl at Andover whom I had ever asked out on a date, which I did by writing her a note and putting it in her school mailbox. The next time I saw her, she looked at me with a pitying face and said that she "wasn't interested in me that way." I was hurt and relieved.

We ended up moving into a six-bedroom house in the heart of Capitol Hill with five other people—including a crunchy couple from Oregon, a gay ginger from a Midwestern state, a mousy blonde from Seattle, and a laconic aspiring massage therapist. I was proud of myself for living with a gay person, and glad that he was leaving. I liked him, but didn't want to become friends. During the one substantive conversation I had with him, I asked if it was difficult to be gay, and assumed he was lying when he said it wasn't. I stayed on alert for any look he might give me implying that I was like him, but he seemed as uninterested in me as I pretended to be in him.

We were all dirt poor. Through my various temp jobs, I made enough money to pay my $300 rent and buy food and beer. Mia invited me to join her coed soccer league. I had grown up playing soccer in Bermuda, but hadn't started learning until I was eight, so was usually relegated to the position of the oversized defense person who was supposed to intimidate the smaller players coming my way. I ended up in the same position in this league, while Mia took center stage as forward, having played all throughout boarding school and into college.

The soccer league was enormous, and through it I met an army of people my age. They shared an optimism and athleticism that I lacked, but somehow what had been a barrier to entry before now seemed to matter little. They were competitive but never critical, and when I inevitably let them down by not running down a ball or falling for the "ball through the legs" trick one too many times, they expressed a flash of disappointment followed by a "nice try" or "next time."

I had grown up in an environment where disappointment was permanent, so at first this attitude seemed inauthentic. I waited after the games for evidence that the team was turning on me. I was in awe of their ease. They laughed freely, and spoke without worrying how they might be perceived. My inner bureaucrat bogged down my system so thoroughly that people had moved on from topics before I felt confident enough to contribute.

After every game, we went to a bar nearby to drink beer and eat. After my fifth beer or so, I reached a magical place where I didn't care what others thought about me, and I felt the ease that I assumed others usually had. I dazzled in the moments that followed, able to hold the attention of a table full of people, sharing stories and witticisms that had been constructed in my extended silences. This magical release would last a half hour before I would get quiet again. I rarely appeared drunk, so most people didn't notice what was happening to me. I had internalized my father's stern proclamation from years before that "gentlemen hold their liquor," and marshaled my resources to maintain some level of awareness and composure as I drank.

There was usually one friend who completely lost control and dissolved into a puddle of drunken ramblings by the evening's end. I perked to life when this happened, suddenly feeling like part of a larger judgmental organism that had identified the weakest link. We rolled our eyes and made subtle gestures to one another as the offending party went on an angry rant, laughed at nothing, or had trouble maintaining an upright position.

Monty exhibited the same glassy blankness I saw in most of the drunks I met. My family had been making fun of him for drinking too much since he was fifteen years old, thinking that ridiculing him would condition him to drink less. That strategy had worked on me when my mother mocked me for being "too sensitive." I had grown a steely exterior in response, on high alert for any slight from my family and ready to give as good as I got. It was having the opposite effect on Monty, whose drinking only got worse, and his responses to us more venomous.

My brothers and I were visiting my father and Barb one Christmas, when the topic of Bill Clinton came up. My older brother and father were making bold, Rush Limbaugh–esque statements about how treacherous, corrupt, and misguided the Democrats were, and I was standing like Rambo on the proverbial liberal mountaintop, mowing their points down one by one, only to find when vanquished that they opened up another front on the eastern flank. We had been engaged in political warfare for years, and I had learned to pick my battles carefully.

"Clinton's going to be impeached, I can guarantee it," my father said. The Democrats had just taken a beating in the 1994 midterm elections.

"You just don't like him because he's smart," I replied, "and I don't understand when that became so awful for the person who is responsible for leading the free world."

"Hillary's a dyke," Robin said.

Monty's chin was resting on his chest and his eyes were closed. He let out an exaggerated laugh, his head fell back, and his eyes opened and looked at the ceiling. "This conversation is so . . . stupid."

"Amen," I said. "That Hillary's a dyke is completely irrelevant." I looked over and smiled at Robin.

"So, Monty, what do you think of Bill Clinton?" Robin asked.

"Like it matters." Monty's head rolled toward Robin in full disdain and leveled a stare in his direction. "You think this stupid conversation matters and it's so stupid that you think that."

"Why is this conversation stupid, do you think?" Robin asked.

Monty scoffed. "Never mind."

"No, tell me, I want to know."

"It doesn't matter who the president is!" Monty yelled. "Are you a fucking idiot?"

"Here we go," my father said.

"It's not nice to call your oldest brother an idiot," Robin said lightly. "You hurt my feelings." Robin's face dropped into a contrived frown.

"Robin, stop," I said.

Monty's head whipped around to me. "You're an idiot too."

"Robin, continue," I said.

I yelled to my stepmother. "Barb, come in here. You're not going to want to miss this."

"You think the president has any power?!" Monty continued. "It's all the fucking FBI."

"The FBI?" Robin said, aghast.

"And the CIA. They control this whole fucking country and nobody fucking sees it!" Monty was leaning forward now and speaking into the middle of the room.

"That's so scary, Monty," Barb said warmly, walking in from the kitchen. "Would anyone like smoked salmon?"

"I'll bring it in, Barb," Robin said and got up. "Monty, can I get you another beer while I'm up?"

"What?" Monty's eyes had closed again.

"It may go into your FBI file," I said. "They profile people who drink more than twenty Heinekens a day."

"Good thing I only drink gin," my father said.

"Oh my *God*." Monty shook his head, a derisive smirk on his face. "You people make fucking jokes and this country is going to shit!"

"You have deeply offended me. And this great land of ours," Robin said, pretending to clutch pearls.

"Fuck off, prick." Monty's head fell back on the couch and he started to snore.

"By the way," I looked at my father, "if you're insane enough to think that Bill Clinton is going to get impeached, let's make it interesting. I'll bet you two hundred and fifty dollars that you're wrong."

"You're on," he said.

Part IV

Chapter 11

I traveled back east to see my father, stepmother, and brothers the first Christmas after moving to Seattle. My father had moved to south Florida a few years before and had reinvented himself as a successful Realtor for a firm specializing in homes on Jupiter Island, an exclusive enclave. It was the winter destination for the elite, peppered with people with whom my father had grown up, providing him a ready-made list of contacts. The most prominent of these was the wealthiest matriarch on our Adirondack lake. She owned several lots on the ocean side of the island and was a fixture of Jupiter Island society. She knew the owner of the real-estate firm well and served as a reference for my father, whom she viewed as a combination of son and partner in crime. They shared a perspective that the main benefit of growing up rich is not giving a shit what other people think about you.

Jupiter Island wasn't a gated community, but when driving down the main road on the ocean side of the island, there was a sense that you were being watched by a sophisticated surveillance system. If you weren't a white person in a polo shirt, or holding a piece of gardening equipment, the ever-present security force would stop and ask what you were doing. Most homes had two signs in front of two distinct driveways: the main entrance bearing the name of the homeowner, and the second entrance labeled "Service," indicating the back driveway for household staff, caterers, and landscapers. The top-tier houses were on the ocean side, followed by those on the inland waterway. The bottom-rung houses sat without water views between the two. Several families owned second second homes in the middle of the island, for overflow guests.

My brothers and I had spent a few Florida Christmases with my father, and each time, being there during the holiday felt as if somebody had arranged a Make-A-Wish celebration in the middle of summer. The town was decorated with evergreen wreaths, Christmas trees, and scenes of Santa on his sleigh being pulled through the snow, while people walked around in shorts and tank tops in eighty-degree weather. My father and Barb lived in a new development called Loblolly Bay—known as the Jupiter Island of Catholics, or Protestants who couldn't afford to live on the island. Many of the houses sat on stilts, nestled amid the large swaths of mangroves, and connected by elevated wooden walking paths. My father's house was built next to the golf course. It had a pool and a separate guesthouse, as well as an enormous open floor plan that connected the living room, dining room, and a separate sitting area.

I was the first to arrive for Christmas 1997, the year I turned twenty-nine. My father and Barb weren't speaking to each other, and I didn't know why. Through Al-Anon, I had learned that you were "only as sick as your secrets," and decided this gave me the power to cure any conflict by encouraging people to talk about what was going on. At dinner that night, my first step was to apply copious amounts of alcohol to the situation, to get us all primed and ready for confession.

"You two are quiet tonight," I said.

"Are we? I hadn't noticed," said my father.

Barb looked down and dabbed at her mouth with the cloth napkin. When she was eating, she often looked like she was having her own little-girl tea party with imaginary friends, even when other people were around. She focused on something out the window and sipped from her glass of wine while humming to herself.

"Is something wrong? It seems like the two of you are mad at each other," I said. I leaned forward and looked back and forth between the two of them.

"Do you like the new house?" my father asked.

It wasn't the answer I was expecting. "It's beautiful," I said.

"It is, isn't it?" He pushed his chair back and pointed to the foyer. "Did you notice the side table by the front door with the lamp on it?" he asked.

"I came in the back door, so I haven't seen that yet."

My father looked at Barb and tilted his head like a confused husky, though his look indicated vindication more than mis-understanding. She kept looking out the window, humming to herself and sipping her wine.

"That's interesting, what you said about the back door," my father said, standing up. "I too have noticed that almost everyone enters the house through the back door."

"Fascinating," I said, my eyes darting back and forth between the two of them.

"Don't you want to see the table and lamp?"

I did not. "I guess so."

"Please, come take a look," he said, stopping at the edge of the foyer. A wall blocked my view of the table and lamp in question, but he was pointing in their direction and summoning me forward.

"Deh do dee dah deh do do," hummed Barb.

"Must be quite a table and lamp," I said nervously, getting up.

"Oh, *it is*," my father said, nodding his head up and down as his eyes grew wider. "You've never seen a table and lamp like this before, I can guarantee you."

I walked toward the foyer, looking back to see Barb staring at me, with a tear rolling down her cheek.

The table was four feet tall, with what looked like a marble top, three feet long, and three-quarters of a foot wide. The lamp was metal and molded into the shape of a palm-tree trunk, with green and brown markings. Instead of a typical lampshade, green metal palm leaves surrounded the light bulb.

My father smiled at me. "Do you like it?" he asked quietly.

"I do."

"The table cost seven thousand dollars. The lamp was three thousand dollars. You are looking at ten thousand dollars' worth of table and lamp," he said, staring at Barb, "so you might want to think about coming in the FUCKING front door every now and then."

I looked at my father, but he had stopped talking to me. He fixated on Barb, who got up from the dining room table and walked into the kitchen. He raised his voice as he walked toward the round table in the middle of their great room and pointed at a two-foot-high wooden pineapple.

"This COCKSUCKING pineapple? Four thousand dollars. You see that chair over there? Five thousand dollars. The pillow *on* the chair? A thousand dollars."

"I think I get the idea."

"People say you're the smart one."

"Easy now."

"I'm glad that incredibly expensive education I paid for introduced you to the basics of supply and demand."

"I hated economics."

"You learned how to add somewhere along the line, I hope."

"And I totally failed finite math. I failed it so badly I'm not even sure what it is."

"Let's just agree that it's not buying a wooden pineapple for the price of a Yugo."

"I don't know why you're getting so mad at me. *I* didn't buy the damn pineapple."

"Where did Barb go? I didn't get my coffee."

"To be fair, didn't she buy part of the pineapple? Didn't you buy this house together?" I didn't know the details of Barb's finances before she met my father, only rumblings that she had inherited money from her family's media business. My mother was certain that he had jumped his sinking financial ship to commandeer her more stable one, but she was certain of a lot of things related to my father.

"We could have purchased an orchard of pineapples. We could have purchased an army of Mexicans to pick pineapples all day!"

"And while we're on the subject, didn't I pay for part of my incredibly expensive education?"

"Where is my coffee? Did you see her leave the kitchen?"

"I don't think pineapples grow in an orchard, just FYI."

"I told you to go to community college, didn't I? You decided you wanted to stay at Tulane, so you took out loans so you could stay. If I could have paid for it, I would have."

His anger triggered my own. It reminded me of when my horse had spooked during a cross-country ride when I was eight years old and galloped uncontrollably for five minutes before ending up halfway up a mountain of logs on our farm. The horse and I both found ourselves stuck someplace that we didn't know how to get back down from.

"I'm not talking about the loans. I'm talking about the trust fund that your father set up for us," I said.

What I didn't say, but wanted to, was: *the trust fund that you tried so hard to keep from us, that we needed so that we could buy food and clothes and not be looked at with pity by the people my mother looked down upon.* A montage of scenes in which my mother didn't have money to pay for things played in my head, triggering memories of the nonspecific but persistent anxiety that everything could fall apart at any minute.

There's a look that a divorced parent gets when confronted by an accusation of the other parent through one of their children. My father's eyes grew big, and his mouth pursed, as if he was physically holding back words that he knew, if they escaped, would damage something fragile. "I wouldn't assume your mother's perspective on that is entirely accurate," he said.

"What's yours?"

He looked down, and his voice got low. "If I could have afforded to pay the entire college tuition, for all of you children, I would have," he repeated, in a way that let me know this conversation was over.

His dismissal elicited a familiar feeling of anger that accompanied any talk of money in my family. I wanted somebody to blame for how my brothers and I had grown up with the bare minimum to survive, while my father was arguing over $4,000 wooden pineapples and my mother complained about too many deckhands on her yacht.

I looked at the pineapple and then back at him.

"Smells like your coffee's ready," I said.

WHILE MY FATHER AND BARB argued over their décor, my mother and John were navigating some issues of their own. I called her a few months after Christmas to check in, trying her numbers in Florida and Bermuda before reaching her at their London flat.

"I'm upset," my mother said. "John's in the hospital. The helicopter took him there."

"He's what?! Is he okay?"

"No, he's not okay!"

"He's alive, though, right?"

"He's alive for now! At least, he was the last time I saw him."

"Start at the beginning. What happened? Where are you?"

"He fell out the window!"

"What do you mean he fell out the—"

"He walked out the window, actually. I don't know, Kirkland. I'm a wreck. I've never been so upset."

"Can you start at the beginning please? I'm having a hard time understanding what you're—"

"We were having a lovely evening. We had just arrived in Paris the day before, after a horrendous trip. I told John I am *never* going on British Airways again. We finally get to our place on the Champs-Élysées, and I'm *exhausted*, so we go to bed early, because John has, of course, invited the queer to dinner the next night, which I am *not* happy about. He's as 'no come-from' as they get, you know. But he comes over the next night, and we end up having a lovely evening. Angus is telling stories. God knows if any of them are true. He's flailing around with his arms. You know how they are. I've never laughed so hard in my life."

"Okay."

"But I'm still *exhausted* from the travel, so I left them both downstairs, deep in their cups, and I took to my kip. You know how I love my kip."

"I do."

"So I'm sound asleep, having a wonderful dream about Tom Selleck, and I hear 'Missy! Missy!'"

"John calling you?"

"Well, I think it's Tom Selleck at first, but it happens again—'Missy! Missy!' So, I eventually come to and get out of bed and I can't figure out where it's coming from. I knew it was John's voice, but it sounded far away and nearby at the same time. So, I'm walking around the bedroom saying 'John, where are you?' and he keeps calling my name. I check the bathroom, the closet. I lean over the railing to see if he's in the living room.

He's nowhere. I walk back into the bedroom and head over to the window, and his voice is getting louder. And I look down onto the street, and there he is, naked as the day God made him, and I say 'What the hell are you doing down there?' and he's telling me to get help, and I'm asking him what happened because I don't understand what he's doing down there."

"Holy shit."

"You're damn right, holy shit!"

"He fell out a *window*?"

"He thought it was the bathroom."

"He . . . wait . . ."

"He was doing his *toilette* before he came to bed."

"And walked out the window? How do you walk out a *window*?"

"It's a French window."

"French windows don't have, like, a balcony with a railing?"

"He fell out of the fucking thing! What do you want me to tell you?"

"I'm just saying. It seems like France would be raining drunk people on any given Saturday night with windows like that."

"Believe me, I'm not happy about it, and I told him. Once I figured out what was going on, I let him have it. I said, 'What are you doing on the street, you drunk pussy? I should leave your fat ass right there for waking me up in the middle of the night and scaring me half to death!'"

"You were *yelling* at him? Were you on the street at this point?"

"*Les gendarmes* were on their way, and I told him, 'How could you do this to me?' We had just arrived. I had just had a perfectly lovely evening. I was looking forward to doing some shopping and now I'm going to spend the whole bloody time in the hospital."

"He's still naked—"

"My entire vacation 'out the window,' you could say."

"—and by himself on the street?"

"Don't laugh, Kirkland. It's not funny."

"I'm not laughing."

"He was airlifted to London. He's in a full-body cast with a broken back—little fat thing with his arms sticking out. I told him he looked like that floating doggy balloon in the American parade. They say six months until he's right again."

"Snoopy?"

"They're not even sure he's going to walk. He could hardly walk before he fell out a three-story window, for fuck's sake."

"Are you okay?"

I asked the question unsure whether I wanted the answer. My mother flaunted a tough veneer that was paper-thin and easily punctured. There was a long pause on the other end of the line, then a sniffle, followed by a deep inhale and a muffled cry.

"I was so scared," she whispered.

"I know."

"What am I going to do?"

"It's going to be okay."

"I love him so much."

"I know you do."

I didn't know she did.

*   *   *

I WOULD LIKE TO SAY that I called her every day after that to make sure she was okay, but I waited for three weeks before I checked in again. She answered the phone drunk, her words slow, slurred, and tinged with anger.

"How's John doing?"

"What do you want me to tell you?"

"How John's doing."

"Pfft. Tell me something about your life," she said.

"I just got back from the Greenbrier with a group of friends," I said. "My friend Lee's mother has a house there."

"The Greenbrier?" She scoffed. "*Jews*."

"Okay then. About John?" I said, my voice rising.

"He's in a bloody bed all day. He's shitting in a bowl." I heard the clinking of ice as it moved toward the phone, then a soft slurp, followed by the receding of the ice as she brought her glass back down. "You try getting a fat cinder block to take a shit. It's not pretty, I can tell you that."

"About his back—do they think he'll be able to walk again?"

"They don't know anything. I've got my own problems. People have tried to bring me down my whole life, but I won't give them the satisfaction."

I sighed audibly.

"I called my psychic last night," she continued.

"Your what?"

"Her name's Brenda, or Betty. Why the hell do I have to know what her name is?"

"Why are you calling a psychic?"

"I've had a hemorrhoid that's been bleeding for weeks. I've been worried about it."

215

"Have you gone to a doctor?"

"How's your weather? It's been raining here all week."

"When was the last time you went?"

"They don't know what they're doing."

"And your psychic does?"

"We'll see, won't we?"

I CALLED AGAIN TWO MONTHS LATER. I had been keeping track of how John was progressing through Robin, who was in more regular touch. I didn't check in more often because it was expensive to call Europe, but mostly I didn't want to hear how horrible John's broken back was for my mother. And I didn't need to spend money discussing the weather.

My mother picked up on the first ring.

"Hello, darling. How's your weather?"

"It's fine. How's John?"

"It's just been awful here. I hate London weather. When it's not raining, it's bloody hot and sticky. I'm sweating like an Indian all day."

"Is he still in the hospital? When was the last time you saw him?" I had heard from Robin that she was traveling the forty-five minutes to the rehab center less and less often.

"It's been a week or so. Who knows? He's a cranky little fucker. He doesn't like being in bed all day. And so I finally told him after he had yelled at me one too many times that he could shove it up his ass. I said, 'Well, if you hate this so much, you shouldn't have walked your fat ass out a window.'"

I laughed.

"It's not funny, Kirkland."

"That was kind of funny."

"I was dressed to the nines, with the fur and the jewelry, and he wanted to know where I was going all gussied up."

"No wonder you're sweating like an Indian, whatever that means. Who wears a fur coat in August?"

"And I told him I had just met a thirty-year-old doctor and was leaving him. And he said, 'Good for you,' and I said, 'Damn right, good for me.' I said, 'I'm still a hot sexy mama and I don't need to be stuck with a broken old man who can't get it up anymore. I need a real man!'" She laughed. "That shut him up."

"So I'm going to have a new stepdaddy now? One who can prescribe meds?"

"Hah!" She scoffed. "It'll be a cold day in hell before I get married again."

"I think that's probably for the best," I said. She laughed.

"You've got to laugh to keep from crying, Kirkland. That's what your mama always says." Her laughter ebbed. She paused for a second or two before she spoke again. "You've got to laugh to keep from crying."

ROBIN MET CHARLOTTE on an American Airlines flight to Seattle, where she worked as a flight attendant. He was on his way to a work event before spending the weekend with me. He never mentioned Charlotte to me that weekend, perhaps because he slept with my roommate Lisa soon after arriving.

Robin had good reasons for not telling us about Charlotte sooner. His history with women was mixed enough that even the indication that he was dating somebody new put the family on full alert. Robin preferred his women sassy and damaged, with enough daddy issues to match his mommy issues, ensuring a never-ending cycle of anger and reconciliation packaged as passion.

My father and Barb met Charlotte when they hosted an engagement party for the couple at our Adirondack camp. I had heard rumblings that my father was uncomfortable sanctioning my brother's marriage when he hadn't met his fiancée, but by this point he approached almost everything in relation to his children with a shrug. I was unable to attend the party, but guessed that it hadn't gone particularly well when Robin told me that my father and Barb had sat them down for lunch the day after the event and said that their marriage wasn't going to work and they should call it off. I never received a thorough debrief from my father as to what had so alarmed them about the pending nuptials, but it was sufficiently out of character for him to intrude in such a direct manner that I figured there was something about Charlotte that concerned him. Not surprisingly, after the lunch, Charlotte did not feel welcome at my father's house. She wanted to leave. In the end, my father acquiesced to Robin's request to apologize to Charlotte that same afternoon. They never spoke about that weekend again.

I met Charlotte for the first time at the Adirondack wedding of one of our childhood friends, the evening of the rehearsal dinner and cocktail party. She was getting ready when I arrived, and by the time she descended from upstairs to join us we were an hour late. She greeted me much the same way a supermodel might greet her cameraman's assistant. She seemed to view our annoyance as temporary, soon to be replaced by a collective awe at her beauty and charm. I can't speak for Robin's experience of this particular entrance, but my first thought was that she had an outsized sense of self-importance. My second thought was that she was just like my mother. I soon recognized that Charlotte had no intention of auditioning for my approval, expecting instead that I would be motivated to secure hers. She wanted all love for Robin to be filtered and curated through her, and she would be the judge as to its authenticity and utility.

Robin and Charlotte started building a life together based on a foundation of mutual admiration for each other's unique brand of self-promotional ambition, coupled with a healthy dose of seventies-throwback pop-psychological conditioning. She introduced Robin to "the Forum," a three-day intensive seminar based on Werner Erhard's est trainings. The Forum taught that you could create an identity for yourself by challenging assumptions and altering your personal narrative. Trainings encouraged you to be "coachable" and active observers of your life. There was a strong evangelical component, requiring those who had been transformed to preach the gospel of the Forum to others, especially family members. They believed it would be easier to continue living in your truth if others were living in your truth too.

I noticed the slogans first. "You have a 'need to be right racket' going on" or "Can I coach you on this?" peppered every conversation between Robin and Charlotte. I received multiple impassioned phone calls from Robin during which he offered to fly me to the next Forum seminar and pay for all my expenses.

Because of Al-Anon, I was familiar with the temporary euphoria of having discovered a new way of looking at the world. The biggest difference was that Al-Anon believed in "attraction rather than promotion" and suggested that any evangelizing on the program's behalf was an indication that you weren't focused on your own growth, and were therefore off-track. Further, although many people in Al-Anon experienced a "conversion" moment, it was only the beginning of a much longer process to change bad habits and patterns. The Forum, as described to me, erased your clogged psyche in seventy-two hours, outfitted you with a new vocabulary of jargon, and required that you then impose your new beliefs on everyone around you.

After multiple attempts to get me to go to the Forum, Robin was fired from recruitment duty, and Charlotte stepped in. I had recently moved to Washington, DC, from Seattle, having secured a job as an elementary-school computer teacher over the phone through a friend of mine who worked at the school. I didn't know how to use a computer, but educational technology was so new that I assumed I could learn enough to surpass sixth-grade-level proficiency before the kids noticed that I didn't know anything about technology. I was proven wrong when, the second week on the job, an advanced third grader looked up at me with innocent, confused eyes and said, "You don't know what you're doing, do you?"

I traveled back to Bermuda for the Christmas holiday and met Charlotte and Robin at a pizza place for dinner one of the first nights I was back. After a few glasses of wine, Charlotte focused on me, leaned forward, and said, "I really need you to do the Forum."

"I think I'm good," I said.

"I love your brother *so much*." Her eyes glistened.

I side-eyed Robin, who was looking adoringly at Charlotte. I had seen his weepy look directed at most of his girlfriends, but there was a surrender in this one that was new.

"I'm glad."

She leaned back in her chair, and her face hardened. "I don't understand why you won't do it."

"Because I don't want to."

Charlotte looked up and bit her lip. Her face cycled through hurt, anger, resignation, defiance, pity, and sadness—searching for the slot machine combination that would get her what she had come for. I didn't know if there were official stages of southern belle male manipulation, but I was keenly aware that we were moving through some version of it.

"It's okay," Robin said, reaching for her hand. He had yet to realize that our conversation was no longer about him.

She brushed him off and leaned forward. "We are going to be a family," she said, her eyes filling with tears. "You're all going to be a part of *my* family." She pulled back again and placed her hands over her eyes, her shoulders shuddering with muffled sobs. I wasn't sure if she was crying because she was frustrated that I was missing out on an opportunity for enlightenment, or if she was horrified by the realization of what she was marrying into. Charlotte wasn't interested in integrating into our family. She was here to change it.

"He's not going to change his mind because you're crying," Robin said.

I smiled at him, and he smiled back.

*   *   *

THEIR WEDDING TOOK PLACE the following February in Bermuda. It was a small affair, self-funded by Robin and Charlotte at a humble venue in St. George's, on the east end of the island. The guest list included immediate family, Robin's Bermuda friends, and our joint Adirondack friends. Charlotte had her parents, her sister, and a handful of close friends.

As the best man, Robin told me it was my job to keep my mother separated from my father, stepmother, and stepsister, and that Charlotte's father and stepmother needed to be kept away from her mother. Robin and Charlotte negotiated the seating charts for both the rehearsal dinner and the reception like the opening event of a United Nations summit.

The rehearsal dinner went smoothly, until the moment my mother decided she wanted to say something. She had arrived late to the event, with John, obviously drunk. She wore an elaborate full-length white suit and hat with blue-tinted sunglasses that stayed on all evening. My father had just finished his own toast, which uncomfortably referenced his early trepidations about the marriage in an effort at humor that fell flat. The audience picked up on his not-so-subtle implication that Charlotte was marrying my brother for his money.

"I would like to say something," my mother said, standing up. She had trouble managing the dual action of rising from her chair and holding on to her glass.

"Oh God," I whispered.

"I love my son!" she said angrily. "My children are the *best* thing that ever happened to me."

There was a murmur of *awws*, and eyes moistened as my mother's face contorted with emotion. They had no idea what was coming, but Robin and I knew this preamble well, and shared a quick *Oh shit* look.

"Their *father*, if you want to call him that . . ."

"Okay, Wendy," said John, tugging at her sleeve.

". . . wasn't there. *My* father should be here. He loved my boys." She slapped John's hand away. "Stop *pawing* me."

John dropped his hand, grabbed his drink, and sat back. He had recovered from his broken back but still looked uncomfortable no matter where he was sitting.

"I'm sure Charlotte is a *perfectly* nice girl, but you can do better than this, Robin. I brought you up better than this."

"Okay, Missy," said John, chuckling in embarrassment, "let everyone eat now."

"You do *not* tell me what to do."

"I know, darling."

"No man tells me what to do anymore. Hold my glass. Don't *touch* me."

John took her glass as she steadied herself to sit down.

"Your mama loves you more than anybody. You *know* that," she said, a slight weep in her voice as she descended back into her chair.

Whenever my mother said something outrageous, she followed it up with an expression of personal pain, so that people were confused as to whether they should be concerned or angry. As the reception guests looked around awkwardly, our Adirondack friend Mr. Jameson quickly rose and gave an elegant toast that redirected attention from my mother.

The wedding ceremony, held the next day, was short and simple. Midway through the reception, at a modest social club overlooking the north shore of the island, Charlotte's step-mother sidled up next to me.

"Can you do me a favor, darlin'?"

Linda looked like Alice from *The Brady Bunch* if Alice had been stripped of her maid's uniform and dressed head to toe in fancy rodeo attire, complete with a big turquoise belt buckle.

"Do you see my husband over there talking to Charlotte's mom?" she asked.

Across the room, I saw a couple talking amicably. Charlotte's dad was tall and skinny and had also donned Sunday rodeo wear. I couldn't tell if they dressed this way at any wedding or as a show of Texas-style pride to combat the army of preppy snobs surrounding them. Charlotte's mother evidently had no such need to look the part of a Texan, having chosen an elaborate ensemble like my mother's, metaphorical armor for the battle they were both still waging against their ex-husbands.

"I don't like it," Linda said. "I would appreciate it if you went over there and broke them up."

"Broke them up?"

"She keeps touching his arm. Do you see that?"

I hadn't noticed. To me, they looked like every other chatty couple at the reception. I was more confused that they were speaking at all, given that I had been warned about how much they hated each other. I would have thought a thaw in relations was good, especially as I compared them to my own parents, who occupied opposite sides of the small reception room. My mother was focused on my father, which she communicated by never once looking in his direction.

"What do you want me to do, exactly?" I asked.

"Just go and be your charmin' self," she said. "Go on now." She waved me toward them.

As I walked up to them, Charlotte's mother, Martha, turned slowly toward me as if I were a creature who became fascinating only because I had drifted into her orbit. She had bleached-blond hair, cut short, and striking eyes framed by heavy makeup. I immediately recognized her as the kind of woman who thirstily absorbed male attention even as her larger goal was to control it.

"Well, look at this tall drink of water coming my way," she said, smiling seductively at me.

"Are you having fun?" I asked them both.

"So handsome," Martha continued.

"We're having a nice time," Charlotte's dad said.

"And so tall. I have always loved tall men," she said.

"It was a beautiful ceremony, don't you think?" I continued.

"That's what attracted me to Jeff," she said, "his height. There is nothing more attractive in a man."

"It was a very nice ceremony," Jeff responded.

"If a short man even tries to ask me out, I am just not interested."

"Can I get anybody a drink?" I asked.

"And believe me, they've tried. It must be horrible to be a short man in this world," she grabbed my arm and pulled me in, "and not just for the obvious reasons," she said, winking.

"I'm fine with my beer," Jeff said.

"That was never our problem, was it, Jeff?" Charlotte's mom said, turning to Jeff. "Nothing small on you."

"Sounds like everyone's all good, then?" I said.

As I walked away, I spotted Linda from afar, looking in my direction, but I avoided catching her eye. I went to the bar, grabbed a glass of wine, and noticed my younger brother and my stepsister, Lola, and her husband, Neil, on the deck outside the main reception room. I arrived in the midst of their conversation.

"... I'm not sure what you want me to say," Lola said. Monty was looking at her, a beer in his hand.

"I want to know what happened between you and my father."

"I already told you."

"When did it first happen?"

"What are you talking about?" I said. I knew what they were talking about.

"Did you know?" Monty turned toward me.

Lola and I had never talked about it. I didn't even know if she knew I knew.

"Yes," I said.

"Why didn't you *tell* me?" He said it like I had betrayed him.

"Who did tell you?"

"Mommy was upset just now, and I asked her why, and she told me."

"She's always upset."

"When did you know?"

"I was fourteen, I think."

Monty shook his head, smiling slightly in disgust.

"Tell me again," Monty said to Lola. I realized I wanted to hear it too.

Lola looked at her husband, Neil, who was sitting nearby. Lola had always talked about how much Neil reminded her of me: tall, blond, and quiet. They had, no doubt, talked through her affair with my father, as Neil didn't seem disturbed by Monty's questions.

"I honestly don't know how it started. I was only nineteen and I was fucked up most of the time. It was the seventies, for Christ's sake." I smiled, feeling a combination of wanting to protect her and wanting her to be accountable. "I think your father wanted to get high one day at the farm, and we got high. We were in your house for some reason. He kissed me. He told me he and your mother were getting divorced because he didn't love her anymore."

"She said they got divorced because of you," Monty replied.

"That's not what your father told me," Lola said. "He told me that he had already told your mother he didn't love her and wanted a divorce."

Hearing a third party talk about my parents like they were characters in a story felt disorienting. Even after all of these years, the intimacy of our family wound felt like something that shouldn't be spoken out loud.

"Did you sleep with him?" Monty asked.

"Monty . . . ," I said, tilting my face toward him with a warning look.

"No, Kirk, I want to know. I have a right to know," he said. I wasn't sure that was true, but didn't say anything.

"Yes, I did," Lola said. "It was the biggest mistake of my life. I regret it every day."

Monty kept asking Lola questions about where they got together and how many times, and why. When an answer didn't satisfy him, he asked the same question differently. Monty was drunk, as was I, as were Lola and Neil. It was the kind of drunk where you feel close to resolving something that has haunted you for a long time, but you don't quite get there. I knew Lola was sorry and ashamed for her role in my parents' divorce, even as I was coming to recognize, as she repeated the same answers over and over, that she too was collateral damage of a larger conflict.

Robin and Charlotte cut the cake and took to the floor for their first dance while the guests gathered to watch. When they finished, Robin decided it was important to honor tradition by insisting that my mother and father share a dance. Charlotte's parents were already complying, much to Linda's chagrin, but my father looked skeptical as he approached my mother's table and asked if she would do him the honor of joining him on the dance floor "for our son." It was unusual to see my parents in the same frame, let alone referencing anything in relation to the good of their children. My mother looked at me with a bemused smile as she ignored my father's request.

"Just one dance, Mommy," Robin said.

My mother kept her eyes on me as she stood up, resigned to the entreaties of her eldest son. She allowed my father to lead her to the dance floor, maintaining a stoic impenetrability even as my father beamed. She allowed my father to join her right hand with his left and placed his right hand on her waist as the music played. My mother still refused to look at him, preferring to stare off somewhere over his right shoulder, as if there was a bad smell that she was willing away. It had been fifteen years since I had seen my parents in the same place, let alone next to each other, touching each other.

After a few moments, my mother stepped back and turned her gaze to my father, the first time she had looked at him that night. I realized that without her sunglasses on, even though the rest of her body had been taken over by the drinking, her bright green eyes looked the same as they always had, the ones that had captivated my father when she was only nineteen years old. My father stopped dancing and looked back at her, and for a moment the air vibrated with possibility. I wondered if my mother might finally let some of her pain go.

"Look at you," she said. "You're fat, you're gray, you're old—what the hell happened to you?" My mother turned back toward her table and walked off, leaving my father standing alone as Frank Sinatra's song about love reached its final note.

I QUIT TEACHING AFTER TWO YEARS. I realized I wasn't outfitted for the profession after spending five minutes each day with my head out of my classroom window, breathing in and out slowly, in an effort not to murder children. To this day, I can't hear "Mr. Hamill!" yelled in a high-pitched voice without tensing. Nineties-era computer game sound effects make my palms sweat. I will never again help a child find a missing window behind the ten other open windows on a computer screen.

I took a job in Roanoke, Virginia, at a fledgling educational-software consulting company run by the sister of a colleague. Two of my closest friends—a couple—lived in Roanoke, and the thought of getting out of DC was appealing. I didn't have much of a social life, and no dating life at all.

Downtown Roanoke was a movie-set town—with an open-air produce market, people waving from bicycles, and young mothers pushing strollers. I rented a place owned by my new boss that used to be a beaten-up old house before it became a beaten-up old office, and was now a beaten-up old apartment with fluorescent lighting and industrial carpet. I drove my sensible Geo Prizm to work every day past people who never waved, and worked for a woman who looked at my coworker and me with the suspicion that we were ripping her off. We didn't understand how she could charge $1,500 a day for our time and yet pay us only $23,000 a year, so the suspicion was mutual. She was the first (but not the last) boss I had who believed that constant and sustained criticism of one's work constituted effective mentorship, and that it would somehow inspire Gillian and me to greater heights, when all it did was impress upon us that there was nothing either of us could do to secure her approval, so why try at all?

At first, my social life revolved around my friends Lee and Ruth, who were both born and raised in Roanoke and were engaged to be married the following September. I would wait for them to call me, having learned over the years that my intense loneliness was betrayed by a repellent neediness, so I spent a good bit of my psychic energy pretending that I was just fine by myself. If I didn't hear from them, I left a carefree

Thursday message asking if anything was going on that week-end. If this yielded no response, I watched bad movies on cable all weekend. Eventually, I also became friends with my coworker Gillian and her husband, Bill, spending many week-end nights eating, playing games, and drinking too much wine at their house.

I analyzed my friends' relationships closely, looking for evidence that supported the supremacy of my singledom. Whenever there was a disagreement, or any indication that either of their personal freedoms was being curtailed by the other, I made an invisible checkmark in the "single" column. Asked by your partner to do something you didn't want to do? Check. Partner says something counter to your personal view of the world? Check. Partner wants you to go shopping with them? Visit their parents? Invite a sad single friend to dinner? Check. Check. Check.

I was building the case against marriage, because I couldn't see that it was in my future. I had come to believe that love was either like a lightning bolt that hadn't struck me yet or a compromise that people made not to be alone. I had been surrounded by beautiful, intelligent, and funny women all of my life, and I had been told that some of those women found me attractive. But I couldn't see it when it was happening, and I was only attracted to women who were unavailable or showed no interest in me.

The most striking example of my paralysis occurred a few weekends before Lee and Ruth's wedding, when a law school friend of Lee's came to visit. Danielle was strawberry-blond, brilliant, fit, and funny. We clicked soon after she arrived, connecting on multiple levels in a way that eventually led her to my apartment late that Saturday night with a bottle of wine, soft lighting (I turned off the fluorescent overheads), and the two of us sitting next to each other on the couch. Danielle turned her body toward mine, and as we bantered back and forth her hand found my knee and traveled farther up my leg. She flipped her hair, tilted her head, and touched my arm. I felt nothing but abject terror and confusion.

After it became obvious that I was not responding, Danielle left, confused and surly. The next day I told Lee and Ruth what had happened.

"I don't think she's ever been rejected before," Lee said, laughing.

"I didn't *reject* her."

"I can't think of a single man she's wanted that she hasn't gotten." He scrunched up his face in deep thought.

"You saw through her bullshit," Ruth said.

"Not responding the way she wanted isn't rejection."

"Yes, it is," they said in unison.

"I can't be held accountable for turning down something that I didn't want in the first place."

"I would have loved to have been there," Lee said giddily.

"She wanted it. You didn't give it to her. *Rejection*." Ruth pounded the table for emphasis.

"I don't like it," I said.

"Did you ever want her?" Ruth asked Lee.

"Oh, fuck yeah," he said.

*   *   *

MY MOTHER'S WHEREABOUTS were a perpetual mystery to me at this point. She and John split their time between Bermuda, Boca Raton, the new yacht *Bermudiana*, and their flat in London. Monty was just finishing up at the College of Boca Raton, where he was studying "hospitality," a major I had never heard of. Robin thrived as a high-paid executive of a Bermuda reinsurance firm. He slicked his hair back and wore power glasses. He looked like a member of a secret preppy murder club where one smoked cigars and drank scotch while a young, beautiful blond nymph was trussed up in the background, mewling for her release. He played golf, hunted, joined private clubs, and settled into the life he had dreamed of, the one my father had let slip away.

My mother came to visit me my second year in Roanoke. To this day, I'm not sure how she got there, given that I can't imagine her navigating the process of boarding one of the small commercial planes that flew into the valley. She only traveled first class, which wasn't an option coming to Roanoke. She no doubt would have worn a fur and dark glasses and expected several members of the airline "staff" to help her to her seat and stow her carry-on luggage. What she would have discovered was a lone ticket agent hustling people into a cramped fuselage, chirping an inauthentic and weary "Good morning, y'all" to a country crowd, a good portion of whom were likely wearing overalls, NASCAR T-shirts, or polyester blends.

I'm sure John encouraged her to come, a suggestion she bristled against because it implied she was neglecting us or that he didn't want her around or, more likely, both. Instead of feeling like she was happy to see me, I had the sense that she was formulating a response to John's arrogant presumption of neglect, not realizing that her internal rejection of his presumption proved his point.

I was excited that she came, mostly because it gave me the opportunity to prove to my friends that my stories about her were not exaggerated. I had bonded with a small group of UVA grads my last year in Seattle. We stayed in touch as we each moved back east, the small group growing into a cadre of twenty, all of whom lived within a few hours of each other in DC, Roanoke, Richmond, and Charlottesville. Many of my new friends had navigated their own unconventional upbringings. Lee remembered his mother, as they were driving the narrow streets of Ireland, seeing a toddler on the side of the road precariously close to traffic with no supervision and eerily giggling "Bye-bye, baby" as she drove by, before the parent came running out to keep it from getting run over. Ruth described the note she received from her mother, pointing out that her "fuck knots" (the tangled hair knots that formed presumably after having sex with Lee) were unladylike, and warning that she was heading for an adrenaline crash. She had written the note in a spiral shape, so that Ruth had to keep turning the paper to read the warning, the final word, "DESTRUCTION," highlighted at the bottom of the illustrated vortex.

Lee and Ruth invited my mother and me over for a drink before dinner. Several friends who lived nearby came as well, eager to see if the caricature I had drawn was even close to true. I think my mother knew she was being presented as a novelty act for everyone's entertainment, but by this point, it was the only way for us to connect. She was uncomfortable in front of people she didn't know, and responded to that discomfort by wearing expensive jewelry and elaborate outfits. As with any good actress, I think the costumes helped her access the character.

My friends were noticeably excited when we walked in the front door.

"This is my mother," I said to a group of beaming faces. I pointed out each of my friends by name as my mother followed, stony-faced and uninterested.

"I would like to sit down, please," she said.

Lee showed her to their largest upholstered chair, which she occupied like a throne.

"It's so nice to meet you, Mrs. Hamill," Lee said. "We've heard so much about you."

"It's Mrs. Outerbridge."

"I'm so sorry. Mrs. Outerbridge."

"Can I get you something to drink?" Ruth asked gently.

"A white wine would be lovely."

"We're huge fans of your son," Lee said.

My friends Mimi and Roger stood in the back of the room, smiling. "We love Kirky!" Mimi said. It sounded like an unexpected hiccup.

"Did you have a good flight in?" Lee asked.

"I wouldn't say that," my mother replied, scanning the room with an eye toward finding something objectionable about it.

"It's not the easiest place to get to, that's for sure," he said.

"You think?" my mother said, looking at Lee like he was an escaped mental patient peeing in a planter. "Did the other one go to France to get the wine?"

"Her name is Ruth. She is one of your hosts," I said.

"Who's this one?" my mother asked, waggling her finger at Mimi, whose face was paralyzed in a clown-like smile of terror.

"That's Mimi. You can ask her yourself, you know. She's with her fiancé, Roger."

"They're good-looking too," she said suspiciously. "Why are all of your friends so good-looking?"

"They speak English. Everybody here speaks English, and they can hear you."

"You weren't a good-looking baby."

"We're all dying to know what Kirk was like when he was younger," Mimi said.

"You turned out okay, but you were one ugly baby."

"Here's your wine," Ruth said, returning from the kitchen. "I hope Chardonnay is okay?"

"Thank you, darling." My mother looked at Ruth, acknowledging her for the first time. Ruth didn't realize that she could have brought my mother paint thinner and she would have been just as grateful.

"I can't tell you what a pleasure it is to meet you," Roger said, moving forward. "It is truly an honor."

"I raised three boys on my own," my mother said to nobody in particular.

"I can't even imagine," Ruth said. "I don't think I could do that. I really don't"

"It wasn't easy," she said, her face hardening in a memory.

"Impossible," Ruth said.

"But I did it."

I wanted to add a caveat or two about her roaring parental success, but thought better of it.

"If Kirk is any indication of your ability to raise good people, you have a rare and precious talent," Roger said. Roger was the friend of mine who always spoke as if his biographer were nearby jotting down his insights.

"We love Kirky!" Mimi repeated.

"Good thing this one is pretty," my mother said, a slight smile appearing on her face for the first time.

"Mimi."

"What?"

"'This one' is called Mimi," I said.

"Oh please; I'm too old to care," my mother said.

My friends laughed harder than they should have, including Mimi. Either my mother was the Don Rickles of the drunks or they were treating her as such because they loved me, or a little of both. She loosened up more and more with each round of laughter, to the point where she started telling the stories that they said they wanted to hear about my childhood: about how I only wanted to eat hot dogs and Frosted Flakes until I was eight years old, or about when I threw up on the airplane landing in a thunderstorm at JFK when I was six. They were all the same stories I had heard before, many times. I noticed for the first time that all of her stories of me took place when my parents were still together, as if the story of us ended when we moved to Bermuda. In the middle of her stories I caught glimpses of who she used to be—when her laughter was unguarded and her joy irrepressible—and held my breath to cling to the moment as long as I could before the shadows moved back in. I started to see my mother as somebody caught in darkness, doing whatever she could to steal glimpses of light, knowing they wouldn't last for long. I saw how brave that was, and how sad.

A YEAR LATER, I WAS IN PORTLAND, Oregon, for work when Robin called to tell me that my mother had been in a car accident and was in the ICU. She had pulled out into traffic and driven drunk into one of Bermuda's iconic pink buses. According to my brother, when the paramedics arrived, she was pinned in the car and was fighting the rescue workers trying to extricate her.

"They say she smelled like somebody had poured a bottle of scotch over her head," Robin said.

"Do I need to come?" I asked.

"I think so."

She had a massive concussion and broken ribs, and had shattered her leg. She didn't open her eyes until two days after the accident.

"What are you doing here?" she slurred when she saw me.

"I enjoy the beach."

"Where am I?" She started to move around, not realizing that every part of her body was connected to a tube, monitor, or traction device; the saddest marionette you'd ever seen.

"Don't move."

The nurse came into the room and checked her eyes and adjusted dials and tubes. "You're a lucky woman, aren't you, Wendy?" she said with a strong Scottish lilt. "You smelled like a bloody distillery when they brought you in here, didn't you?"

"Fuck you," my mother replied.

She closed her eyes and turned her head. The nurse looked at me with raised eyebrows.

"She says that to everybody," I said sheepishly.

"At least she's got her fighting spirit on," the nurse said matter-of-factly. "She'll need it."

"She sounds like that all of the time, actually."

"Stop talking about me."

"Thank you," I said to the nurse as she walked out the door.

"What happened?"

"You drove into a bus. You're in the hospital." I listed her injuries and the long recovery the doctors had outlined for Robin, John, and me.

"Am I going to be okay?"

"They think so."

"Shit."

Chapter 12

"D o you think you might be gay?"

I had just turned thirty and was hanging out with my friends Wendell and Jessica at their house in Georgetown in Washington, DC. I knew Jessica from Seattle, having met her and her two best friends from Miss Porter's School. They all loved hard-core rap, gay porn, and skinny boys with stringy hair and budding drug addictions.

Wendell was the one asking me. He and Jessica had been married for a few years and had recently relocated to DC for his work. Throughout our heavy night of drinking, the questions had become more intimate, so I wasn't immediately put off.

"I don't know," I said.

I honestly didn't know. It was the first time anyone had asked me directly. I had been gently confronted several years earlier by the only gay person I knew—a friend of my father's growing up, who offered himself up as a resource should I ever need "somebody to talk to." He told me that my friend Kevin—the friend I lived with in Boston right after college who had "stolen" my non-girlfriend, Avery—had said something to him about the possibility I might be gay. I don't know if it was the memory of the betrayal, or that I was suspicious of my father's friend's motives as he swayed drunkenly in front of me, but I vehemently denied that I was gay and let him know that I didn't need his help.

"I'm going to think about it," I said, after a short pause.

Once I had let the possibility that I might be gay into my brain, it set up shop, and memories of my past started to make more sense. The flashes started at four years old, watching my brother and his friend Andrew sword-fighting with sticks and climbing trees while I sat and built little cottages with moss and bark, wincing when one of them would scream too loudly. I remembered seeing my mother needlepointing in the corner chair in our study, and how I admired the intricacy of each stitch and the way, little by little, the tiny bumps transformed into a story, knowing, without being told, that I wasn't allowed to do what she was doing, even though I so desperately wanted to. There's a picture of my brothers and me taken when I was thirteen. Robin is sitting up straight to my left. Monty is slouching on my right. I am posed coquettishly in the middle with my legs together, as if I don't want somebody to look up my skirt.

I hated war movies, and buddy cop shows. I never played with toy soldiers. I didn't think the Marx Brothers, Benny Hill, or the Three Stooges were funny. I thought burping was gross, and farting unforgivable.

I loved the Carpenters, the movie *Beaches*, Wonder Woman, Judy Blume books, Stevie Nicks, Madonna, the smell of hand lotion, talking about my feelings, Air Supply, dance routines, and movies where men fell in love or cried.

I loved Ethan. I had been in love with Ethan.

"I think I might be," I said to Wendell.

A few years earlier, I had noticed that the voice inside my head was feminine and didn't belong to me. The voice wasn't my mother or anyone I knew. It wasn't necessarily even a personality. But it was distinctly feminine, and it felt like it didn't belong, like some genetic wire had crossed in my brain and my life's narration had been assigned to the wrong actor. She wasn't accusatory or self-destructive, nor was what she said inconsistent with who I was, yet she wasn't me. As soon as I admitted to myself that I was gay, she disappeared, replaced with a voice that was male and mine, and integrated in a way that the female voice had never been.

Within a week, I had told my closest friends. I had never kissed a man, and besides the awkward fumble in the Tulane library bathroom ten years earlier, I had never touched another penis. But I knew. Around this same time, Ethan called, having tracked me down in Roanoke. He told me about his career as an international businessman that took him to London and Europe, and how he had lived in Russia for a while. It didn't take long for us to find the rhythm that we had shared so many years before. Just one exhale and we were right back to it. I told him I was gay, and reminded him of our conversation in my dorm room so many years before. He apologized and said that he wasn't that same person anymore, and he hoped I was happy. "I miss you, Kirk," he said before hanging up. In some ways this was the first time we had met.

ONCE I HAD TOLD THE PEOPLE who I knew would be supportive of the news, it was time to tell my family. Harboring a secret felt like holding a hot potato in my hand. I knew the relationships I had with them were going to be strained in some indefinable way until they understood this part of me. I didn't think they would be happy about it, but I never once had the fear that anyone would cut me out of his or her life because of it. My family members weren't disciplined or concerned enough with the lives of others to exert the energy for such a campaign. As luck would have it, it was already late fall, and I was traveling to Florida for the holidays in a few weeks to stay with my father and Barb through Christmas Day, before spending Boxing Day with my mother and John.

Robin and Charlotte picked me up from Palm Beach International Airport. I sat up front with Robin. "Let's play a game," I suggested when the conversation lulled. "It's called Who in This Car Thinks They Might Be Gay?" I kept my eyes forward, not wanting to look at them. "The winner is the first person who raises his or her hand."

I shot up my hand before they had time to think about it.

Robin got a confused look but kept his eyes on the road. It took him a minute to respond.

"You are?" he offered eventually. "That's *great*."

He didn't say much after that, but the confused smile never dimmed as he kept driving. He tried to mask his bemusement with questions: When did I know, did I know for sure, did I have a boyfriend, and was I going to tell everyone? Charlotte sat defiantly quiet, stabbing her needlepoint needle into the Christmas stocking she was working on, as if she could cure our family dysfunction with holiday gifts. My one-year-old niece, Piper, sat in her car seat, looking around with big, curious eyes.

We arrived at my father's house after forty awkward minutes. In retrospect, it would have been smarter to wait until we had almost arrived to tell them. I had underestimated the impact of my announcement. Robin looked queasy, and Charlotte seemed angry. Robin had always made cracks about gay people—he would exaggerate an effeminate gesture, or make a gerbil reference here and there—but I never sensed any animosity in his remarks. Instead, I think he thought of gay people as "other"—similar to how poor people, Jews, or black people were "other"—and therefore never imagined that one of them would enter his orbit.

Monty was already at the house when we pulled into the driveway, so I waited until we had a quiet moment on the couch before I played the "Do you think you might be gay" game with him. He looked at me with the same expression that Robin had given me, then leaned over and started laughing. Hard.

He was hunched over on the couch, looking at his feet, a Heineken still dangling from his fingers, quaking with the vibrations of silent hysteria. Anybody walking in would have thought I had just told him his entire family had been killed in a car crash. After thirty seconds, he hadn't moved, so I looked around the den and noticed that my father and Barb had installed a new television. It was off, which was unusual, since they had become the type of Floridians who kept it on all day. There was a vague smell of beef cooking in the kitchen. I heard muffled voices in the guest room, where Robin and Charlotte were setting up Piper's travel crib. *Barb must be walking the dogs*, I thought to myself.

A minute elapsed. Monty had tipped over to the side, his shoulders still shaking up and down. He held out his arm, looking for a perch on which to place his beer, so I gently took it from him and put it on the coffee table in front of us. My father wasn't around, and it crossed my mind that he was still at work, which also seemed a little weird, since it was already dark and he would normally have been excited enough to see us that he would have been home already. Once freed from his beer, Monty placed his second hand over his face, and I heard a series of sharp intakes of breath followed by muffled howls. He was now fetal, twitching like a Pentecostal congregant who had just been struck with the Holy Spirit.

After a good two minutes, he looked up at me, wiped the tears from his eyes, and asked, "So, does this mean that you like to suck cock?"

"I guess so," I replied. I didn't know.

I shared the third installment of the "Who thinks they might be gay" game that night—Christmas Eve—right after we had finished dinner. Monty spit out his red wine and fell forward once again, almost face-planting into his gravy-drenched green beans.

"There he goes," Robin said.

Neither my father nor Barb looked amused.

After an awkward pause, Barb said, less casually than her words would suggest, "So what? Lots of people are gay nowadays. It's almost passé not to be. And they look good, and cook beautifully." She got up from the table and cleared the plates.

My father sat silently for a long time, looking everywhere but at me, as he processed the information. Finally, he said, "Kirkland, I love you no matter what. But I'm not going to believe that this is true until you actually bring somebody home with you. And then I can begin having trouble accepting it." My father was always manufacturing mind-twisters in response to difficult news. I didn't know what to say, so I looked over at Robin, who was staring at my father, his face scrunched up in confusion.

"He doesn't know if he likes to suck cock!" Monty blurted, wine once again spraying out of his mouth.

"He better," Robin said. "Guys like that."

"I don't think you should drink any more wine, at least until this gay thing doesn't send you into hysterics," I said to Monty. "You're making a mess."

Charlotte bolted up from the table, grabbing Piper and whisking her out of the room as if a tsunami warning horn had gone off.

"Watch the teeth," Robin continued.

"Oh God," my father said, lowering his head.

"You better end up with somebody rich," Robin said. "You're the Hamill family's last chance at a private jet."

"Hey, I'm not married," Monty said.

"I think you're looking at this all wrong," I said to my father. "My boyfriend might like golf, or racist jokes."

"I need to get out of here," my father said, getting up from the table and grabbing the keys to his car. "I'll be back later."

He had never left our dinner table like that before. Robin and Monty watched him leave with the same surprised expression that I did, and then looked over to make sure that I was okay. I didn't want to show anybody that my feelings were hurt; the whole plan was to make my being gay as normal as possible, so that my life wouldn't change any more than necessary. I would rather be teased mercilessly about sucking cock than endure polite and insincere tolerance.

"Where did your father go?" Barb asked, returning from the kitchen.

"ARE YOU SURE YOU WANT TO DO THIS?" Robin asked. It was the day after Christmas. We were pulling into a parking space next to my mother's new convertible Rolls-Royce, a car she had never driven. The person who sold it to my stepfather told him it once belonged to Barbra Streisand.

"I'm kind of excited about it," I said.

"This is going to be so good," Robin said, giggling.

"More money for me!" Monty said, clapping his hands. They were both convinced that my announcement would oust me from the will, assuming John died before my mother and there was something to inherit.

Years earlier, we had decided that the best way to mitigate the hurt my mother felt that we chose to spend Christmas with my father was to offer to have lunch with her on Boxing Day. It was an English holiday, providing minimal justification for why it might hold some meaning to her when it didn't hold any to my father. A flimsy excuse, it provided an out that we all needed. As much as my mother felt slighted that we chose my father over her, she was relieved that we didn't come to her place for Christmas. The holiday had been ruined for her many years earlier because my grandfather died on Christmas Eve, not long after he and my grandmother left Bermuda for Australia. (Her birthday had also become a time for mourning because our dog, Lady Diana, died during her birthday week the year after she lost her father.)

John answered the door. As usual, my mother was nowhere to be seen. For the past few years, she didn't appear from her bedroom until the last minute, looking as if she were recovering from massive surgery.

A few minutes later, she shuffled out of her room behind a walker, with a forced smile that came out like a grimace. She hid her eyes behind her ever-present blue-tinted sunglasses.

"Hi-i," she said to us without looking up. My mother was the only person I knew who could infuse a single word with equal parts judgment, betrayal, and sadness.

"Hey," I said lightly. "You look . . . good."

"No, I don't," she said.

She walked straight through the dining room and into the sunroom. She had abdicated the responsibility for interior decorating to John, who had festooned the dining room with a seven-hundred-pound Lucite table and chairs with matching grandfather clock, surrounded by deep red Chinese wall hangings and side tables.

My mother sat down in the sunroom and asked John to get her a drink.

"How about some tomato juice, darlin'?" he said.

"Fuck your tomato juice," she replied.

"What can I get you boys?" he asked, waddling to the bar. "I have gin, vodka, bloody mary mix, whatever you want."

"Whatever's fine," Robin said.

"How about a bloody bull?" he continued. "It has a little bit of beef broth in it, and some Clamato. Your mother loves it,

although I try to tell her to, you know, dial it back a little bit."
He grabbed a Campbell's can from the cupboard and walked
back into the kitchen to retrieve whatever else he needed to
make the drinks.

Someone had placed a bowl of Planters Cheez Balls, a small
dish of M&M's, and a platter of caviar and toast points on the
table. As we settled in, drinks in hand, there was an awkward
silence. I took a large gulp. Robin and Monty looked at me
expectantly, devilish grins on their faces.

"I have something to tell you," I said to my mother.

"What is it?" she said accusingly. "I don't want to hear any
bad news today."

"It's not bad news. Well, *I* don't think so, anyway."

Monty hiccupped into his drink.

"If it's not one thing with you children, it's another," she said.

"I haven't even said anything yet," I said.

"What is it?"

"I just wanted to play a game."

Monty hiccupped again, lunging forward just in time to
catch an ice cube rocketing from his face. Did he ever not have
anything in his mouth?

The game thing had become lame, but I wanted to communicate playfulness rather than misfortune. When I was done, hand
waving solo in the air, my mother narrowed her eyes at me. The
same confused smile I had seen on my brothers swept her face. It
occurred to me that all of them had thought I might be kidding.

"Shut up, Kirkland."

"No, it's true."

Monty dropped his drink on the table and ran out of the room.

"Robin, I need another drink."

"He's not kidding," Robin said.

"A mother like you should have a gay son," I said lightly. "My God, a mother like you *makes* a gay son."

My mother looked out the sunroom window wistfully, brought a hand to her face, and watched as a fifty-foot pleasure yacht made its way through the intracoastal waterway below. My comment had landed where I wanted it to, bonding us together in my gayness, so that she couldn't judge me without judging herself. I was no longer the little boy who would do anything to make her laugh, or the teenager who tried to stop her crying, or the young man who turned every negative feeling in on himself until his heart stopped beating. I had fought hard to claim myself, and if being that person caused others pain, I hoped for them the resilience I had found to endure it.

"I got you a book," I said, handing her a copy of Andrew Sullivan's *Virtually Normal*, which I had kept tucked away in my lap during our conversation. "It's supposed to help people understand what it's like to be gay." This was only partially true; the book was written by a gay conservative who used an intellectual argument to help convince people who were opposed to homosexuality why it was in society's best interests to accept it.

My mother looked at the front cover, turned it over, looked back at me, and in one swift motion tossed it over her shoulder into the potted palm behind her. It landed with a dull thud.

"That's what I think about your book," she said.

She refused to talk about it after that. We sat through lunch with Monty snickering and my mother occasionally looking my way with an inscrutable expression. I wondered if she was trying to formulate the combination of words that would shame me out of who I was, as she had done when I was younger. But I had become too much like her now, certain in who I was and unwilling to bend for anyone.

I WENT ON MY FIRST GAY DATE when I was thirty-two years old, two years after I came out. His name was Josh, and he worked as the head librarian of the local library. A mutual friend set us up in the same way that most gay people are set up on dates in small towns, which was that we were the only two gay people my friend knew and we were single.

Josh wasn't my first choice. Not long after I had come out, I had been introduced to Lawrence—Roanoke's most high-profile gay man, from a prominent family, who spent much of his time in New York City when he wasn't managing the local family business. I was so starved for any entry point into the gay world that I had been desperate to meet him. I was so used to living a sexually dulled life that this newly discovered power felt like a fully loaded Uzi placed in the hands of a child.

Lawrence invited me over to his apartment on a Saturday morning somewhat reluctantly, explaining that he only had a few minutes to spend with me before he was scheduled to fly to New York. I was confused and a little annoyed by this, having assumed he would be similar to pop-culture depictions of gay men over thirty-five in small towns, desperate for validation and nursing an open wound of societal rejection. I assumed he would try to seduce me, so I didn't shower or brush my hair, and wore the baggiest clothes that I owned.

Lawrence buzzed me up to his downtown apartment. When he opened the door, I noticed that he was unmistakably handsome in the effortless way that I never was, with a captivating smile and a self-possessed aura. He was dressed casually, yet impeccably, like it took a lot of work and no work at all.

I walked into a meticulously decorated apartment outfitted with modern décor in monochrome black and white, with tasteful flashes of color strategically placed on uncomfortable-looking leather furniture. He was friendly, but I noticed an undercurrent of impatience, which he explained by saying that he hadn't yet fully packed and would need to do so before we spoke. My immediate thought was that the packing thing was a ruse for him to disappear into the bedroom and return in a shortie robe to pounce on me.

Instead, he emerged from the bedroom a few minutes after I arrived with a roller bag, apologized again, and asked me what he could do for me as he sat down on the couch and checked his watch. I hadn't expected that question, assuming that there was a preset protocol for the onboarding of new gays, so I sputtered through a "just wanting to get to know people" answer while he nodded his head.

"Most of my weekends are spent in New York, so I'm not sure I'll be much help on the social side, but I'm certainly happy to serve as an ear if you need one," he said, not unkindly.

"Okay, thank you. That would be great," I said.

"How is your family taking the news?"

"They seem to be okay. They aren't thrilled, but there's no danger of being cut off."

"That's good."

He paused and pursed his lips, and I could tell by the bounce in his foot that it was time for him, and me, to go.

"Well, thanks for taking the time to see me," I said.

"No problem at all. Don't hesitate to call if you need anything." Lawrence walked me to the door and waved as I stepped into the hall. I barely had the chance to return the wave before the door closed behind me. I realized that I didn't have his phone number, as we had made arrangements through email.

On my way back to my car, I ran my fingers through my oily hair and smelled beneath my armpits, conscious that not only had it not been necessary for me to discourage Lawrence, it was looking more like my shabby appearance had repelled him. In ten minutes, my newly forming gay self-image had plummeted from irresistible temptress to rejected newbie. I realized that I had no idea what being a gay man was about, except that I now understood with humbling certainty that Lawrence was out of my league.

I felt cheated. Having never actually known any gay people, I had adopted society's idea of the insatiable sex predator on the prowl for young, vulnerable flesh. Lawrence was my second example (the Seattle ginger being the first) of a gay man who not only didn't fit this stereotype, but also seemed conspicuously unmoved by my presence. Was it possible that gay people were less one-dimensional than I had been led to believe? I had thought the most difficult part of my journey would be picking the person who would be right for me. Now I wondered if I needed to be more concerned with whether I would ever be chosen.

And so, almost two years later, there was Josh. I didn't want to spend any time alone with him, lest I inadvertently adopt a judgment that might deter me from my newfound priority of getting laid. I still had never had any meaningful sexual contact with a man. By now it was becoming clear to me that not only was I not in danger of being devoured by an army of gay men, I might have to work a little bit at getting one interested in me. So I invited Josh and my friends Lee and Ruth over to my apartment for an after-dinner drink one night.

Josh showed up an hour after Lee and Ruth had arrived, having come from a work event. He was wearing a gray suit and smiled nervously as he entered the apartment. Lee and Ruth greeted him and made small talk about Roanoke to help ease any weirdness associated with my having invited a stranger to my house.

I sat next to Josh the way Danielle had sat next to me, with my body turned toward him and my hand casually playing with my hair. When Lee got up to get himself another drink, I followed him into the kitchen. He asked me how things were going.

"Good, I guess."

"Do you like him?"

"Yeah. I think so."

"Do you think anything will happen?"

I lifted my eyebrows and smiled. If the ice cube Lee was dropping into his glass could have stopped mid-fall, it would have as he realized that the only impediment to sex was their presence.

"Ruth! We have to go!" He dropped his glass on the counter and ran back into the living room, gathering up his jacket as he went. Ruth was confused initially, but caught on, and they both wished us a good night and ran out the door.

Josh was older than me by a few years, and my understanding was that he had been out most of his adult life. As we sat there talking, I mmm-hmmmed and head tilted to signal as clearly as possible that I didn't care about the evolution of the Dewey decimal system, but nothing I was doing spurred him to action. After twenty minutes, I said, "So, I'm new to this gay thing, but if one of us doesn't make a move soon, I'm going to bed."

He looked surprised and paused before saying, "Well, all I can tell you is that I'm not going to do that, but if you do, I won't stop you."

Good enough for me.

As we rolled around on my bed, I assumed that we would progress to penetrative sex, because what else would gay men do? I also assumed since he was older, he would be doing the penetrating. The only sexual partners I had had before were Winnie the Pooh and the handle of my mother's broom, and neither one of them had required consent, so I was a little surprised when Josh was unsure whether he wanted to go all the way.

"I usually don't sleep with somebody until we've been dating awhile," he said.

"How long?" I asked, trying not to sound annoyed.

"It was a year with my last boyfriend," he replied.

That was not going to work for me. In the endless verbal foreplay of the evening, I had determined that I had no interest in learning more about him beyond what noises he made when stimulated. So I did what I needed to do to help separate him from his better judgment. It didn't take much, and when it was over, I knew without a doubt that I was gay and that I wanted Josh out of my house.

Chapter 13

My father divorced Barb after twenty years of marriage, a few months after I came out to them at the Christmas table. He told her that the divorce was a formality meant to lessen their tax burden, without giving her any financial details and without mentioning that he was in the midst of a torrid affair with his secretary, Samantha.

"He went to see her that night, you know," Barb told me on the phone.

"What night?"

"Christmas Eve. Remember when he got up and left the table after your announcement? He went to see her."

Barb discovered the affair the following spring, after overhearing a conversation my father had with Samantha on the kitchen phone.

"He didn't seem terribly concerned about hiding what he was doing," Barb said. "When he got off the phone and I confronted him about it, he said, 'We're not married anymore, so I can do what I want.'"

"But he told you the divorce was for taxes?"

"Yes."

I was silent on the other end of the line, not knowing what to say. Didn't marriage *lessen* your tax burden?

"He wanted her to move in," she said.

"What do you mean?"

"He wanted us all to live together—the two of them would sleep in our room, and I would move into the guest room."

I didn't understand what she was saying.

"He said it would save us all money, he considered me a good friend, and he liked living with me. He just wasn't in love with me anymore," she continued.

My mother, I thought, had heard the same words twenty years earlier.

"I'm devastated," she said.

"I'm so sorry. I don't know what to say."

My brothers and I were furious at my father for tricking Barb into divorcing him. He had left her with little legal recourse, so we told him that he had to do right by her or we would never speak to him again. Under pressure he eventually agreed to pay her alimony. He seemed confused by our anger, not registering that he had done anything wrong.

"You can't help how you feel, Kirkland," he told me on the phone. "I thought you of all people would understand that."

"Oh no you don't."

"You love who you love."

"*No.*"

"Barb and I had twenty wonderful years together."

"Do not turn this into the same thing. It's *not* the same thing."

"Our marriage had run its course. It happens."

I sighed. "It seems to happen to you more than most."

I had come to realize over the years that my father maintained his mostly upbeat demeanor by not thinking about how his actions affected other people. I had asked him a few years earlier if he was relieved when we moved to Bermuda after the divorce, since he then didn't have to worry about the day-to-day drudgery of raising children. He looked at me and said, "Yeah, I guess so."

We had met Samantha a few times before, when my father had invited her over to his and Barb's house. They served as her support system when she was going through a divorce. She was short, with short, bleached-blond hair. Her clothes were an endless combination of white and yellow. She looked as if she were always heading either to or from the tennis court. She laughed at everything anybody said with unnerving intensity.

My brothers and I were not ready to get to know Samantha better, but my father insisted that we give her a chance, so that Christmas, we once again convened in Florida for the holidays. He invited Samantha to lunch on our first day together.

My brothers and I arrived at the restaurant to find my father and "Sammie" already at the table. After we sat down, she took a big gulp from her glass of white wine, turned to us, and said, "You know, your father is so excited to have all of his boys here with him. He really misses you during the year and wishes that you were in better touch. He just loves you all *so much*."

She looked at each of us with a concerned and disappointed half smile on her face, grasping my father's hand under the table. My brothers and I shared a look. Clearly, she was going to be one of those people who viewed winning over their significant other's children as a competitive sport.

"Well, it's good to be here now," I said curtly.

"And I live here," Monty said, "and I actually see you both every day."

"Oh, that DOESN'T COUNT!" she said, laughing manically.

Monty had been working with my father for a while, doing odd jobs at some of the houses he managed while working on getting his real-estate license.

"Shall we order?" my father asked.

"I don't know *what* your father would do without Monty," Samantha continued. "He can be so helpful until that tenth Heineken, and then it's, 'WHERE DID HE GO?'" Her laughter went up an octave as she winked at Monty and continued. "But sometimes he just needs to get away from that fiancée of his." She leaned in closer to Robin and me and put her hand to her mouth, continuing in a stage whisper, "And can you really *blame him*?"

Samantha harbored a distinct grudge against Monty's fiancée, Tonya. The source of this grudge would become clear only some years later, when she drunkenly stuffed her tongue down Monty's throat, proclaiming, "You've always been the one that I want," after he'd been charged with seeing her safely home from my father's house.

"I hope the roast beef is rare today," my father said, studying the menu intently. "Where is that damn waitress?"

"So, Kirkland," Samantha continued, "your father tells me that you're doing remarkable things at your new job." She

leaned forward again, looking like she was about to cry. "I just think you are so smart and good-looking. I really do. I just love tall, sexy men."

"We are hard to resist," I said drily.

"Too bad you're a huge homo," Robin said.

"The guy I fucked last weekend seemed to be okay with it," I replied.

"I could always have the cheeseburger," my father said.

"Good for you, Kirkland!" Samantha yelled, lifting her wineglass. "You tell him!" She continued laughing, her wild, hungry eyes never turning from me. "You are so funny, just like your father!"

"He's definitely a funny one," I said.

"I'm so glad we're doing this, you guys," Samantha said. "I just want you to know that you can ask me any question you want and I'll answer it. Go ahead and ask me; it's really okay." She looked at the three of us, waiting.

"I don't think we have any questions," Robin said. "Do you guys have any questions?"

"I just want you boys to know that I love your father, and I really think Barb is great. And *nothing* happened while they were married."

I turned to my father. "So, how's business going?"

"Don't do that, Kirkland!" Samantha interrupted, and for the first time I noticed a glint of genuine and intense anger in her eyes. "I know you boys have questions for me, and I want to answer every one. Go ahead, let me have it!"

She had clearly not studied the Hamill handbook as part of her preparation to win us over. We were immune to whatever her charms might be, having already placed them in the category of dangerous weapons that had destroyed something we valued. She would have been more successful had she acted like she didn't care what we thought. Hamills appreciate strength of character, even if that character is shit.

I looked Samantha in the eye. "Are the crab cakes good here?" I asked.

Samantha, in the end, would not prove to be the balm my father sought to his relationship woes, though she did turn out to be his last relationship of any notable length. Although we weren't aware of it at the time, her erratic behavior at our first lunch together was an early indicator that Samantha had a serious drinking problem, which was at odds with my father's more comic drinking problem. My father and Sammie broke up for good seven years later, soon after an incident in which she passed out at the top of her stairs with a .3 blood alcohol level after having told him she had stopped drinking. When it was over, and she was out of my father's life for good, we asked him why he had stayed with her for so long. "She was taking care of me," he said. "Who's going to take care of me now?"

MY MOTHER ROLLED UP to Monty's wedding in dramatic fashion, exiting her stretch limo like Whitney Houston, my grandmother and stepfather tagging along behind. As at Robin's wedding, she came to Monty's with an audience of one in mind, preparing for that cathartic moment when she planned to stand in front of my father and watch him crumble to dust before her. I assume she believed such a confrontation would replace the fairy-tale ending that had been denied her—the last revenge of the wronged princess, releasing her from the self-imposed spell that had kept her confined in her prison tower.

My father had a .32-caliber semiautomatic strapped to his waist. Ever since his divorce from Barb three years earlier, he had taken to wearing a sidearm, usually at cocktail parties and family picnics, I assume to ward off predators. A wedding like this was a metaphorical walk through my father's past, with more and more ghosts lining up to remind him what a shitball he had been: There was Barb, still stinging from her humiliation and having developed a hatred for my father that matched my mother's; Barb's daughter, Lola, who was justifiably resentful that my father had lassoed her into his dysfunctional marital narrative at the vulnerable age of nineteen, and had divorced her mother twenty years later; and my mother, who remained a walking experiment in how much alcohol could be applied to a person before anger overcame social convention. He might have also been anticipating a confrontation with my stepfather, John, whom my mother had certainly talked to about my father's various misdeeds. What my father didn't know was that John had long ago tuned out my mother's endless complaining. Samantha was not present, likely because she hadn't been invited.

Instead of confronting each other, my father and John both sidled up to the martini bar that had been erected on a small foot-high platform in the middle of the reception. They chatted about yachts and made the occasional crack at my mother's expense. Robin, perhaps thinking that things could go sideways at any moment, propped my one-and-a-half-year-old nephew, Lyon, on the bar between them as a buffer.

John and my father both adopted the same coping mechanisms for the wedding: avoid my mother and drink excessively. As the two-hour pre-wedding cocktail reception went on, John became the unofficial caretaker of my young nephew, challenging him to eat a handful of strawberries for every martini John drank. After ninety minutes, Lyon was crying with stomach cramps and my father was holding on to John to keep him from toppling off the platform.

"Have you seen our mother?" I asked Robin, while nursing my third martini. "She can't have been thrilled to see Bobo and John chitchatting like old war buddies." ("Bobo" was the name we had given my father when he became a grandfather. It was derived not from a cute story of my niece having trouble saying his name, but rather from his children thinking it would be hilarious to name him after a gorilla. He had resisted vehemently, which only made it more fun for us to make sure Bobo stuck by having my niece Piper repeat it over and over again, until she had no idea his name wasn't Bobo.)

"She was sitting with Grandma at one of the tables," Robin replied. "I don't see them now."

"Was anybody with them?" I asked.

"I don't think so."

"Poor Grandma," I said.

I watched as my father navigated John down from the martini platform. John managed to stay upright as he wandered off in the direction of the lake, as if he were responding to an innate call. My father and Monty walked over to join Robin and me. I heard organ music playing in the distance.

"Is John okay?" Robin asked my father.

"At the end there he was teetering like a one-legged penguin. I don't know where he went."

"You seemed to be getting along," I said, eyeing my father suspiciously.

"I like him. If it wasn't for your mother, we could have been friends."

"That bitch," Robin said.

"What's going on down by the lake?" I said. "Is there some kind of organ concert?"

"There better not be," Monty said. "We reserved the whole space."

"Where are you seating everyone at dinner?" I asked Monty. "There are fewer people and more contentious divorces than at Robin's wedding."

"Table spacing," Monty said, gesturing to the seating area with his beer. "That's why they're all twenty feet apart."

"I don't understand where everybody went," Robin said, looking around. "Is the party over?"

"And we decided against place cards. People can sit wherever they want," Monty continued.

"Nothing could possibly go wrong with that plan," I said, thinking about how my father got much more forgiving the more he drank, while my mother got more vindictive the more she did.

"Music stopped," Robin said.

"I'm kind of shit-faced," I said.

"Spoke too soon; there it goes again," Robin said, as the unmistakable first notes of the wedding march started.

"I think there's another wedding here," I said to Monty. "I would check with your—"

"Fuck!" Monty yelled, interrupting my thought. He dropped his beer and took off full tilt toward the lake.

Robin and I looked at each other, each processing what was happening through a gin haze. Monty's wedding had begun, and as the groomsmen, we were a potentially important absence. We took off behind Monty, the three of us arriving just in time to meet Tonya at the altar.

"I really need to sit down. Who has a two-hour cocktail reception *before* a wedding?" I whispered to Robin, catching my breath as the minister started the ceremony.

"Who starts a wedding without the groom?" Robin whispered back.

AFTER THE CEREMONY, people wandered back up the hill from the lake for the reception. My mother reserved a seat for John on one side of her, and I sat on the other. My grandmother had opted for a less hostile space next to Robin, a few tables away. Almost immediately after we sat down, my father approached us, held his hand out to my mother, and said, "I just wanted to say hello and pay my respects to the mother of the groom. You're looking lovely this evening, Wendy."

As at Robin's wedding, my mother refused to look at my father and instead stared at me with the same deadpan expression, cocked her head in contempt, and replied dismissively, "So you've said hello. Now go away." Each time she saw my father, her confrontation always fizzled, proving more satisfying in the planning than the execution.

I gave my father an *Oh well* shrug and an apologetic smile as he backed away, his hand resting lightly on his holster.

A few minutes later, I noticed John weaving in our direction, looking unsure about where he was going. "Over here, you drunk," my mother called. John responded to the sound of my mother's voice but didn't look up, seemingly unable to lift his head. He stumbled from side to side like the last survivor in an action-adventure movie emerging from the wreckage of a flattened building. When he got to the table, he looked skeptically at the small wooden chair next to my mother, grasping the back of it uncertainly and slowly navigating his body into a position so that he was stable enough to sit. My mother chuckled lightly and said to me, "This should be interesting."

I don't know why, but I didn't get up to help him. Perhaps it was because my mother didn't seem to care, or because I was curious to see what would happen. As he grabbed one side of the wooden chair and tried to maneuver his large body in front of it, images of the chair tipping over and John going with it flashed through my mind.

It took a while, but he found his way to a seated position, like a helicopter landing on an aircraft carrier in a storm, while my mother and I watched, transfixed. Once it was clear there was no imminent threat of disaster, we returned to our conversation as John swayed in his chair.

"I hope your brother knows what he's doing, getting married."

Over her shoulder, I saw John pick up each piece of silverware and study it as an archaeologist might examine ancient fossils.

"They seem to love each other, and I think she's good for him," I replied.

"Good for him, is she? She's old enough to be his mother," she said bitterly. "Like father, like son, I guess." Tonya was ten years older than Monty, the same age difference as my father and Barb.

John put down the silverware and extended his hand out in front of him, in search of something. As far as I knew, he hadn't been struck blind in the last few hours, but he was clearly having trouble distinguishing what was right in front of him.

"Maybe she snagged him with some hot old-lady sex moves," I said.

John's hand bumped into a martini glass filled with ceviche, the first course that had been preset at the table. His fingers fumbled around the stem and gripped the main part of the glass.

"Don't be so disgusting," my mother said.

"I'm just saying: He seems happy, and they're now officially married, so I'm not sure why you're all worked up about it now."

John pulled the glass toward him, still swaying in the chair, and lifted it to his lips. He tipped the glass back slightly, removed it from his lips, and studied the contents of the glass, his head tilted in confusion.

"Happy, is he? Pfft. We'll see how long that lasts."

"You and John seem to be going strong."

John brought the glass to his lips again and tipped it a little farther, dislodging a piece of raw fish that tumbled down his front and onto the ground. Once again, he seemed confused about what was happening and held the glass back out in front of him, narrowing his eyes. With a determined look on his face, he tilted his head back as far as it could go and brought the glass to his lips one last time. The entire contents of the martini glass rained down around him, hitting his nose and forehead, tumbling down his cheeks, and bouncing like spongy hail on the grass around his feet.

"It's *fish*, John," my mother said. "You don't drink it."

John looked at the almost-empty glass, then at my mother and me, and placed the glass back down on the table like an obedient child, a slight frown of recognition on his face. She turned back toward me.

"That's marriage for you," she said, shaking her head slowly. "I don't know what the fuck people are thinking."

Chapter 14

My mother could pull herself together for important events, but the majority of her time was spent in close communion with a Mason jar full of rotgut vodka in the small master bedroom of her Boca Raton condo. Her decline came rapidly after Monty's wedding, as if she had been her own dam holding back a raging river and it had breached. Once my brothers and I were in lockstep, agreeing that she needed help, and started lobbying our stepfather about it, he agreed to an intervention, partly because his life had shrunk along with hers. Monty, who saw them regularly, reported that John increasingly fled the premises as soon as he awoke and returned only to check that my mother was still alive. It wasn't entirely clear whether he wanted her to be.

We arranged for an intervention counselor to meet us at their apartment. I flew in from Roanoke and Robin from Bermuda. The counselor told us ahead of time to think about what we wanted to say to her that would help her understand how much we missed who she used to be, and how much we wanted her back. We were going to take turns reading our statements, finishing up with a "Will you please get help" pitch once we were done.

My body was rigid as I wrote, as if twenty years of cumulative emotion had seeped into my sinews and calcified. Al-Anon had taught me well, but no matter how I worked the program, I could never accept that my mother was probably going to die and I couldn't do anything about it. I still wanted to say something that would compel her to get help, but I didn't want to craft anything that would drill too deep, lest I strike a deposit of unexpressed feeling that would spew up and out of me when I had no means to channel the energy or contain the spill.

When the time came, we gathered in the living room, and John went to get my mother from the bedroom. She walked out like she had been freed from a bunker, squinting and confused as to why we were there. In the past few years, I had always felt a little pang of hurt whenever we came to see my mother and she could barely summon the energy to greet us, let alone show any excitement at our presence. It may have been because the last time we had showed up unexpectedly was when she was in the ICU after her car crash. For her it only meant bad news. As she took her seat on the couch amid the circle of chairs that we had created around her, she was decidedly annoyed that she had been pulled out of her room for what was shaping up to be the equivalent of a bus hitting her head-on.

My brothers talked about our early years in Bermuda—about going to the beach, and the decathlon course that we set up around the house. John told my mother that he loved her, although he said it like he was fulfilling a court order, and that she had to get her "tipping under control—it's too much." He cleared his throat and stammered, and I couldn't tell if he was trying not to cry or if the expression of a genuine emotion, for him, was like starting up an old car that had been sitting in the garage for decades.

"Do you remember when we would play gin together?" I said to my mother, who smiled sadly from across the room but didn't look at me. "We would sit on the couch, and while I dealt the cards you would tell me that you were going to win, and you usually did. And every time you did, you sang the 'gin' song—do you remember that? *Ginny gin gin, ja gin gin gin, ginny gin gin, ja gin gin gin*—and you would be so happy that you won. And there were those times, after I dealt out all the cards, that you would be arranging your hand and you would start smiling like you were thinking about something funny. I never knew what you were smiling at, but then you would chuckle like you were remembering a funny joke. I never asked you what you were chuckling about; I just started smiling and chuckling too. And your smile would get bigger, and you'd let out a giggle, and my smile would get bigger and I would giggle back. And then you'd start doing that whining thing that you do before you start laughing, and I would make the same sound, and your whine would turn into a laugh, and we would go back and forth until we were both laughing so hard that we couldn't catch our breath, and we would fall back onto the couch because the cards were falling out of our hands and we had no idea what we were laughing about but we couldn't stop, and we didn't want it to stop, and even when it did, if one of us even looked at the other later in the game it would all start happening again. In those moments, laughing with you, I've never been happier, because I knew there was somebody in the world who I could laugh with about nothing and know that it was everything."

My mother pursed her lips but didn't look at me, probably knowing that if she did she would break my heart further. She had chosen the alcohol over us long ago.

An intervention works in the same way that it works for the trapped mouse to be carried off by the cat, so after each of us had spoken, the counselor asked if she was ready to get help, and she shrugged her shoulders, looked away, and said, "I guess I don't have a choice." The only clothes that fit her at this point were large, billowy muumuus, so we packed a few of those and found the only pair of slippers that fit her blue and bloated feet.

"When I was a little girl, my daddy used to take me to the beach," she said.

"You never told us about that," I said.

"I had friends. I wonder where they are now?" She cried softly.

"You have us," I said.

"I only ever wanted to be a mother, and I failed."

"You were a fantastic mother. Didn't you hear us tell you how great a mother you were?" It felt like an elephant was sitting on my chest.

"I'm a bad mother."

"We love you."

"Well . . . ," she whispered, not finishing the thought. She looked at the wall and didn't say anything. The small pillow that she was holding, her favorite, dropped next to her on the bed. I picked it up and put it in the suitcase.

My mother didn't look at any of us as we escorted her to the door of the van dispatched to take us to the rehab facility. "I want my own room," she said.

"Of course." I didn't know if she was going to get her own room.

My mother held my hand for the forty-five-minute ride to the rehab place and commented on what she saw out the window.

"You should just drop me off here," she said, as we passed a "Girls, Girls, Girls" sign underneath the silhouette of a busty lady.

"You've always liked to dance," I said.

"I could shake my huh-huh for dollar bills."

"There's a type for everybody," Robin said.

"Ah so! Flied lice!" my mother said as we passed a Chinese fast-food restaurant.

"Where exactly is this place?" Monty whispered to Robin and me.

"I have no idea. Knowing John, he probably found a fifty percent off coupon in *Reader's Digest*," I replied.

"What are you filthy beasts whispering about?" my mother asked, looking scared.

"Monty was calling you a racist. I was defending you, knowing how much you respect Chinese culture," I said.

"Ching-chong chiney!" my mother said, laughing. Her face dropped again as we passed a series of abandoned warehouses. "Where the fuck are you taking me?"

"I hear it's the best rehab center in south Florida," I said.

"I'm not doing this," she said, turning toward me with tears in her eyes. "I want to go home. Please, Kirkland."

"It's going to be okay," I said. "We're going to make sure you get help."

"Please don't leave me there." She was crying, holding my hand tighter. "I'm scared. Please don't leave me there alone."

"They're going to help you. I promise you'll feel better," I said.

"You can't make me do this. I want to go home. *Please*." She sounded like a victim pleading with her kidnappers. For a moment, I wondered if that's what we were.

"I know you're scared. I promise you it's going to be okay," I said.

"We love you, Mommy," Robin said.

She turned and looked back out the window. "You're not listening to me," she said. "Nobody listens to me." She let go of my hand.

We pulled up to an industrial-looking concrete facility near a strip mall. John spoke to a woman behind a glass partition to arrange the finances, and a stern intake person started going through my mother's bag to make sure she hadn't smuggled in any booze. Generic "One Day at a Time" posters covered the cracking beige walls. Overhead fluorescent lights flickered. I had pictured more of a birds-singing-in-a-secluded-compound kind of vibe. My mother looked around in disbelief.

"I want to go home," she said.

"You can't go home," I replied. "You're going to die if you don't get help."

"I'm going to die here."

My resolve was wavering.

Once my mother checked in, the nurse brought us up to her concrete-walled room, with its two single beds and low-light lamps. She sat on one of the beds and looked around tentatively, her hands folded in her lap, like a little girl being left at camp. She was trembling. Outside the walls of the condo, I noticed for the first time how sick she looked. I wondered why we hadn't seen a medical doctor. Was one coming by after we left?

After each of us had kissed her on the cheek, we stood at the door to her room for a final goodbye. I flashed back to seventeen years earlier, when I was the one being left at boarding school, and wondered if the ache in my chest and the overwhelming feeling of sadness was what my mother had felt as she watched me walk to my dorm. I wanted to talk to somebody who could assure me that she was going to be okay, but I also wanted to get out of the building before the feeling that something wasn't quite right bubbled too far up, to the point that I would have to do something about it.

JOHN SPRANG MY MOTHER FROM REHAB after three days. She had been calling daily with increasingly dire tales of how cruel "the staff" were, as if she had been sentenced to a real-life Cuckoo's Nest, with Nurse Ratcheds looming over her at every turn. It was hard to know if her stories had any truth to them or were just the most effective strategy to get back to her Mason jar of vodka in her curtained bedroom. John was an easy target. He hated being alone and lacked the internal fortitude to deny her anything. I heard everything secondhand, having chosen to let John and Robin take point for no other reason than that I didn't want to be responsible for any decision.

I had survived my mother's decline by finding the humor in the character that it spawned, but there was always the shadow of dread creeping closer—a time when the comedy of who she had become would be played out and all that would be left was the tragedy. I comforted myself by repeating the Al-Anon refrain that I didn't cause her alcoholism and couldn't cure it, and on my better days, I even believed that it was the height of arrogance to judge her life based on my idea of how she should be living it. But the emotional truth of what was happening couldn't be assuaged by a slogan, and whatever philosophical wave I was riding related to her autonomy always crashed on the shore and left me with the realization that one day she would be gone, and in the remembrance of who she was there would be only profound loss. That day was getting closer.

By the fall of 2003, the year I turned thirty-five, communication with my mother had grown sporadic, limited to times when I felt strong enough to weather the unpredictable nature of our conversations. Speaking to her on the phone was like calling back in time to the green room of a Hollywood talk show in the 1940s and not knowing if Joan Crawford, Marilyn Monroe, or Greta Garbo would pick up the receiver. No matter what time of day it was, or which Golden Era diva she was channeling, they were always well into cocktail hour, and one of them had just thrown a metaphorical drink into Clark Gable's face.

John had somehow convinced my mother to travel to Bermuda that August, to take up residence in a condo they had built on the golf course of a new luxury resort. The resort was located on the old Castle Harbor Hotel property in which my father's family had once owned a stake—the same place where, twenty-five years earlier, my mother had pulled up to the front door and claimed that her young children were still the owners. The hotel had struggled over the years, falling into disrepair before switching owners a couple of times. This latest incarnation was a return to the five-star concept that my father's family had invested in long ago, with premier accommodations and top-notch service for the main resort and hotel, plus new lots for luxury condos. John was an early investor. He had always been annoyed by my mother's nostalgia for her life with my father, and it wouldn't have surprised me to learn that his decision to claim a piece of land that my father lost was his way of claiming a final victory over her past.

In September of 2003, Bermuda was hit by Hurricane Fabian, a Category 3 storm with sustained winds of 120 miles per hour. John was off the island at the time, and Robin was scrambling to get his house prepared for a direct hit, while my mother insisted that she and her full-time nurse (employed not long after rehab had failed) were going to be fine—shrugging off Robin's pleas that she relocate to his house. When the worst predictions of the storm's intensity started coming true, he made a last-ditch effort to get her out of her condo by calling our cousins on my father's side, who were renting the old Porter/Hamill house near my mother's condo, the place where my parents had met the same year the last big hurricane had hit Bermuda, forty years earlier. When my cousins—Chip and Tiger—knocked on her door as the winds started to pick up, she ignored them, telling my brother that she would rather die in her own place than spend one minute with "those people."

I called her just as the hurricane made landfall and was surprised when her nurse, Judy, picked up the phone.

"Well, hello, Kirkland," Judy said, in a chipper tone. I had never met Judy, but thought of a stiff-upper-lip Brit who might casually knit a sweater as bombs rained down on London. "Hold for your mum." There was a long pause before my mother got on the phone.

"Hello, darling." My mother's voice was whiskey thick and slurred. She spoke as if she were juggling cockroaches in her mouth.

"How's it going over there? I thought I would hear wind in the background." Bermuda had managed to escape a direct hit by a hurricane during my time on the island, but I had heard enough about them to assume that the wind would sound like a freight train barreling through your house.

Her response was slow and tinged with the contempt of the perpetually annoyed. "We're in the closet, Kirkland. We're not on the fucking roof."

One of my classmates had told me that if you didn't open the windows on the leeward side of the house as the hurricane hit, the pressure would build and the house would explode. My mother's response caused me to question the veracity of this claim while, simultaneously, her bitchy delivery momentarily quelled my concern for her well-being should it be true.

"You're in a closet?"

"It's an upstairs walk-in. I'm not amongst the bloody brooms."

"I didn't think you were."

Whenever my mother was this drunk, our conversations resembled the dance between a ringmaster and an angry tiger. My questions were meant to keep her occupied without sparking a violent attack.

280

"It's actually lovely. Judy has set up two very comfortable lawn chairs. We have a bottle of vodka, a bucket of ice, and some nibbles."

"Of course you do."

"You're damn right." I heard the familiar advancing and receding of clinking ice cubes.

"Well, it sounds like you're hanging in there okay."

"You know your mother. I've been to hell and back before."

"So, what's happening there? Can you tell from the closet?"

There was another long pause as she took another swig of her drink. "What do you think is happening here, Kirkland? It's unadulterated hell. Like the hinges of hell."

"I can only imagine."

"You're damn right you can only imagine. I wouldn't wish what I'm going through on my worst enemy."

"Uh-huh."

"The electricity's out. The shutters are blowing around like billy-be-good. The phones are down."

I paused for a minute to make sure I had heard her correctly. "Well, I don't know about the electricity, but I'm pretty sure your phone's working."

"Oh, you think so, do you? You haven't been through what I'm going through, Kirkland. None of you kids have. You've been damn lucky."

"I'm just saying that we're talking on the phone, so . . ."

"And your brother? You think he gives a shit? What comes around comes around again."

"Goes around."

"What?"

"Didn't he want you to come stay with him?"

"Why would I do that?"

"I'm just saying, I think he *is* concerned about you. That's why he sent Chip and Tiger."

"Hah! Those two . . ."

"Never mind. You nailed it. Robin doesn't care about you. Good thing you have me."

". . . couldn't find their way out of a paper bag. *Drugs.*"

"Anyway, it sounds like you're doing okay. I just wanted to check on you."

"So now you care—when your mama's about to be blown out to sea."

"It felt cruel not to at least say goodbye."

"You laugh. You'll see."

"All right, I better go. I just wanted to call and see how you were doing. But since the phone's not working, I guess I'll have to try later."

She held a beat before continuing. She knew I was mocking her for something but couldn't quite figure out what that was.

"I'll probably be dangling from a tree with my privates hanging out for the world to see on CNN."

"Okay, then. I'll be sure to tape it—show it to the grandkids."

"You do that."

"I love you." I always told her that I loved her at the end of every conversation now, knowing that each time we spoke held the real possibility that it would be our last.

"I love you, darling. Thanks so much for calling."

I called the next morning, and once again a chipper Judy picked up the phone and handed it to my mother.

"You made it!" I said.

"Of course I did. We're making French toast. It's a lovely morning."

MY MOTHER ENTERED THE HOSPITAL for the last time eighteen months later, a few months before her sixty-first birthday. She had fallen down while waiting outside of their hotel for John to pull the car around so that they could go to lunch up the street at the Mid-Ocean Club. John had sold the Bermuda condo soon after the hurricane, and they had come to the island only for a short visit, to attend my grandmother's memorial service.

My grandmother had died of the heart condition that she was always complaining about, the one my mother had no patience for, at ninety-one years old. A few years earlier my grandmother had visited my mother at her and John's sound-side house in Bermuda, and complained that climbing the stairs to the parking lot was going to strain her heart. "Listen, you old bag," my mother replied, "you have two choices. You can either get your ass up these stairs or I can throw you out this window and you can swim for it. What's it going to be?"

Her memorial service was held that next week, at which time both hers and my grandfather's ashes would be interred in the family's burial plot. My mother was annoyed that she was once again whisked away from her Floridian vodkatorium to the homeland that she couldn't seem to escape. She had no interest in venturing out of the hotel room for anything but the service. But John, having now grown intolerant of her complaints, insisted that they go out to lunch.

Robin called to tell me she was back in the hospital.

"What for this time?" I asked.

"She fell down."

"Again?"

"Yup."

"Is she going to be able to go to Grandma's memorial service?"

"No."

"I knew she'd find a way out of it."

I flew to the island the following week for my grandmother's service and went to see my mother in the hospital the day I arrived. She was sitting up in bed as much as she could, clearly in great pain. Every time I had seen her the last few years, I couldn't imagine that she could look any worse, but each time it was like another part of her had fallen away. Every once in a while, I saw in her eyes the person she used to be, and when I walked into her hospital room on this day, I saw it again, just for a flash.

I shuddered at the mainline injection of pain I felt when our eyes met. I looked away. The change in her face in the year since I had last seen her was startling, the final vestiges of her beauty having at last been stripped away. For the first time, I saw a resemblance to her mother.

"How was your flight, darling?" she asked. Her voice shook, and her body trembled, the pain radiating off her in waves. She had spent decades pretending that she was fine and now she had reached a point where the mechanics of proving that she was okay seemed too difficult to muster. She didn't wait for me to answer before asking for her sunglasses.

She put them on and looked away from me, toward the hospital room wall. My brothers attempted a joke every now and then, hoping, just like when we were young, that somehow if they caught the right wave of funny, it would lift us out of where we found ourselves and into someplace new.

Gail was on the island for my grandmother's service with her partner, Maggie, and came to visit my mother in the hospital the next day. They hadn't seen each other in many years. The only time we had spent any time with Gail was decades before, when I was twelve and Gail came to visit for a week. She spent most of the day smoking and watching TV while sitting on my spot on the couch, so my mother's distaste for her had seemed justified at the time.

Before she walked into her hospital room, I asked Gail about their upbringing, and she scoffed at my implication. "We had an ideal childhood. Your mother was given everything she could ever want."

My mother cried when Gail entered. She held my mother's hand, and they talked softly to each other before Gail ran out of the room and fell into Maggie's arms, crying loudly. "I didn't think it was so bad," she said. "I don't recognize her. She's in liver failure. I just can't believe it." Gail was a nurse, but we hadn't heard from the doctors that my mother was in liver failure, and I was angry at how dramatic she was being. My mother could hear Gail, making me panicky and livid. I stifled an urge to run into the hallway to tell her to shut the fuck up, to explain that those of us who had watched my mother over the years had learned to hide our shocked reactions, to let her live with the illusion that everything was okay.

Eventually Gail pulled herself together and returned to my mother's side. Maggie went to the other side of the bed and held my mother's hand.

"What are we going to do with you, Wendy?" Maggie said sadly.

Gail and Maggie spent a couple of minutes by her side and then told her they had to leave.

"But you just got here," my mother said, in a timid voice that I hadn't heard before.

"We'll be back tomorrow."

"But I haven't seen you. Please don't go."

"We'll be back tomorrow, love."

Gail and Maggie kissed my mother and left the room.

My grandmother's memorial service was a quiet, staid affair, much like my grandmother. There were a handful of older Bermudian women who came, people who had gone to church with my grandmother when she lived on the island. I didn't know any of them, except for one or two whose faces I remembered from when my mother dragged us to church when we first moved to Bermuda. After the ceremony, the minister asked Robin and me to lower both my grandmother's and grandfather's ashes into the family's plot at the top of the hill on the church grounds. He and his assistant had rigged a piece of twine to either side of each urn. He gave us each an end of the twine and instructed us to lower my grandmother when he began the prayer. Halfway down, the twine snapped, and my grandmother hurtled into the burial plot, dangling on her side with the top of the urn propped open. None of her fell out, and she was quickly hoisted back to the surface, the proceedings were halted, and the minister and his assistant frantically jury-rigged another device. Robin and I looked at each other and smiled wickedly. My grandmother would have been mortified. My mother would have loved it. It was the only reason I was sorry that she was not there.

After the service, Robin invited the attendees to a small gathering at his house. My grandmother's brother, Uncle Keith, and his wife, Mary, arrived unexpectedly; they had always planned on attending the funeral but had initially refused the invitation to the house because they assumed my mother was going to be there. During our first year in Bermuda, we spent many a weekend day at Keith and Mary's pool because we begged our mother to take us there, even though she never wanted to call and ask if they would mind if we came. She would always relent. She didn't know Keith and Mary that well, and she knew that we were imposing and that they said yes only because they felt bad for her and for us. She sat in the sun in one of their lounge chairs, while Keith, Mary, and their kids walked in and around the house, ignoring us. My mother spent those days with her nose turned up to the sky and her eyes closed.

Many years later, my mother bumped into Mary in the grocery store, flashed her the large diamond ring that John had just purchased for her, and told Mary that she was fat and needed to lose weight. Mary never spoke to her again.

* * *

When the trip was over, I returned to my home in Portland, Maine, where I had moved a few years earlier. I figured New Englanders would be more welcoming to a single gay man than people in Roanoke, even if it just meant they couldn't care less about you.

I kept up with my mother's situation over the phone with my brother. We had been told by professionals for many years that my mother was very sick and was going to die if she didn't get help, but having heard that for so long, I had come to view it as an exaggeration. I figured that this hospital stay would go much like the others—she would be there for an inordinately long amount of time, drive half of the doctors and nurses crazy, charm the other half, and then demand release. But when I talked to her on the phone a few days after I got home, something seemed different. Her voice was shaky and her manner was uncommonly resigned. Robin told me later that day that the doctor had told him that she had damaged her liver, but they hadn't told her yet.

When the doctor finally gave my mother the news about her condition, she waited until he had left and then said to my brother, "Well, that's a relief. At least I haven't damaged any of my organs."

"What are you talking about?"

"What do you mean?"

"The doctor just told you that your liver is damaged. Didn't you hear him?"

My mother apparently didn't talk for a few minutes, and then looked past my brother and out the window and said, "How stupid."

I spoke with my mother a few days after the news. She had a hard time following what I said. My brother had warned me that she had begun to hallucinate and occasionally didn't know where she was. She tried hard to sound present and with it, but the seams were showing. She was able to get a few of the catchphrases down, like "How is your weather?" and "Your brother can go to hell," but for the most part the conversation was a wobbly ramble.

A few days later, my brother called and told me that my mother had aspirated and been moved to the ICU. I had always imagined my mother's death as the most tragic moment of my life. When I was young, I had lain awake and pictured her being thrown out of a boat and drowning in front of me while she screamed for help. It was my greatest fear. Now that it was happening, I felt hopeful that this time her head might stay down.

I flew back to Bermuda a few weeks after my mother was admitted to the ICU. Before I entered for the first time, Robin warned me to prepare myself for how she looked. She lay on the ICU bed with tubes and wires coming out of her arms and neck. The respirator tube stuck out of her throat and was wide enough that it forced her face into an openmouthed scowl. Her brown teeth were showing, and her tongue was visible, flopped to one side of her mouth. The machines around her were beeping and wheezing—the heart monitor kept going off because her heart rate was fluctuating rapidly from 50 to 170 beats per minute. The respirator inflated her chest mechanically and artificially. Every breath was a sharp inhale, like the one a normal person would take if they were shocked or surprised, and each one felt like her last. Her hair was matted down and stringy, like that of an old doll. I stood beside her bed and touched her yellowed hand, from which liquid was seeping out of her skin in small droplets. Her whole body was bursting with fluid, a consequence, the doctor explained, of her failing kidneys. Unless her body started processing that fluid, she would continue to inflate and toxify until she died. He explained that she was also in constant danger of going into cardiac arrest because of her fluctuating heartbeats. Her liver was not working correctly, and they had discovered an enormous ulcer in the bottom part of her stomach that was causing internal bleeding.

And she had herpes. I don't know why he mentioned that.

We asked the doctor if she was going to die. I had always thought that was an easy question, but we didn't get a straight answer the entire two months she was in the hospital. *It depends*, they kept saying. I came to understand that there were so many parts of her body that weren't working, it was like a dike that had sprung twenty different holes, and plugging one could make the one next to it bigger.

She was in and out of consciousness and unable, because of the respirator, to communicate except by looking at us with what could be interpreted as terror, pleading, or regret. As a result, we started projecting what we thought someone in her position would want to say. *What is happening to me? How can I tell you how sorry I am? Am I going to be okay? How can I make this up to you?* Every time she tried to mouth words through the tube coming out of her mouth, one of us just kept repeating, "You're in the hospital; you have some things wrong with your liver and kidneys; we all love you and we're all here for you." That wasn't what she wanted to hear, so she closed her eyes, shook her head, and turned away, frustrated and exhausted. I became convinced that she wanted to tell us something important, perhaps a deathbed confession that might fill in the missing pieces that could explain how she had ended up in this place, how any of us had ended up in this place.

We came up with the idea of writing the alphabet on a big piece of paper so that I could stand by the bed and point to each letter, and she could nod or shake her head to spell out what she wanted to say. After numerous attempts, the closest we could get was a "C" and an "O" before she would look confused, unsure what letter came next. Was she in touch with the after-life, perhaps being summoned to "come closer" to the light?

She stabilized enough for me to go back to Portland, and soon thereafter received a tracheotomy so they could remove the breathing tube and she could mouth what she had been trying so hard to say.

"Remember the 'C' and the 'O'?" Robin said on the phone.

"You figured it out?" I asked, terrified at what he might tell me. As much as I wanted to understand my mother better, that whatever we now learned wouldn't change anything made the idea of knowing almost too painful to bear.

"She wanted a Coke," he said.

MY BROTHERS AND I, her three beloved filthy beasts, each of us having navigated his own path through her slow and complete self-destruction, made the decision to remove her from life support even though she was still in and out of consciousness. We had finally understood what the doctors weren't saying—that she was never going to get better. Her organs were failing, and there was nothing they could do but try to keep her comfortable until she died.

I flew into Bermuda on the last day of her life. When I got there, Robin explained that the doctors had told my mother that they were going to disconnect the machines keeping her alive. Her eyes darted open when I walked up to her bed. I told her that I loved her, and she mouthed back that she loved me. I was grateful when she told me she wasn't afraid to die. If she had broken, after thirty years of telling the world to fuck off, I would have broken too.

Gail called from England to say goodbye. They put the phone up to my mother's ear and my mother nodded her head as Gail spoke with her.

The air in the room grew still and electric when it came time to shut the machines off. The nurse gave her a shot of morphine. Robin and Monty started crying and turned away from her bed. I asked John if he wanted to stand next to her and hold her hand, and he said, "I'm not very good at this kind of thing," and also turned away, flicking a tear from his eye. I was simultaneously annoyed, aware of how horrible being with my mother must have been for John, and grateful that he had stayed with her. My brothers held each other in front of the ICU window and sobbed. I didn't cry.

I sat next to her and told her it was okay to go, but she shook her head back and forth, and scrunched up her face like she was trying to wake from a bad dream. Her forehead beneath my hand went cold and she turned blue. After five minutes her lips opened and closed like a fish dying on a hot pier. I prayed for them to stop moving. When she was gone, I kissed her forehead and walked out of the room. Robin thanked her for being his mother and kissed her goodbye. Monty placed his forehead on her hand and cried softly. John kissed her cheek. She was sixty-one years old. I was thirty-seven.

Epilogue

My brothers and I worried that nobody would come to my mother's funeral. She had grown up on the island, but we knew little about her social life before she married my father and moved away. She occasionally recognized somebody passing us in a car or walking down the street. She didn't provide details of her remembrances, just made a small comment about having known that person before, and then it seemed the memory, like a wisp of exhaled smoke, would disappear.

On the day of the funeral, my brothers and I gathered at the entrance to the church with five of Robin's closest friends who had agreed to serve with us as pallbearers. Just as at my grandmother's service, most of the people who filed into the church were older women who looked familiar, and I started wondering if they attended every funeral regardless of who was being laid to rest. Only one woman came up to us and said that she had grown up with my mother and had loved her and was sorry for our loss. I didn't recognize her. Robin's friends stood among themselves and laughed, recounting something that happened the weekend before.

When we dragged the casket out of the hearse, it was heavier than we'd anticipated. The funeral director had suggested that we roll it up the aisle to the altar, but Robin had in his head a more Kennedy-esque send-off, complete with personalized escort to her final resting place. We got her to the entrance of the church, only to discover that the narrow aisle could accommodate the coffin comfortably but not the people conveying it to the altar. As a result, our mother's journey to the front of the church resembled the maneuvering of an oversized couch up a narrow stairway. As we bumped and weaved our way forward, whispering apologies to the congregants who were pushed back lest their hands get crushed against the pews, the spray of flowers came loose, dangled to one side, and fell to the ground as we heaved the casket onto the platform before the altar. Instead of an array of white lilies, a large strip of white Velcro adorned our mother's oversized coffin for the rest of the service. My brothers and I took our places in the front pew drenched in sweat.

After the service, we hoisted my mother to make the long trek to the gravesite, which sat at the top of the hill overlooking the rest of the cemetery. The congregants gathered around the burial plot and along the route, creating a path for us to walk. We had made it halfway up the hill, heaving and jostling the casket as we went, when my back and left side numbed. I whispered to the other pallbearers that I couldn't go on. I let go of part of the weight, which dipped the coffin in my direction and stopped the procession. I was tired of carrying her. She was too heavy.

Just as I was about to let her go, I heard her speak to me in the voice that she had used so many times before when I was ready to give up on something. "Get your skinny white ass up that hill," she said. "This is the last thing you're ever going to do for me, so do it." I flashed back to my NOLS trip eighteen years earlier, when I had sat in a kayak unwilling to move forward. I reclaimed the weight and continued up the hill. We placed our mother on top of the gravesite into which we had lowered her parents just a few months earlier.

That night I lay awake in the guest room of Robin and Charlotte's house and pondered if my mother could hear what I had said to her as she was dying. I looked at the white chiffon curtains blowing in the window and imagined her materializing before me. I began to regret the invitation I'd extended, realizing that I didn't want to hear from her again. What would I say? Our conversations when she was alive had deteriorated to detailed recaps of the weather, so what would we talk about now?

Each year of my life, since I was eight years old, a new part of my mother went missing. As I have tried to make sense of who she was, I've bumped into walls and windows where I didn't remember them being. There were happy memories to which I had immediate access, but they're often the twins of ones whose meanings are more complicated, like the way she laughed joyously, with her full body, but when she watched me parade in front of her friends dressed up like a girl, her joyous laughter could also conceal a warning. I know that I absorbed her sense of justice, and her long memory when it came to those who had slighted her. I remember asking my mother about Jamie a few years before she died, and how she screamed and hung up the phone and called my father to demand that they have him arrested, and how my father told her it was too late and too long ago to do anything about it now. And she hung up on him too, perhaps realizing that Jamie wasn't the only person who had escaped justice. I remember my mother's deep affection for me, the warmth of her hugs, and the inevitability of her love; I recall kneeling in front of her chocolate-brown chair and holding on to her to feel the certainty and security that she offered. But the recollection is always paired with the memory of when I turned my back and she showed affection in a way I didn't recognize and could never forget.

I DON'T KNOW IF MY FAMILY'S TROUBLES began with the divorce, my mother's drinking, or my father's infidelity—or if it was all written generations before that, each decision made leading to the next and the next until this was the inevitable outcome. History, it turns out, is easier to transcend when you are building toward something new as opposed to living for what's already lost.

Over the next ten years after my mother died, Monty's alcoholism worsened to the point where it was no longer a family joke, except to my father, who never recognized, or perhaps cared, what was happening to his son. The first time I heard he had been admitted to the hospital with pancreatitis was right after he returned from a trip to Bermuda to see friends and visit my mother's grave on her birthday, though his wife, Tonya, told me then that it wasn't the first time this had happened. He quit drinking off and on over the next few years, but it never lasted. He refused to seek help until the Tuesday after President's Day,

2014, when he called and told me that he had taken my father's handgun and placed it against his temple, not wanting to live anymore. My husband, Dave, and I were driving back from his vacation home on Cape Cod as I listened to Monty cry and say that he needed help, that he wanted his son, Crawford, to have a father. Dave dropped me off in Newark, where I caught a plane to Florida and helped Monty enter a rehab facility in Fort Lauderdale for a thirty-day program.

He was in and out of rehab over the next couple of years, each time waiting until he was close to death before admitting that he needed help. During that time Robin and I received drunken, bitter harangues about how we had ruined his life, and didn't protect him, and didn't care about him. I listened and apologized and helped financially with what he and his family needed, until one day I told him that I was no longer available as a receptacle for his endless anger. We didn't speak for months, after which we agreed that we would try to rekindle our relationship with less anger and more understanding. "I can't talk to Robin yet," he said, which I understood. Robin had yet to apologize to him for anything.

Robin and his family moved from Bermuda to Aspen, Colorado, up valley from Lola and Neil's house in Basalt. The 2008 recession had helped tank the start-up he cofounded, and the wealth that he had accumulated started to dwindle as he struggled to find a job in a part of the country that was more popular with people who had money than with those needing to make it. Somewhere early in the Aspen days, Robin and Charlotte found God, the culmination of the journey of self-discovery they had each been on starting with the Forum. They joined a church that believed gay people were sinners in need of redemption. Long before they ever moved to Aspen, I had been taken out of their will as the guardian of my niece and nephews because, as Charlotte said, "It's not that I care whether you're gay, it's just that I don't want my children exposed to the revolving door of men in your life, and I really want grandchildren." She apparently believed my homosexuality was contagious. I didn't argue, even as their rebuke stung. Robin peppered his emails and phone calls with pledges to pray for me, and even though he meant them as statements of support, they felt like judgments.

Shortly after Robin and Charlotte renewed their wedding vows on their twentieth anniversary, Robin told Charlotte he no longer wanted to be married, just as my father had done to Barb soon after their own lavish twentieth anniversary celebration. He quit drinking for months at a time upon discovering that his liver was in distress, but always started again. He called me one Friday afternoon when I was in Denver officiating Dave's son's wedding, and I didn't pick up the phone. Later that night he sat with a pistol on his lap and sent a suicide text to his three children, telling them he could no longer live with his pain, and that he thought God was ready for him. The police arrived at his apartment before he pulled the trigger. His two older kids flew home from college, and we conducted an intervention that Sunday where he broke down and said he needed help. He went through a thirty-day rehab program but, like Monty, started drinking again soon thereafter. He's currently sober and living with Dave and me until he decides where on the east coast he wants to relocate.

Charlotte called me a year ago and said that my fifteen-year-old nephew, Sloan, had asked if I would be his guardian should she and Robin both die (his older siblings, Piper and Lyon, were already legally adults). I said I would be happy to be.

The Christmas after my mother died, I was up late one night with my father when he told me he was sorry about my mother, and asked if I was doing okay. I told him yes, and didn't say anything else until I heard him crying softly. "What's wrong?" I asked, and he told me that it was his fault, what happened to her, and that he was sorry and wished that he could go back and make better choices. "It wasn't your fault," I said, not knowing if I believed what I was saying but needing him to stop crying because I had yet to cry the way that he was now, and there was a part of me that felt he had lost the right to be sad for her, or for himself.

His business started to fail as clients abandoned him one by one—some because of what he had done to Barb and others because they could smell the booze on him when he took them to tour houses. Sometime in 2008, he stopped paying Barb's alimony, or bills of any kind. He hid his financial situation from us for years, until his credit cards maxed out and his reverse mortgage company threatened foreclosure because of overdue tax payments. A few months after discovering the financial hole he had dug for himself, I received a call from one of his oldest friends—Monty's godfather—asking how he was. I told him that my father was having a hard time and we were doing our best to figure out how to take care of him. He listened empathetically, and then confessed that he was calling to collect my father's overdue home owner's association balance. It was the first I'd heard that one of my father's closest friends from Cedarhurst, my childhood home on Long Island, lived in the same development. I don't know if my father even knew he lived there.

My father was held in contempt of court for not paying alimony and thrown in jail in mid-2013. A former colleague of his bailed him out a few days later. We asked him what jail was like, and he said that he enjoyed his roommate and that the "staff couldn't have been nicer." My brothers and I joked that jail could be the long-term living solution we had been looking for, and wondered if they might take him back.

When Monty and Tonya lost their house to foreclosure, they moved in with my father to look after him as he was rapidly descending into alcohol-induced dementia. Monty was regularly awoken late at night to the sound of my father turning on the stove's gas burners to cook himself dinner. He had forgotten that he'd already eaten. My father quit drinking, only because when he asked Tonya to get him a bottle of gin every morning she would respond "Are we out?" and promise to pick one up after work. She never did, and they repeated the same routine each morning until he forgot to ask. Tonya moved out of the house as Monty's drinking worsened, and checked on my father every now and again, knowing Monty was increasingly incapable of caring for him. She arrived one day to find my father eating cat food out of the can, thinking it was pâté. He had also stopped taking his little Pomeranian (whom he'd named "Pomme Frite") outside, so the house was peppered with dog feces and yellow carpet stains. The hygiene situation resolved itself when my father rolled over onto Pomme Frite during one of his afternoon naps, and the dog had to be put down because it couldn't walk properly anymore. That's the story we heard anyway. Robin and I didn't discover most of the details of my father's final years until much later, since we had stopped visiting, and weren't communicating with Monty. When Monty got sober, he reminded us that my father had a second small dog, Jethro, who had also died young and under sketchy circumstances.

Barb died of alcohol-induced dementia in 2014. We had lost touch with her the last few years of her life, partly because of her illness, and partly because her son was aggressively going after my father for $50,000 in unpaid alimony, to the point of threatening to have him thrown back in jail if he didn't pay. We were fortunate that my father's south Florida condo, hit hard by the economic downturn, increased enough in value for us to sell it. It was weeks from being foreclosed on. We used the small amount of money that was left after paying off Barb's estate to place him in a five-bedroom retirement home in Port St. Lucie, Florida. He slept in a single bed next to a stranger.

He would escape the facility often, be picked up by the local police, and I would receive a late-night call asking to calm him down. He would tell me that he had been "shanghaied," was being held captive, and beg me to rescue him. He believed he lived with Robin in Colorado. I told him he was already home, which confused him, and made me feel guilty. I loved him, but I didn't want him to live with me, and I didn't want to spend my own money to put him into a nicer facility. I had already given him more than I wanted to.

After two years, the care home's proprietor called to tell me my father couldn't breathe and they were taking him to the emergency room, where they discovered he had stage-four lung cancer. My brothers and I gathered together in his hospice room and said goodbye to him over the course of a week in mid-July 2017. On his last night, I slept next to his bed and listened to the rhythmic rattle of his breathing, until the nurse told me that it was almost time for him to go. I held his hand and watched as he took his last breath, peacefully unaware, leaving the world as nonchalantly as he had lived in it.

My brothers and I never learned if there was a trust fund set up by my grandfather to take care of us, or who won control of it, or how it was used. I graduated from college with student debt that took fifteen years to pay off. Andover forgave my loan when I explained that I'd had no knowledge of it being taken out in my name. I never asked my parents for money. I stumbled into a career as a nonprofit fundraiser because it was the one skill my upbringing had prepared me for. I felt comfortable around wealthy people. I spoke their language, and knew their rhythms. My job taught me that there were rich people who found joy in giving and viewed their wealth as an opportunity to make the world a better place. My family lost what we never learned to share.

I moved to Washington, DC, from Maine a year after my mother died. I met Dave in the summer of 2010, five years after her death and right when my father began descending into poverty and dementia. I dated a lot of men in the years after I came out, but nobody longer than three months. The last man I was with before Dave was driving me home from a movie one night when he turned to me and said, "I'm not sure that you're good enough for me." I felt something in my psyche shift, as viscerally as if I had been struck by a closed fist. I asked him to stop the car. I walked the rest of the way home, deciding that I would never again let somebody make me feel unworthy—a feeling I had struggled with in my love relationships, even as I had lived assertively in other aspects of my life.

I shared my life story with Dave over time and in small chunks, watching as his face registered more disbelief, concern, and eventually horror with the unspooling of each harrowing tale. "I wish I knew your mother," he told me recently, a sentiment shared by many of my newer friends. "She would have loved you," I told him, "but she would have hated you first." We moved to Baltimore, and split our off time between his vacation house on the Cape and the Adirondack preserve where my brothers and I had spent our childhood summers, though my father sold our family camp decades ago. We rented small cottages now.

During one of the early dinners I had with Dave's family, the conversation turned to the dashboard of the new Toyota Corolla, which ignited a half-hour-long conversation about car dashboards—past and present. They prayed before dinner, as observant Catholics do, and it was all I could do not to run screaming from the room in protest over how ordinary my life had become. "This is how normal family conversations go sometimes," Dave said to me when I complained about it later, and I wondered if that could be true.

I stopped thinking about my mother soon after she died. I don't acknowledge her birthday, or her deathday. I don't post heartfelt remembrances of her on my Facebook feed or make my friends indulge me in long conversations about how much I miss her. Dave and I recently went to Bermuda and visited my mother's grave, although I wasn't sure she would still be in it. The church had called a few months prior to say that rent was due, and if we didn't pay, her site would be assigned to somebody else. I didn't know that burial plots were rented. I told them no. Her grave marker was still there when we visited, but apparently it's only a matter of time before she won't be. I didn't ask where she would be going.

I was present for Monty as he navigated his nightmare journey through alcoholism. I became a resource for Tonya when Monty was absent, or Crawford needed new sneakers. I became Robin's confidant as his life crumbled. I was the liaison between Barb's estate and my father as we tried to keep him from going back to jail. There were nights I would get quiet, and Dave would ask what was wrong, and I told him nothing, because every version of the conversation that I played out in my head ended up in the same place. I felt like I was, in many ways, the last survivor of a family system that had disintegrated little by little until there was nothing left. But somewhere along the line my joy had disappeared, and now it seemed coping was all that remained.

One night not so long ago, Dave and I started watching a movie about a twelve-year-old boy, Conor, who lived with his mother in rural England. The mother was sick, and the boy dealt with her illness by summoning a monster who told him fables that had unexpected twists and turns meant to show that life wasn't simple, or sometimes even to be understood.

Dave found the premise ridiculous and retired to bed. The boy didn't want to talk to his mother, or anyone, about what was happening and became angry and withdrawn. Toward the end of the movie, the monster told the final story in which he forced Conor to confront a recurring nightmare that he had about his mother falling over the side of a cliff. In the dream, the boy holds on to her for dear life, until he can't hold on any longer, and she falls. I remembered a recurring dream I had of my mother walking over a cliff, and how I had to save myself by cutting the rope that attached us. In the final scene of the movie, the monster demands that the boy tell him the truth of what happened in his nightmare, and the boy admits that he wanted her to go, that he could no longer hold on. He could now accept that his mother was going to die, and he draped himself over her in her hospital room as she took her last breaths. The monster narrated the end of the film: "Conor held tightly to his mother, and in doing so was able to let her go."

I started crying. I cried because the movie was sad and I related to the boy. I cried for my brothers, who learned about life from parents who shone so brightly but didn't know what to do when the light dimmed. I cried for myself, for the doughy little boy with the floppy blond hair, the confused teen, the young man with the broken heart, and for the grown adult who held it all in and held it all together because that's all he knew how to do.

And I cried for my mother. The tears catapulted me off the couch and onto the rug, where I heaved and sputtered and placed my hand over my mouth so as not to wake Dave.

Whenever I thought I was done, another wave would hit, each one coming up and out from places that I didn't know existed. And in missing my mother, she started to come back to me, as if the now empty spaces where I had kept the tears created a vacuum where the love I once had for her rushed in and was welcomed back home.

THE END

Acknowledgments

I would like to thank:

My mother and father, who had no idea that their lives would be reduced to my limited and biased experience of them, and then put to paper for all to read. That's what happens when you die young and encourage your child's snarky humor.

My brothers, Robin and Monty, who have encouraged me to tell our story and my truth. I am aware that these are not the same things. You have been my biggest cheerleaders.

To my niece, Piper, and my nephews Lyon, Sloan, and Crawford. I adore you. If this book sells, then I will have money and no children of my own. Just remember that when I am no longer able to use the bathroom by myself.

Aunt Joan and Uncle Bob, Aunt Anna and Uncle John. Thank you for being hilarious, even if that wasn't your intention.

My husband, Dave. The constant, off-tune singing of '80s tunes on eight-hour car trips should be grounds for divorce. I love you. I realize how lucky I am to have you.

My stepmother, Barb. You taught me how to love quietly.

Trey, Lindsey, Corcoran, and Pat. You are the second family

that I never thought I would have. I publicly, and with great fanfare, take pride in your dizzying accomplishments even though I have had nothing to do with them.

Emily Bernhard, my first reader, who gently told me I had an outline of a book, not a book.

Mollie Lindley Pisani, my first editor, who helped me take that outline and turn it into a first draft. And then a second, a third and a fourth one. You made me believe.

Farley Chase, my agent, who saw the diamond in the rough and helped me shine it up. You were thorough, caring, and direct. "I don't like that at all" is a very helpful reaction when you think you're being clever.

Ben Loehnen, my editor, who pounced on the story like an alley cat (he would say that was a clichéd description), and who taught me that you could say things in one sentence rather than two, and without adverbs—or dashes.

The team at Simon & Schuster and Avid Reader for taking such great care of my book—Alex, Meredith, Morgan, Carolyn, Wendy, Tracy, and the entire sales team.

My *Open Salon* blog friends and readers who loved my stories and encouraged me to keep writing. And to the editors of the blog who saw their value before I did.

The memoirists who have been brave enough to share their pain and make it funny. You taught me how to write this book.

My early readers: Katherine Walker, Karen Brockenbrough, Cabell Youell, Kristina Catto, Diz Hormel, Dave Downey, Anne Seay, Louise Gaylord, and Toddie Findlay. You gave me so many insights, even with the things you weren't saying. This book is better because of you.

Acknowledgments

Beth Macy, Steven Rowley, and Amy Sutherland—writers who took the time to read and blurb. I admire your work. I am honored to know you.

Cindy, Rob, Brian, Chase, Alex, Shelly, Dwight, and Sharon. My extended Al-Anon family. You gave me back my life.

My amazing friends who laughed at all the right times and cried with me when I couldn't find the funny. You became my family.

About the Author

Kirkland Hamill is the author of countless witty emails to friends, coworkers, and clients who have, no doubt, at one time or another, rolled their eyes and said to themselves *enough already*. He was born in New York City, raised in Bermuda, and has lived all over the United States. He and his husband, Dave, split their time between Baltimore, Maryland; Cape Cod, Massachusetts; and the Adirondack Mountains. *Filthy Beasts* is his first book.

www.kirklandhamill.com

Filthy Beasts

Kirkland Hamill

This reading group guide for Filthy Beasts *includes an introduction, discussion questions, and ideas for enhancing your book club. The suggested questions are intended to help your reading group find new and interesting angles and topics for your discussion. We hope that these ideas will enrich your conversation and increase your enjoyment of the book.*

Introduction

Gripping, thought-provoking, and equal parts hilarious and wrenching, *Filthy Beasts* is the story of a once-wealthy family whose gilded lives fell to pieces. Following a rancorous split from New York's upper-class society, newly divorced Wendy and her three sons are exiled from the East Coast elite circle. Wendy's middle son, Kirk, is eight when she moves the family to her native Bermuda, leaving the three young boys to fend for themselves as she chases after the highs of her old life: alcohol, a wealthy new suitor, and other indulgences. Kirk learns to maintain appearances and bury his inconvenient truths from the world, until he leaves the island, falls in love for the first time, and begins to discover the freedom of telling his truth.

Topics & Questions for Discussion

1. After Kirkland's mother moved to Bermuda with her children, she would wake them for breakfast by shouting, "Wake up, you filthy beasts! It's time to face the beauty of a brand-new day!" (page 79). Why do you think Kirkland chose *Filthy Beasts* as the title of the book?

2. How does Kirkland's sense of self change over the course of the book? How is he finally able to come to terms with his sexuality at the age of thirty, and what does he gain from doing so?

3. In the book's acknowledgments, Kirkland offers his thanks to "My brothers, Robin and Monty, who have encouraged me to tell our story and my truth. I am aware that these are not the same things" (page 309). What does he mean by this? What might the boys' childhood look like from Robin's or Monty's point of view? Do you have any memories from growing up that differ from those of your family members?

4. Kirkland's acknowledgments also thank "My mother and father, who had no idea that their lives would be reduced to my limited and biased experience of them, and then put to paper for all to read" (page 309). What could be the concerns of publishing a memoir that portrays other people in some of their worst moments? Do the ethics change when the people Kirkland writes about are no longer living, like his parents, versus living subjects, like his brothers? Where does Kirkland admit to, and attempt to transcend, his biased view toward the people in his life?

5. How do the themes of blame and forgiveness play out in *Filthy Beasts*? Is it possible to find closure without the comfort or satisfaction of blame? Is it possible to find peace without forgiveness?

6. What choices does Kirkland make, consciously or unconsciously, for the sake of self-preservation? What does he sacrifice? How does he later regret or affirm his decisions?

7. Kirkland chooses to attend Tulane University for college without ever visiting the campus. He writes, "I was on a quest to find a place that fit. . . . Why not head south?" (page 127). How is Tulane, in New Orleans, different from the places in the Northeast or on Bermuda where Kirkland had previously lived? What foundational lessons does Kirkland learn from this environment? If you've

lived away from home, what lessons did you learn from your experience?

8. How does Ethan, the object of Kirkland's confused feelings in college, compare or contrast with the other primary object of Kirkland's feelings, his mother? How do they each treat Kirkland?

9. Kirkland sees a counselor in Bermuda who refers him to Al-Anon group meetings for friends and family of alcoholics. He remembers, "I walked out of her office with the Al-Anon pamphlet held against my chest, feeling the first flicker of hope in as long as I could remember" (page 161). What kind of insights does Kirkland hope to hear when he first seeks out Al-Anon meetings? What realizations does he ultimately find from the group, and how do they affect his life?

10. Kirkland describes how, when talking to his college friends about his unusual family, he "started to sell my mother as a character for public consumption, a larger-than-life throwback to another time, a late-era Bette Davis" (page 189–190). Which of her tendencies does he exaggerate and which does he downplay or disguise? How does his caricatured characterization of her serve to mask the pain her behavior causes to him?

11. How do you think Kirkland's life might have played out differently if his family had never been forced to reduce

its means? Did the family's problems originate with their loss of income?

12. How do Kirkland and his brothers cope differently with their mother's behavior and the scars it inflicted, both as children and as adults?

13. In the book's dedication to his mother, Kirkland writes, "You taught me how to survive you." Did you get that sense from reading the book? In what ways do you think Kirkland's mother taught him "how to survive her?"

14. Do you think that the epilogue concludes on a hopeful note? What challenges lie ahead for Kirkland and his family?

15. As Leo Tolstoy wrote, "All happy families are alike; every unhappy family is unhappy in its own way." What parts of the Hamill family's story can you relate to from your own experience? What is very different from your family?

Enhance Your Book Club

1. Divide your book club into groups and have each group discuss the events of the book from a perspective other than Kirkland's: one of his brothers, his mother, and so on.

2. Reflecting on the title of the book, go around in a circle and have each member think of a different title for Kirkland's memoir. Then go around and ask each member to think of the title they would give their own memoir.

3. Kirkland writes powerfully about the physical and emotional suffering that alcoholism can cause for alcoholics and the people they love. For your next book club read, choose a memoir by an author who has battled alcoholism and then discuss how it changed your understanding of this condition.